The Model Prisoner

The Model Prisoner

Tracy Kirby

with Tony Thompson

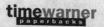

A *Time Warner* Paperback

First published in Great Britain in 2002
by Time Warner Books

*All the events described in the book are true,
but some names have been changed to
protect the privacy of certain individuals.*

A CIP catalogue record for this book
is available from the British Library.

ISBN 0 7515 3334 3

Typeset in Bembo
by Palimpsest Book Production Limited,
Polmont, Stirlingshire
Printed and bound in Great Britain by
Clays Ltd, St Ives plc

Time Warner Paperbacks
An imprint of
Time Warner Books UK
Brettenham House
Lancaster Place
London WC2E 7EN

www.TimeWarnerBooks.co.uk

To my family, who have always
been there for me.

Prologue

The plate came flying through the serving hatch, missing my head by a fraction of an inch. Mad Mandy, fresh out of the punishment block and halfway through a two-stretch for GBH, was high on crack and after my blood. 'I'm gonna fucking kill you,' she screamed in her thick south London accent. 'I'm gonna rip your fucking face off, you dirty bitch. You hear me? You're dead, you're fucking dead.'

I could feel the eyes of dozens of inmates burning into me as they gathered round to see how I'd react. Whatever happened in the next few seconds would have a dramatic effect on the rest of my time at Holloway: to show even the slightest sign of weakness would be an open invitation for every other prisoner to walk all over me. I couldn't let that happen – my life wouldn't be worth living.

Mandy was by far the toughest girl on the wing, a vicious brawler who'd beaten both men and women with equal ease. She looked completely indestructible, but I had no choice. 'Come on then, you bitch,' I spat back, 'come on then.' Ripping the thick black kitchen gloves from my hands, I sucked in a deep breath and charged out towards her . . .

There are few things in the world scarier than a prison fight. There's nowhere to run, nowhere to hide, and trying to talk your way out of trouble only makes things worse. You can't ask the screws for help – you just end up being labelled a grass. The only thing to do is stand your ground. And pray.

You pray that, if you're winning, her friends don't suddenly join in to even things up; you pray that the screws on duty like you enough not to turn a blind eye as your teeth are being kicked in. Most of all you pray that the person you're up against isn't tooled up.

The plastic knives in the canteen are too brittle to do any real damage, so the girls have learned to improvise. They stamp their heels down on to the cheap razors we use to shave our armpits and retrieve the thin metal blade inside. Stuck to the end of a toothbrush, it becomes a 'shank', a device easily capable of slashing someone's throat. Other weapons are equally ingenious, equally lethal: a plastic spoon, softened by melting and then shaped and sharpened, can poke a hole in a house-brick; three big batteries in a pillowcase make a cosh that will crack a skull like it was eggshell.

Even without weapons, the violence at Holloway is horrific. I saw my first fight on my second day inside and it's stuck with me ever since. Two girls stood toe to toe, trading punches like heavyweight boxers until their lips and noses split and dripped with blood. When one was felled with a head butt, the other grabbed a metal chair, raised it above her head and smashed it down on her opponent's spine. I thought that would be the end of it but the girl was so off her head on drugs she simply got off the ground and carried on fighting. By the time the riot bell sounded, alerting screws from all over the prison, the pair were rolling on the ground, tearing at each other's faces with their fingernails.

The first screw on the scene was a tall, muscular woman whom we nicknamed Tarzan. She got to the doorway, saw what was going on and ran towards the mêlée to break it up. The next thing I knew she was sprawled on the floor – someone had tripped her – and three girls with messy dreadlocks and heavy boots were kicking her senseless.

A male PO arrived a split second later but froze with fear when he saw the attack on Tarzan. It was only when more reinforcements arrived that the fight was finally broken up and the injured PO hauled away to safety. The troublemakers were dragged away screaming – arms behind their backs and thumbs bent back double – getting a right earful from the screws as they were taken to the punishment block. And as I stood watching from the corner of the room, I remember making a promise to myself that I'd never let prison turn me into an animal, that I'd never let it get to me the way they had. But deep inside I knew it was inevitable that some day it would.

I'd arrived at Holloway thinking that all I'd have to do was be polite and make people laugh and then they'd all like me. I couldn't have been more wrong. One of the first lessons you learn in prison is that the only way to survive is to stand up to every challenge and fight every battle, no matter how scared you are.

You can never get used to it, but eventually you learn to accept it. You realise that the violence is an outlet for all the frustrations of prison life. People fight because they're pissed off that they spent twenty-two hours

locked in their cell the previous day due to staff shortages, or because the slop they had for dinner the week
before made them sick, or because the friend who was
going to visit them cancelled at the last minute.

Violence in prison hangs in the air like a bad smell.
It's there to greet you the moment you wake up in the
morning and follows you around all day until they lock
you up at night. It's with you from the moment they
shut the gates behind you and sooner or later, no matter
how hard you try to fight it, it gets into your blood.

I reached the short corridor that separated the serving
area from the main dining room and kicked open the
door just in time to see Mandy's bulk fill the doorway
at the other end. There was no longer any fear, only
anger and adrenalin. The plate Mandy had thrown at
me had been piled high with a sticky mix of stewed
chicken and rice that had spattered all over my face and
hair. On top of everything else I'd been through, everything that had happened since I'd got to prison, it was
the last straw. As I ran down the corridor I heard someone nearby shouting and screaming, taunting Mandy
with every name under the sun. It took a few seconds
before I realised it was me doing the shouting. I'd
completely lost control. I no longer recognised myself.

Two screws appeared from nowhere and ordered us
to stop, which just made me even angrier. The first flung
himself at Mandy, locking his arms into her elbows and
desperately trying to pull her back on her heels. The
other darted around her and headed straight for me.

'Back in the kitchen, Kirby.'

'Bollocks to ya.'

I launched myself into a crazy dive and gasped with shock as I realised I'd managed to force my way past him. Mandy was now just within reach. We both lashed out with punches and kicks but managed only a few glancing blows before I felt myself being grabbed from behind and hauled away.

I was dragged back to my cell to calm down. As soon as the POs shut the door I collapsed on the bed and burst into tears. I hated what I'd become, hated what was happening to me. There was no way I could cope with this for the next eighteen years. I didn't see how anyone could.

There had been two suicides since I'd arrived at Holloway and I soon found myself thinking about taking my own life. I sat curled up on the bed, my knees up tight against my chest, my face red and puffy with tears, looking at the top of the window and wondering how easy it would be to make a noose out of the sheet and fix it up there.

Had it really come to that? How on earth had I ended up in such a mess? How had I gone from a top Page Three girl to a key figure in an international criminal syndicate that included members of the Chicago mafia, Colombian drug cartels and some of the best-known faces in the British underworld?

With hindsight it seems obvious: the clues were there all along. But, just like the character in *The Truman Show*, I had no way of knowing that everything I was being shown, everyone I met, was in on the big lie. There was no way to know what to believe.

It was then that I started thinking back over my life, about every decision I'd ever made, every person I'd ever met and everything I'd ever done. In the end I came to one inescapable conclusion that was so ridiculous and utterly stupid, I couldn't help but smile. I sat huddled on the bed, giggling and sobbing myself to sleep with one thought on my mind: all this trouble, I decided, could have been avoided if . . . if only I'd kept my top on.

Chapter One

I never wanted to be a model.

I left school at sixteen with a handful of O-levels and vague plans to go to business college at some point in the future, but no clear idea of what I wanted to do with my life.

A series of dead-end receptionist/typist/dogsbody jobs soon taught me that being stuck in an office all day didn't really suit my temperament, so I started looking for some kind of career where I could be my own boss. Nothing felt quite right until one day, out of the blue, the perfect solution seemed to fall into my lap.

I was working for a small marketing company close to my home in Broxbourne, Hertfordshire, when a smartly dressed, slightly chubby middle-aged man with round spectacles, a scruffy beard and a large canvas bag turned up early for a meeting with one of the executives. While he was waiting in reception, I noticed that he was staring at me intently.

'Can I help you?'

He grinned, stood up and walked over, perching his flabby bottom on the corner of my desk. 'Actually, love, the question is whether or not I can help *you*. I know this is going to sound like the oldest chat up line in the book, but have you ever thought about becoming a model?'

I'd never blushed so quickly in my life. Then I let out one of those stupid girly giggles – I just couldn't help it. 'What, me? Are you serious?'

'Dead serious, love. I'm a professional photographer,' he said, tapping his canvas bag with two fingers, 'and I'm absolutely certain that if you let me do some test shots, I could get you work all over the place. My name's Nigel, what's yours?'

As I reached out to shake his hand alarm bells were ringing in my seventeen-year-old brain. It was all too good to be true. 'Nigel. Look, listen, I don't mean to be rude but . . .' Nigel's shoulders slumped. He looked like someone had let all the air out of him. He started shaking his head and held his hand up to interrupt me.

'Tracy, you don't need to say another word. I know what you're thinking, and I've heard all those stories too. Believe you me, those few bad apples in the industry make life for us professional photographers so much harder. You're right to be concerned but let me assure you there's absolutely nothing to worry about.' He reached into the bag and pulled out a black plastic folder full of pages from glossy magazines and catalogues. There were a few covers, lots of close ups of hands and nails and a few fashion spreads for teen magazines, showing skinny girls with big hair in a variety of glamorous outfits. 'This is the kind of thing I do and let me tell you there's good money in it. I can give you references from people I've worked with – top models all over the world. Ask your boss, he's seen my work. Here, let me give you a card . . . oh, damn, I've run out. Tell you what, let me write my number down for you. Give me a call and we'll set something up.'

Nigel was true to his word. The pictures were fabulous and within a week I had my first professional engagement and was well on the way to my debut Page Three appearance . . .

At least that's the way I'd like to remember it. The reality, sadly, was a little less fanciful.

I spent a couple of days checking Nigel out and he seemed genuine enough so I agreed to meet with him. He picked me up from work a week later and was full of apologies as he explained that the studio he had booked had been flooded when the pipes in the building above had burst. Not to worry though, he said, he had cleared some space in his flat and we could do the shoot there.

He lived in a split-level Victorian conversion on the outskirts of Waltham Cross. His flat was clean, tidy and nicely decorated and had absolutely everything you'd expect to find in the home of a professional photographer – except for any sign of cameras, lights or photographic equipment. He saw me looking around suspiciously and answered my question before I had a chance to ask it. 'All the gear's set up in the spare room,' he said. 'But I don't want to rush you into anything, let's get you relaxed first. If you're too tense it will ruin the pictures, the muscle tone will be all wrong.'

'Relaxing' me meant trying to pour as much wine down my throat as he could in the shortest possible time. When I refused to do anything more than sip at my glass, he finally lost patience and pounced, lunging at me and trying to force his tongue down my throat while clamping me in the corner of the sofa with his big belly. I'd made sure I'd kept my wits about me and managed to squeeze myself out of the way, his pouting bearded lips crashing harmlessly into the seat cushion as I jumped up, dashed into his bathroom and bolted the door behind me.

For the next two hours he tried everything he could to get me to come out. He played it nasty – 'What the fuck do you think you're playing at you stupid cow, get out of there right now before I break the door down' – and when that failed he played it nice: 'I'm sorry, darling, I was well out of order back there. It's all my fault, I was being stupid. Please come out, I'll behave myself, I promise.' And then back to nasty again: 'Don't play the innocent with me. You know what you've come here for. If you want to get on in this business you've got to play the game. You scratch my back and I scratch yours. I'm telling you, that's the way it works.'

I finally unlocked the door when I realised that I couldn't stay in his bathroom for ever and that my mum – the only person I'd told about going to have my pictures done – would be getting worried. I waited until 'nice' Nigel was back in charge, made him drive me to the nearest station and breathed a massive sigh of relief as I sped homeward. If that's the world of modelling, I thought, then there's no way I want to have any part of it.

I'd never really believed I had much potential as a model but I was still disappointed at the way things had turned out as, for a few brief moments after Nigel had approached me, I'd thought I'd found a way to escape the nine-to-five. My life was going nowhere and I'd quit or been sacked so many times that my CV was starting to look like a bad joke.

* * *

My career troubles had all started soon after I got out of school and began working in a small shop selling clothes for teenage girls. The owner was a tight-fisted old git who paid me just £20 a week, even though I was working there full-time. When my younger sister, Sarah, started looking for a Saturday job he agreed to take her on too, paying her £6 for the one day. That meant that, pro rata, she was earning more than me. I remember talking about it with my dad who said I should stand up for myself, not let anyone get one over on me.

The next day I summoned all my courage and confronted my boss, demanding a pay rise. He scratched his chin for a few moments, mulling it over, and then said he reckoned he could afford to give me an extra £6 per week.

Then he sacked my sister.

I resigned in protest and tried my hand at the corporate world, taking a job with a well-known recruitment company. I quite liked the work but my boss was a horrible woman who delighted in treating me like dirt, humiliating me in front of anyone who happened to be around. I put up with it for six months before I finally snapped.

She was in the middle of a high-powered meeting and buzzed me on the intercom, ordering me to bring her a cup of coffee. I dropped everything and made one as quickly as possible but when I got into the room she started shouting at me. 'What the hell do you think you're playing at? Why have you made it in this cup? You know full well that I don't have my coffee in this cup, I have it in my special mug. I want it in my mug.

Go and do it again and for God's sake get it right this time!'

I walked out of the conference room, fuming. She had gone out of her way to embarrass me in front of everyone, so it seemed only fair that I should have the chance to do the same. With a fresh mug of scalding hot coffee in my hands I returned to the conference room, walked over to where she was sitting, emptied the coffee into her lap and smashed her precious mug to pieces on the table in front of her. 'There's your fucking coffee and there's your fucking mug. I'll be leaving now.'

A few other jobs came and went after similar, if somewhat less dramatic, confrontations with co-workers, but for the most part things failed to work out because, while I could put on a front, I didn't really have much self-confidence. That meant I was useless at dealing with customers and clients, either on the phone or in person.

A few weeks after the Nigel incident I was in a wine bar with a gang of friends when I noticed this drop dead gorgeous guy at the other end of the bar. Tall and muscular with really good legs, a nice tight bum and lovely dark wavy hair he was just my type. By the time my eyes returned to his face, he was looking at me too. I was really embarrassed at being caught checking him out so blatantly but then he smiled sweetly and I felt butterflies fluttering in the pit of my stomach. I spent the next ten minutes praying for him to come over and talk to me, and just when I was ready to give up, he finally did.

'Hello, I'm Gus.'

'Hi, I'm Tracy.'

'Sorry to bother you, I just wanted to ask . . . have you ever thought about being a model?'

He almost blew it there and then but luckily I soon realised that Gus wasn't offering to take my pictures or anything like that; he just genuinely thought I had what it takes to do that kind of work. We chatted for the rest of the evening and got on like a house on fire. He called me a couple of days later to ask me out on the first of a string of wonderful dates. It was all picture-book perfect; at a time when my self-confidence was at an all-time low, Gus made me feel incredibly special. After only a few weeks, I knew I was falling in love with him.

Six months earlier I had split up with a guy called Finn, my first real boyfriend, who I'd been going out with for a couple of years. He'd started out treating me well but towards the end turned into a violent, obsessive bully who made my life an absolute misery. Gus was the complete opposite. He didn't have a bad bone in his body and everyone that met him liked him enormously. My parents had not been very keen on Finn but welcomed Gus in the family home with open arms.

During the day Gus had a job in the print business, but his real passion was football. He had masses of talent and had been signed up by the local semi-professional team. I loved going to watch him play – he looked great in shorts – and before too long we were spending virtually all of our spare time together.

Almost every time I saw him, Gus would tell me I should try my hand at modelling. I'd told him all about my experience with Nigel and he understood my reservations, but he also knew that at the back of my mind I'd always regretted not giving it another chance.

A few weeks before my twentieth birthday and just after our first anniversary, Gus took me out for a romantic candlelit dinner and asked me to marry him. I said yes immediately: there was no doubt in my mind that this was the man I was going to spend the rest of my life with. And now we were going to stand up in front of all our friends and family and make it official.

We decided to wait at least a year before even setting a date. We were both dead keen to become Mr and Mrs, but there was no sense in rushing it. I was still living at home and if we were going to get a place together I needed to find a job I could hold down for longer than three months in a row. Gus also had his ambitions – he was keen to move up a league and play football full time. I wanted the wedding and our life afterwards to be as perfect as everything had been up until then, so it made sense to wait a little.

But big changes were in the air. Gus damaged his knee while playing and was forced to retire. I knew he was deeply upset, but I couldn't help but admire the way he never seemed bitter about it. As far as he was concerned it was just one of those things.

Then, on Christmas Day, it was my turn to see my life go spinning off in a whole new direction. Gus had spent the day messing about, pretending he'd forgotten to buy me anything. Late in the afternoon he finally handed me a thin package wrapped in coloured paper and told me it was my present.

Intrigued, I tore away the sheets of gift-wrap, revealing a brochure about a course run by the Judi James School of Modelling. I was wide-eyed as I flicked through the pictures of budding catwalk queens being put through their paces, read about the kinds of work the graduates of the course had gone on to do and saw that the curriculum included a session with a professional photographer.

Gus explained that he had booked me in for the class that started in the second week of January. Everything was paid for – all I had to do was turn up. I was stunned, excited, delighted and terrified all at the same time. It was by far the most thoughtful and fantastic present anyone had ever given me. The feelings that I'd had a couple of years earlier – that this might be exactly the career I was looking for – came flooding back with a vengeance.

I pictured myself travelling around the world, dressed head to toe in the latest Gucci, striking weird and wonderful poses across the pages of glossy magazines. I imagined myself refusing to get out of bed for less than £10,000 and smiled gleefully at the thought that, in the very near future, the only office I would ever have to step inside would be the one belonging to my agent.

The course took place in a small studio in Chelsea. Within minutes Judi, a tall, strikingly beautiful former model who oozed confidence and sophistication from every pore, shattered each and every one of the illusions that I and the other nine students had been fantasising about. As we sat in a semi-circle around her, she left us in no doubt about the phenomenal amount of work that lay ahead.

'It may look like the easiest job in the world, but becoming a professional model is every bit as difficult and as challenging as becoming a professional actress, dancer or athlete,' Judi explained. 'No matter how good you look or how well you prepare or how many castings you attend, there is no guarantee that any of you in this room will ever find work.'

She left a pause, allowing the cold facts to sink in, and then continued: 'The reason it is so difficult is very simple. Out there in the world of fashion modelling, supply vastly exceeds demand. Everyone wants to be a model but everyone wants to hire the models who are already famous and doing all high-profile shoots. But unless you do a high profile shoot, you'll never get any work. It's a classic Catch-22.'

Over the next five days, through a mixture of lectures and practical workshops, Judi did her best to ensure that our chances were better than most. We learned about body movement and make up techniques; we learned the right and the wrong way to walk along a catwalk; how to exude attitude, charm and sophistication from every pore so that you make the clothes you are wearing look the way the designer wants.

We worked on poise and posture, speaking in public and how to master the audition process. We learned that for cover girls the most important quality was to have naturally clear skin – when you're photographed that close every imperfection shines through and no amount of make-up can help – and spent hours going over tips and techniques to keep spots at bay.

There were also lessons about the seedier side of the industry and how to cope with it. There was advice from Judi on how to deal with men who approach you in the street and offer you a part in their latest film ('Knee them in the crotch'); what to do about 'professional' photographers who expect sexual favours as part and parcel of every shoot ('Knee them in the crotch'); and how to handle newspaper reporters who try to get you to talk about your private life ('Refer them to your agent and, if that doesn't work, knee them in the crotch').

There were plenty of opportunities to dress up and try out various looks and poses in front of the camera, including a full fashion show. I loved every minute of it and by the end of the week I knew I'd found the thing I had been looking for.

Judi had great connections and arranged for a few of the more promising students to get our first paid work as part of a spread for the teen magazine *Jackie*. I still have the picture in one of my scrapbooks, and it makes me cringe every time I see it. I look like someone sacked from the original line up of Bananarama for being too much of a plonker. I try to console myself with the thought that it was the mid-eighties and that when you look back, all the fashions seem kind of strange. Then I remember that even back when the picture was taken, it was still pretty uncool.

What was important, though, was the £50 I got paid for the session. From that moment onwards I was officially a professional model. I quit my job as a clerk with a Japanese bank and set my sights on the catwalks.

Gus and I went out to dinner to celebrate my new career. I spent the whole time telling him about the course and how fantastic it was, going through every detail. By rights he should have been bored rigid but when it came to modelling Gus seemed to get every bit as excited as I did. It was only when he dropped me home that he started looking a little sad.

'What's up?'

'Nothing. I'm just thinking how great it is that you liked my present so much.'

'It's been fantastic, Gus, the best present ever, but something's on your mind. Tell me.'

'It's daft really . . . I just can't help thinking that now you're going to become this really famous model and end up running off with a millionaire. I feel like I'm that bloke who was the fifth Beatle: you're going to dump me as soon as you get famous.'

'Oh Gus, don't be silly,' I said, reassuring him with hugs and kisses. 'I'd never do anything like that. I love you, and we're getting married.'

My ultimate destination may have been Milan, possibly via Paris and New York, but, like so many aspiring catwalk queens before me, I'd have to start by treading the boards at Morecambe Bay, possibly via Salford, Great Yarmouth and a dozen other provincial towns.

The first port of call for many future models is the beauty-pageant circuit. Competitions are held across the country virtually every week of the year and range from the glitzy and prestigious to the weird and downright sleazy. There are so many different competitions it boggles the mind. If you take the name of any county council, any obscure weekly seaside newspaper, car-cleaning product or holiday company and add the word 'Miss' to the start of it, then the chances are pretty high that the competition actually exists.

On top of that there are also countless regional heats for the Miss United Kingdom competition which belong in a class all their own. For some bizarre reason, you don't actually have to live in Norwich to enter Miss Norwich or in Peterborough to enter Miss Peterborough, and so on. It means that the most determined girls end up travelling around the country from town to town, entering heat after heat in the hope of getting through to the next stage.

All the shows follow the same basic format. They start with some kind of cabaret or variety act and then the main host appears and tells a few lame jokes. Then it's time for the contestants, grinning like deranged Cheshire cats, to make their first appearance, either in swimsuits or evening gowns, first one by one and then all together in one long line. We smile big and wide until the muscles in our faces start to ache while the host says something like, 'They're all winners tonight, ladies and gentlemen, let's give them a big hand,' then we head off backstage.

There's another cabaret act and more lame jokes while we get changed and then line up to go on stage again. This time the host asks a few naff questions – 'What are your hobbies? What do you do for a living? What is your beauty routine? What animal are you most like?' – that kind of thing. Then there's a final cabaret while the judges make up their minds.

In keeping with tradition, the results are always announced in reverse order and, no matter who takes first place, we all keep smiling, clap, cheer and hug the winner before she steps forward to receive her crown. After all, it's not the winning that counts, it's the taking part. At least, that's how it looks from a distance.

In reality, with so many of the same girls entering all the competitions, it doesn't take long before you get to know people. And I have to say that if there is a group of bitchier, more two faced, arrogant and downright nasty women anywhere in the world, then I have yet to meet them.

At modelling school we were all in the same boat. None of us had any previous experience and we all shared the same dream so instead of rivalry we went out of our way to help one another as we struggled to learn the ropes. Out in the real world it's every girl for herself and backstage at a beauty pageant is a cross between a war zone and a mental hospital.

A typical exchange between a group of girls passing one another in a corridor would go something like this:

GIRL 1: Darling, Emma, how are you? (Kisses Emma on both cheeks.)

GIRL 2: Mandy, hi, great to see you. What a surprise. Wow, that's a lovely dress, very nice.

GIRL 3: Oh it's gorgeous, the colour really suits you.

GIRL 1: Really? You think so? Ahh, thanks. Well look, must dash. See you on stage. Best of luck.

GIRL 2: Bye, love you, bye.

GIRL 3: Bye, love you.

GIRL 1 walks into the distance.

GIRL 2: Fucking bitch, who does she think she is? Have you seen the size of her thighs?

GIRL 3: Christ, only a cow could love calves like that. And what about that make up? I'll tell you what, you could scratch your name in her forehead and not draw blood, that's how thick the foundation is.

GIRL 2: Gave the judge a blow-job in Plymouth, y'know, that's how she got into the finals.

GIRL 3: Slag. My granny's got that exact same dress. Doesn't suit her either.

And so on.

It doesn't always end with harsh words: some girls are so keen to win they will stop at nothing. There are stories of rivals hiding each other's shoes or evening gowns or 'accidentally' bumping into someone's leg backstage so that the victim walks with a limp during the evening wear section and has a nice big bruise developing when it comes to the swimsuit round. The real professionals also try to play mind games. They snigger and whisper to one another as you're putting on your make up or fixing your hair. It can really eat into your self-esteem and I've seen girls burst into tears, convinced they were about to make fools of themselves.

Before the show starts the dressing rooms are full of hissing catfights, girls having crises over spots and cellulite, bouts of fat anxiety and bad hair days. In the aftermath there is always lots of sobbing, swearing, stamping and stomping around. This is when the claws come out and the true colours start to show because no one has to pretend any more. If the winner is blonde then all the brunettes will claim the judges were biased, and vice versa.

The reason people get so emotional is nothing to do with winning the titles themselves – no one really cares about those – it's the fact that any winner is virtually guaranteed a small amount of promotional work and, when you're starting off, the more stuff you have in your portfolio, the more chance you have of getting other work.

The very first competition I entered was Miss Nine To Five, organised by the free magazine of the same name. I managed to get through to the final twelve and got my picture in the magazine standing alongside motorcycle stuntman Eddie Kidd. I was chuffed and Gus was enormously proud. After that I entered dozens of the Miss UK heats and was runner-up in Norwich and a couple of other places, but never managed to go all the way. I think it was because, while some of the girls used to take the whole thing incredibly seriously, I couldn't help but play it for laughs. When it came to talking with the host I'd make a load of silly innuendoes and instead of wishing for world peace or expressing a desire to help underprivileged children, my ambition would always be to meet Bruce Springsteen or win the pools.

Because I'd given up work to concentrate on modelling, I became increasingly reliant on Gus. He would drive me around the country to the various competitions and cheer like crazy whenever I appeared on stage. It might sound odd, but without Gus I would never have had the bottle to go out there in the first place. There were plenty of times when I would stand in front of a mirror, think I looked like a complete dog and wonder why I was trying to be a model when I would have been better off running around barking and peeing up lampposts. I used to look at the other girls in the competitions, at their hair and skin and bodies, and think that I didn't stand a chance against them. It was only really the fact that Gus was so convinced that I was just as pretty as they were and that I was going to make it that drove me on. His confidence in me made me confident in myself.

And confidence is something you need in abundance if you want to be a model. In between pageants I'd pound the streets with my portfolio, making endless rounds of 'go-sees', where you literally go and see photographers, picture editors, fashion companies and the like so they can bear you in mind for their next project.

I'd also attend dozens of castings, an ordeal which always seemed to involve spending half a day queuing up outside some dingy old studio so that a photographer could spend thirty seconds taking a Polaroid of you and adding it to a pile of hundreds of others. The chances of actually being picked out to do the job or called back from a 'go-see' were always minimal, but you had no choice but to do the rounds.

I soon learned that starting out as a model is all about rejection. You get rejected so many times that you lose count, and sooner or later you can't help but question whether there is something wrong with you. You might think that you're OK-looking, but when you get into a room and there are twenty girls who are all taller, slimmer and prettier than you could ever be, it's quite humbling.

Whenever I failed to get a job I'd try not to take it personally, but there were some girls who had been rejected time and time again and really let it get to them. They'd start to believe they were ugly or fat. Some of them had put everything into the idea of becoming a model and it was heartbreaking to see the effect it was having on them.

Whenever I did have doubts, Gus was there to crush them. He never complained about the hours I spent sewing sequins on to my evening gowns, the weekends I spent shopping for new outfits or the times I went on panic diets and lived on nothing but coffee and cigarettes for days at a time.

My first big break came when Gus and I took a cheap but cheerful break at a Pontins holiday camp and I entered their two in-house pageants, Miss Pontins and Miss Glamorous Legs. Although it sounds a bit naff, the Pontins competitions are actually quite a big deal. The company holds heats every week of the year at each of its camps around the country and the winners of each heat go forward to a big annual competition. It attracts a lot of semi-professional models and I recognised several of the contestants from castings and other pageants.

To my complete and utter amazement I won the weekly heats for both contests. I was so gobsmacked I had to sit down.

When it came to the finals for Miss Pontins I expected to be knocked out at an early stage but for some reason kept getting through to the next round. I found myself among the finalists and listened intently as the host read out the names of the girls who had placed third and second. Having been used to being runner up I assumed, when my name was not read out, that it was all over and that I hadn't got anywhere. Then he called out my name and said that I'd won.

My legs were so wobbly that I could barely walk and mascara was running down my face as the tears came flooding out. Gus was standing up, cheering and clapping as loudly as he could. I could not believe it. I might just as well have won Miss World. I was so happy.

A week later I was back at Pontins for the finals of

the Miss Glamorous Legs competition. A few girls from the circuit were in the dressing room, puffing away on Marlboro Lights, and I made the fatal mistake of greeting them with a cheery hello. A thin-faced blonde with hazel eyes and cherry lips spoke for all of them.

'Tracy isn't it? You look really brown – that's quite a tan you've got.'

'Oh, thanks . . .'

'Fake, I take it.'

'What! I . . .'

'So tell us then. Who are you sleeping with?'

'I beg your pardon?'

'Which one of the judges are you sleeping with?'

'How dare you!'

'Oh come on, you've already won one of the Pontins titles. I don't see what right you have to be here; you're obviously sleeping with someone important. I'm going to complain.'

It wasn't true, of course, but I'm sure their suspicions were only confirmed when later that evening I was crowned Miss Glamorous Legs. This time a group of friends had come along with Gus to support me and as the result was announced they all started diving across their tables, shouting and screaming out my name. I'd never been so happy. I cried buckets.

In the history of Pontins no one had ever won both titles before and my picture appeared in dozens of local newspapers, alongside little stories about my 'historic double victory'. The prizes included a big wad of cash and an all expenses paid week's holiday for two on the beach in Morocco. I took Gus, of course, and it was the best holiday I'd ever had.

I got back from the trip to find dozens of messages waiting for me with offers of all kinds of work. For the next few weeks I draped myself across cars, motorbikes and speedboats while wearing stilettos, a swimsuit and little else. It was nice to be working and earning some money, but I was still only scraping by. My real dream was to be up there on the catwalks.

My portfolio was now impressive enough to get me appointments with top fashion photographers and agencies but everywhere I went I heard the same thing: I was too short and curvy for fashion and would be far better off trying my luck in the glamour market.

At the time I thought glamour modelling was all about top shelf magazines and the kind of shots that you could use to teach human biology. It didn't help that a few of the photographers I met would pull hardcore magazines out of their desks, show me the pictures they had taken and ask whether I'd be interested in having a go myself.

More than once I'd be doing a shoot in a bikini or swimsuit and the photographer would be chatting away casually and then suddenly say: 'Why don't you pull those straps down, love, or take it off altogether?' to which I would always reply, 'No thanks, I'm happy with them where they are.'

Although my confidence was growing because of the modelling, I couldn't imagine ever allowing myself to be photographed naked. Ever since I can remember I've always been painfully shy about nudity – I'd wear a swimming costume in the bath if I could. More than anything I hated the idea of complete strangers knowing what I looked like with no clothes on. The most I had ever done was go topless a couple of times while on holiday with Gus in Spain, but even then I was in a panic the whole time. Some of the girls on the beach were straight out of *Baywatch*, running around and playing volleyball, tits swinging this way and that, without so much as a care in the world. I could never be like that. Once I'd worked up the courage to bare all I'd simply lie on my back, not moving a muscle, hoping that no one would notice me.

Even when I learned that glamour modelling meant only topless, nothing more, it still wasn't for me. I decided to stick to my guns: it was fashion or nothing.

After six months of nothing I figured it was time to review my position. During that time my mum had sent off some snaps and entered me in the *Mirror*'s Dream Girl competition, aimed at finding new modelling talent, and I was thrilled when the paper called me up and asked me to go in for a shoot.

For the first time I was pampered by a professional team of stylists, hairdressers and make-up artists. It was wonderful, a world away from everything I'd done before where I had always had to do my own styling; the shoot itself, during which I crawled around on my hands and knees wearing a one-piece swimsuit and a confused expression, was great fun. I saw a few of the Polaroids and was really pleased with the results. They obviously knew what they were doing.

During the course of the day not just the photographer but the whole team suggested, one after another, that I try out for Page Three and because I respected their opinions I knew I had some serious thinking to do.

I was now twenty-one, close to the upper age limit for new models, and getting nowhere fast as far as the catwalks were concerned. I could give it all up, but that would mean the previous year had been a waste. Besides, what would I do? I'd tried the nine-to-five work thing and that hadn't been much of a success either. I decided that the least I could do would be try the glamour market and if that didn't work out, then at least I would have exhausted all the possibilities.

But first I had some hurdles to get over. My family had always been hugely supportive of my modelling ambitions but moving into the glamour market was something different. I knew Gus wouldn't have a problem with it but I was worried about what my parents, brother and sisters would say. I sat them all down one afternoon, explained the situation and told them of my decision. My dad got up and walked out of the room.

I was mortified but later that evening he came to see me and told me he had needed some time on his own. I had always been his little princess and he didn't like the idea of the blokes he worked with saying, 'Phwoar, look at the tits on that.' He said that if I was sure that it was what I wanted to do, he wouldn't stop me.

Before I took things any further I wanted to be sure I wasn't going to make a fool of myself. I started collecting old Page Three pictures and spent hours standing in front of the mirror with my top off, trying out different poses and getting Gus to take pictures of me so I could see what worked and what didn't.

Once I felt I could be comfortable, I knew I needed

to get an agent. Yvonne Paul, a former Benny Hill girl, ran the most successful glamour agency in the country, representing the likes of Maria Whittaker, Samantha Fox and just about every other top Page Three girl around. I went to see her, hoping she might take me on.

A tall and stunningly beautiful secretary showed me into Yvonne's spacious office and I made for the nearest chair. 'Don't sit there,' Yvonne said. 'That belongs to the cats. You'll get covered in hair.' It was only then that I noticed about a dozen fluffy cats roaming around the office, purring gently. It made me warm to her instantly.

I sat quietly in the only other chair while Yvonne looked through my portfolio. Once she'd finished she asked me how I felt about Page Three work. I told her I was keen to do it, it was the main thing I was aiming for.

'The thing is, Tracy, I'm not interested in someone who just wants to do Page Three. There are dozens of girls who could do Page Three but I take on girls who can do much more. It's not just about how you look. My girls get work in all kinds of areas because they are versatile. Are you versatile?'

I nodded sheepishly, all the time hoping to God that she wasn't talking about pornography.

'There are loads of pretty models out there and girls with nice figures, but to stand out you need a big smile and a chatty personality, otherwise you'll never get on.' So, for the next twenty minutes, we chatted and I did my best to impress her with my witty repartee. I can't remember what was said but it seemed to do the trick: Yvonne agreed to put me on her books.

She wasted no time. Within a week or so she had

fixed me up with a test shoot with Beverly Goodway, the photographer responsible for most of the Page Three pictures in the *Sun* since the late seventies and a legendary figure in the world of glamour modelling.

I arrived at the address, pressed the buzzer and heard footsteps in the hallway. The door opened and a silver-haired man with round spectacles appeared.

'Hi. Is Beverly in? I'm here to do some pictures.'

'I'm Beverly, you must be Tracy. Nice to meet you.'

'Oh. Right. Sorry, I thought you were a woman.'

He grinned. 'Everyone thinks that. Come on in. Do you fancy a baked potato? I'm just about to stick one in the microwave.'

The walls of the studio were filled with pictures of all the top Page Three models but there were also shots of Beverly's wife and children. I immediately felt at ease. We spent the next forty-five minutes eating, drinking hot chocolate and chatting about this and that. By the time it came to posing, I felt like I'd known him all my life.

Beverly goes out of his way to make sure his models feel comfortable. Even if you're completely naked he won't stand around staring, he just fiddles with his camera and adjusts the lighting until you are in position and only then will he look up. Beverly has been doing Page Three so long that tits and arse are nothing to him. It's when you put on a pair of shorts or some lingerie that he gets interested. 'Oohh, that's nice, very nice,' he'll say softly. But even then it's so genuine that it comes across as being flattering, never sleazy.

It was Beverly who first taught me the tricks of the

trade. Before we started shooting he asked me to spray some cold water over my tits and then switched on a nearby fan. As every girl knows, boobs look bigger and firmer when they're a bit cold and it also makes your nipples stand out. Some photographers achieve the same effect by switching off all the heating in their studios.

The session lasted a couple of hours during which time I posed in a variety of swimming costumes, bikinis, waistcoats, scarves and jackets. Towards the end Beverly suggested we try a few themed shots. He asked me to put on an American football helmet and hold a ball up in the air. I ended up in some ridiculous positions and felt like a complete idiot, but we were having such a laugh that I went along with it.

The whole thing was a brilliant experience and I enjoyed every minute. Even though I was topless for the first time, I ended up feeling a lot less naked than I had done with some of the photographers I had worked with before.

I didn't rush out and buy the *Sun* the next day – there was no point because I had no idea when the pictures would be used, if at all. I'd posed for the *Mirror*'s Dream Girl contest more than a month earlier and those pictures had yet to appear. It was all out of my hands. Yvonne assured me that it was all going to happen, I just had to be patient.

A few days after seeing Beverly I found myself posing topless again, this time for a photographer called Richard Fitzgerald, who worked for the *Star*, but once again with no guarantee of when or if the pictures would appear. I was starting to make a little bit of money and developing a portfolio full of shots by some of the top photographers around, but my pictures still hadn't been made public. It was hard not to get frustrated.

Then, on 24 November, the *Mirror* published my picture. It was my first time in a national newspaper and I could hardly contain my excitement. The fact that they had used the picture also meant that I was officially in the Dream Girl competition with all kinds of fabulous prizes on offer.

It seemed that everyone I had ever known bought the *Mirror* that day. I got phone calls from people I hadn't seen for years who just wanted to congratulate me. I felt as though at long last I'd made it.

Someone at the *Star* had obviously seen the picture too, because the next day they published one of Richard Fitzgerald's pictures on page 3. It had been completely unexpected – I had no time to prepare for it or warn anyone. I was particularly worried about how my family would react. Even though we had talked about it, the fact that my picture was now actually in the paper made things a bit more real. I was particularly worried that my younger sister might get some stick at school over it.

I got home to find Mum on the phone, telling all her friends. Then Sarah arrived back from school and came bounding over to me with a big smile on her face. She thrust a W.H. Smith bag into my hands. 'This is for you,' she said. 'It's a scrapbook for you to keep all your pictures in. I know you're going to need it because I just know you're going to be in the papers all the time from now on.'

It was all I could do to keep from crying.

When Dad got home he picked up the paper to see for himself. I put my hand over the page, covering up my tits. 'Don't look, Dad, it's embarrassing.' Although he'd given me his blessing I was still worried about what he really thought about me posing topless. 'Tracy,' he said softly, 'you look great.' I rushed over and gave him a big hug.

They say you have to appear in the papers at least three times before you can say you've really made it. Lots of girls make one or two appearances and are never seen again because they're not considered quite right. I was getting anxious about whether I was destined to join their ranks.

Although the *Sun* hadn't published any pictures of me, they seemed quite keen on me. During December and early January I went back to Beverly's studio twice to do more shots. I kept my fingers crossed that it was only a matter of time.

And then, one cold January morning Yvonne called me. 'Tracy, you're in the *Sun*. You're a proper Page Three girl. Congratulations.'

I called Gus and then rushed out to the newsagent's as fast as my legs could carry me. My fingers were trembling as I gripped the pages and opened them up. And there I was, in all my topless glory, with a football helmet on my head, a ball in my hand and a deeply dippy caption.

KICK-OFF BY TRACY

Terrific Tracy Kirby has chosen Superbowl week for her first appearance on Page Three. Tracy, 19, from Hertfordshire, says she loves American Football – so give her a body check before making a pass!

That same afternoon I was on the tube going to see Yvonne when a youngish bloke sitting opposite me started eyeing me up. I was trying to ignore him when I realised with horror that he was reading a copy of the *Sun* and had my picture spread out on his lap. Surely he couldn't recognise me, not with that helmet on? Suddenly I felt that everyone was looking at me. I checked the map above his head. I only had one stop to go and I was praying that I'd make it. And then he spoke.

'Excuse me, please don't take this the wrong way but this picture, is it you?'

My cheeks were so warm they felt red hot. 'No,' I said sharply.

He looked at the picture again. 'It is, isn't it? It's you.'

I didn't know how to handle it. I just felt so embarrassed. I couldn't get over the fact that there I was, on a train, fully dressed and going about my business, yet this complete stranger knew what my tits looked like.

I opened my mouth and tried to speak but a load of gibberish came out. So much for killing off the idea that all models are stupid, I thought. The train got to my stop and I rushed to the door. But it was his stop too and he followed me out on to the platform. Before I could make a run for it he was in front of me, holding the picture up to my nose. 'I don't suppose you'd sign this for me would you? Make it out to Phil.'

I was mortified. Other people were walking past and

trying to see what was going on, wondering who on earth I was to warrant that kind of attention. I finished signing my name and rushed away as quickly as I could. It was only later that I realised I'd just been recognised in public for the first time, and also given my first proper autograph.

From that day on everything happened so quickly it made my head spin. I don't know how they go about making decisions about who is in and who is out, whether it's based on the amount of fan mail they receive or merely the whim of the picture editor, but for whatever reason, the *Sun* decided they liked me loads and started featuring me every couple of weeks.

I made sure I took Gus out as much as I could, to thank him for everything he had done. I know he appreciated the time we spent together. He was chuffed to bits and incredibly proud of my success but concerned that we were seeing less and less of each other. It was mostly because I was getting so busy, but deep down I knew it was also because I was getting more and more uncomfortable with the relationship. I still loved him lots but it had changed into something different over the years. The passion simply wasn't there any more. But Gus had been so supportive and so wonderful, he'd always been there for me when I needed him. I just didn't know what to do.

I'd spent the afternoon doing a shoot for a lingerie catalogue and it was one of those days where everything goes wrong. Light bulbs had blown out, costumes didn't turn up and the snapper was a complete lech.

That evening I went out to a local wine bar in

Broxbourne with a few friends to unwind. We were getting nicely drunk and I was trying to tell them a few funny stories about my day but it was difficult because there was a lot of noise coming from one corner, where a group of blokes were messing about. They were totally off their faces, challenging everyone in the place to arm-wrestles. It was one of those situations where you are trying to ignore the noise but can't because every now and then it erupts and breaks your concentration.

The main noisemaker was strutting around with his shirtsleeves up over his biceps. I gave him a look that told him to try and keep things down a bit. He caught my eye and obviously read it differently. He smiled and gave me a little wink. That really pissed me off. What an arrogant bastard.

I decided to take the bull by the horns. I walked over to his corner of the room and stood in front of him, hands on my hips.

'Reckon you're man enough to take me on, then?'

He gestured to the chair opposite and one of his friends got out of the way to make room. Close up, I saw for the first time how good looking the guy was. He made a silly joke, which made me laugh. In fact it made me laugh a lot and that annoyed me as well.

We started to arm wrestle and straight away I was in trouble. He was well built and incredibly strong and had a grip like a vice. I won, but only because I cheated, bracing my knees against the table. We both collapsed in fits of giggles when he realised what I'd been doing.

'You're that new Page Three girl aren't you? You're Tracy something.'

'Might be, who are you?'

'I'm Geoff. Geoff Knights. Pleased to meet you.'

It didn't take long for me to decide that I'd been a bit too hasty in my original judgement. He seemed like quite a nice guy. After talking to him non-stop for the next hour, I'd decided he was really sweet.

It was all a great laugh and, as far as I was concerned, nothing more than a bit of harmless flirting. When it was time to go Geoff pulled me close and asked if he could see me again. I waved my left hand in his face. 'I told you, I'm seeing someone, I'm engaged.'

'No, don't get the wrong idea, just as friends, that's all I meant, just as friends.'

'Yeah, right. I don't think so.'

I thought that would be the end of it, but Geoff proved remarkably persistent. He managed to get hold of my phone number even though I was ex-directory and began calling every day, then several times a day. I was a bit taken aback at first, but then I relaxed and just took it as a sign that he was really keen. It was almost romantic.

I eventually agreed to have lunch. I was hoping it was just some silly infatuation helped along by the fact that I'd been drunk when we met, but I knew I was kidding myself. He turned up in a bright red Ferrari which, I'm embarrassed to say, impressed the hell out of me. I was only twenty-one whereas Geoff was thirty-three. It was easy for him to sweep me off my feet: he'd become a millionaire through property and an office supplies company he had set up, and liked to use his money to have a good time. And I fancied the pants off him.

There was no way in the world I would ever have

cheated on Gus. He was by far the nicest man I had ever met and I knew he was more than I truly deserved. My entire modelling career was more or less down to him; without his support I would never have made it. But I had fallen out of love with him somewhere along the way. Although I'd been wearing his ring for more than a year, we still hadn't set a date for the wedding and I knew in my heart of hearts that we were never going to get married. I just didn't know how to tell him.

Eventually I sat him down for the hardest speech I have ever had to make. I told him that I loved him, but more as a brother than a boyfriend. I watched the colour drain from his face and the few remaining hopes and dreams about our future together seep out of his heart. We both cried.

I felt terrible but I knew I had to do it. I couldn't fight the attraction I was feeling for Geoff any longer. I was trying to play it cool but I wasn't fooling anyone. On our first date Geoff had handed me a small gift box. I opened it to find a beautiful diamond and emerald necklace inside. I couldn't believe that he'd bought me something so valuable when he hardly knew me but it was clear that he was becoming every bit as besotted as I was.

Gus's worst nightmare had become reality: I had become famous and left him for a millionaire. I tried to give him the ring back but he told me to keep it. His mother called me a few times and shouted at me down the phone. I couldn't blame her. I knew I'd broken his heart and that he would never forgive me.

But I was following my own heart and at the time

there was no doubt in my mind that I was doing the right thing. As Geoff and I started seeing more and more of each other I felt I was having some of the happiest times of my entire life. I was doing the job I had longed for and going out with the man of my dreams. I simply had no way of knowing that my relationship with Geoff Knights would be the beginning of the end.

Chapter Two

In the weeks that followed my debut as a Page Three girl, my picture appeared in the *Sun* more than a dozen times, yet I was still barely managing to scrape a living.

Having been paid £50 for my first professional photo shoot for *Jackie*, I laughed out loud when Yvonne explained that in exchange for baring my breasts to the nation I would be paid the princely sum of just £90. Her commission was 20 per cent, and after putting some aside for tax and paying my travelling expenses there was hardly anything left.

I soon discovered that Page Three was nothing more than a platform from which to launch yourself into the world of glamour modelling. Just as Judi James had explained two years earlier, everyone wants to hire the models who are already well known. And once it becomes clear that you are going to be a regular rather than a one-week wonder, the door to well-paid work suddenly flies open.

It happened almost overnight. After my tenth Page Three appearance I suddenly found myself besieged with offers of calendars, lingerie catalogues, promotional tours and, best of all, personal appearances. Back in the days when glamour models were considered celebrities, nightclubs, wine bars and a host of other venues would happily pay several thousand pounds, and sometimes a good deal more, simply to have a 'Page Three lovely' turn up for the night. It was money for old rope: all you had to do was turn up in a nice frock, smile a lot, pose for a few pictures with the owner and then hang around to collect an envelope stuffed with cash.

The top girls like Samantha Fox and Maria Whittaker could make up to £10,000 a time and would often attend several events each week. I was only on a fraction of those kind of earnings, but it was still more money than I'd ever seen in my life.

By the time I started going out with Geoff I was feeling pretty flush, though I still had a long, long way to go before I was anywhere near as wealthy as he was. My wardrobe was slowly filling up with a variety of the latest designer outfits and I began to develop a passion for shoes and boots that would soon turn into a powerful addiction.

I found it easy to justify the time and money that I spent shopping for clothes because I considered it an essential part of my work. As well as paid appearances, there were endless invites to film premières, celebrity book launches, football testimonials and countless other events where the organisers were keen to have a little glamour on display. Each outing called for a new outfit, but I told myself that the more I got seen the more work I got, so it always seemed to make sense.

But being a party animal wasn't the only way to raise your profile. My agent, Yvonne, had famously managed to get Samantha Fox off Page Three and onto page 1 of the *Sun* early in her career by getting them to run a story about her insuring her breasts for £1 million. The success of the little ploy – Sam's personal appearance fee virtually doubled overnight – meant that, ever since, Yvonne had been on the lookout for any possible opportunity to get stories written about her girls. It was only a matter of time before it was my turn, and Geoff provided the means.

Halfway through our second week together, Geoff told me he was planning to buy a new car and asked if I'd like to go to the showroom to help him choose it. It wasn't exactly my idea of a dream date, but I was every bit as smitten with Geoff as he appeared to be with me so any excuse to spend time together was more than welcome.

We arrived at the local Mercedes dealership and spent an hour or so looking over a few different models until Geoff finally settled on a gorgeous, top-of-the-range 300 SL convertible in bright red. As Geoff filled in the paperwork and handed over dozens of bundles of notes from his briefcase, he asked me what I thought of the car.

I looked across at it lovingly and ran my hands along the immaculate paintwork. 'It's absolutely beautiful, Geoff.'

'I'm glad you like it,' he said, holding up the keys, 'because it's yours.'

'Yeah, right.'

'Really, Tracy. Here, take the keys.'

'What, do you want me to drive it home for you or something?'

'No, it's yours, I bought it for you.'

It was an unreal moment, the sort of thing that happens in films, not in real life. And I hadn't even slept with him yet.

I was telling Yvonne all about it the following day and I could almost see the light-bulb come on above her head, and the pound signs spinning away behind her eyes.

Within a couple of hours she had arranged for a photographer and reporter from the *Sun* to be dispatched to my mum's house to get the inside story on what was soon to be billed as my 'whirlwind fairytale romance with a handsome multi-millionaire'.

It was difficult to take any of it seriously or believe that anyone in the world would be at all interested, but Geoff and I sat there holding hands and exchanging loving glances as we cobbled together a slightly sanitised version of the truth about how we met. I sighed blissfully as I told the reporter how I'd felt when he had handed over the car keys and about our plans for the future. Then we posed for loads of photographs, including one where we both lay across the bonnet of the car, exchanging a tender kiss.

I guess the following Monday must have been something of a slow news day because when I picked up my copy of the *Sun* the picture of Geoff and me kissing was splashed over the front page, with most of Page Three given over to a picture of me topless and more details about my new love.

I'd genuinely expected the story to be a small item tucked away somewhere towards the back, so I was completely shocked and also a little scared. I was more than used to seeing my picture in the paper, but this was different. Instead of a silly caption, here were details of my private life made horribly public. As I went through the words, I felt a twinge of sickness as I saw they had printed Gus's full name. The way the story came across, it made it look as though Geoff and I had been carrying on behind his back and I knew he'd be devastated when he read it.

I wasn't sure I'd done the right thing, but Yvonne was absolutely delighted. And, to give her credit where credit is due, it certainly had the desired effect. My bookings shot through the roof and dozens of magazines, local newspapers and radio programmes wanted to interview me.

For the most part the other Page Three girls were really happy for me, but I was surprised to encounter a fair amount of jealousy. It wasn't the fact that I had been given a brand-new car that rubbed them up the wrong way; it was the amount of publicity I was getting as a result.

I was still a relative newcomer to Page Three, but in the days after the story my public profile was just as high as that of some of the girls who had been appearing there for years.

The novelty quickly wore off though, and by the end of the second week I was really starting to get bored with talking about the whole car thing – it was as if there was nothing else going on in my life – and I soon learned that a few others were getting equally fed up with hearing about it too . . .

I'd been out shopping in the West End of London with Christine Peake, a leading Page Three girl with whom I'd become very friendly. We had done a few shoots together and really hit it off. She was completely mad but in a good way, incredibly funny and really good company. We were due to meet Yvonne a little later for a casting but still had an hour or so to kill, so we decided to visit one more shop and see if any new lines had come in.

We were on the tube, chatting and giggling away about nothing in particular, when I noticed two girls sitting opposite, pointing and whispering.

I was getting used to people staring – it usually meant they were trying to work out where they recognised me from – but this was different: there was something malicious in their manner that made me feel incredibly uneasy. The shorter girl fixed me with a hard stare and spoke:

'Must have been pretty hard for you to have to lower your standards today.'

'I'm sorry?' I replied, genuinely confused.

'You know, getting on the tube with the rest of us riff raff when you've got that flash car to drive about in. What's the matter? Couldn't find a parking meter?'

I could feel Christine beginning to stand up beside me, but the last thing I wanted was any kind of confrontation. 'It's all right, Chris,' I whispered. 'Just leave it. We're getting off in a minute, let's just leave it.'

But the two girls had other ideas. 'She's just ignoring us,' said the taller one. 'I guess she can't bring herself to talk to ordinary people like us, silly stuck-up tart.'

By now I was getting really scared. My heart was racing, butterflies were churning away in my stomach and the carriage was making me start to feel claustrophobic. The insults continued thick and fast until at long last the train arrived at Oxford Circus Station. I was up and waiting by the doors as the train slowed down, Christine by my side, desperate to get back up to street level.

The two girls got up as well. As Christine and I stepped on to the platform, I grabbed her arm to slow her down and let our tormentors get ahead of us. But after only a few steps they turned and started staring at us once again, hands on their hips and cocky grins on their faces. I could see their mouths moving but could no longer hear what they were saying. And then it happened.

One of them rushed towards me, her fingernails stretched out in front of her like claws. She was trying to scratch my face. I screamed and tried to get away but she was already right on top of me. I felt a whoosh of air against my cheek as her hands moved towards my face and managed to turn away at the last second, screaming again as I felt her nails dig into the flesh of my neck.

Then Christine appeared from nowhere and hit the girl square in the face with the best right cross I have ever seen. She followed up with two more sharp jabs and the girl's head whipped back as her nose exploded in a fountain of blood. I could see the shock and terror on their faces as Christine squared up ready for another exchange – then, as quickly as it had started, it was over and they had run off.

I sat on the nearest bench and tried to control my breathing as Christine comforted me. I couldn't believe what had happened, or that two complete strangers could feel so much hatred for me. I dreaded to think what might have happened if Christine hadn't been there with me.

After a few minutes we found a phone and Christine called Yvonne to tell her what had happened. Yvonne wasn't generally known as the most sympathetic person in the world but the crisis seemed to bring out a whole new side of her. She wanted to know if either of us was hurt, whether I had any cuts or bruises – I had some deep scratches down my neck which were starting to weep blood – and whether anything had been stolen. Seemingly satisfied that we were more or less OK, she told us to jump in a cab and make our way straight to her office. She even offered to pay for it. We couldn't help thinking that perhaps we had misjudged the woman.

Yvonne's real motivation became clear as soon as we arrived. Still shaky and almost delirious with shock, I opened the door of her office to find Geoff waiting inside. The second she got off the phone to us she had called him, told him what had happened and asked him to come over to comfort me. But that wasn't the only surprise in store.

'The press will be here in a minute,' she explained cheerfully. 'A couple of photographers and reporters. Oh, and I've called the police as well.'

The following day the story was in virtually every tabloid, complete with pictures of Christine's bruised knuckles, my scratched neck and Geoff looking all concerned and protective.

I was pretty pissed off – the attack left me traumatised for days and the last thing I needed was to be posing for photographs less than an hour after it happened. For a few days I was absolutely furious at Yvonne for pulling a stunt like that, but it *was* difficult to argue with the bottom line. As had happened with the car story, the demand for my services grew and my personal-appearance fee climbed even higher.

It all meant that I couldn't and didn't argue when Yvonne told me that the *Sun* wanted to write a feature about her agency, including a picture of her with a couple of her girls. She explained with a smile that she had chosen me and the girl she knew was my heroine, Maria Whittaker.

Although I got on well with lots of the girls on the glamour circuit, something special happened the day I met Maria. Sitting in Yvonne's office and watching her arrive, I started to feel incredibly nervous and quite intimidated. Ever since Samantha Fox had stepped down from topless modelling, Maria had become the biggest – no pun intended – Page Three girl around. Hugely successful and in constant demand, she had become a role model for me – I wanted to be just like her.

There was also the fact that she had always seemed really lovely whenever I'd seen her interviewed. I guess I really wanted her to be just like that in real life and thought I might end up disappointed.

I needn't have worried. We hit it off immediately and after we had finished with the photo session we went out shopping at Harvey Nichols together. I remember walking down Brompton Road and not being able to travel more than two paces without someone stopping Maria to ask for her autograph. It soon started to get on my nerves but she dealt with it really well and had a smile for everyone.

I think one of the things that drew us together was her sense of loneliness. She was surrounded by hundreds of people who claimed to be her friend but were only hanging around to see what they could get. She had started doing Page Three at sixteen, soon after leaving school, and had been an overnight sensation. It meant that all the friends she had made since she had become an adult had first been drawn to her fame and fortune. She was incredibly generous – if she was in a group she would almost always end up paying for everyone, and she was always buying people presents – which meant it was easy for people to take advantage, and hard for her to tell the genuine friends from the frauds.

Although she was far more famous and far wealthier than I was, she knew I didn't want or expect anything from her. The friendship that developed between us was deep and genuine and within the space of a few weeks we had become virtually inseparable.

As my profile and the amount of work I was doing increased, so did the amount of fan mail that poured through my letterbox. In the first few months I had been thrilled to receive around twenty letters each week – I couldn't believe so many people had taken the time and trouble to write to me. That all changed in the weeks after the stories about the car and the fight when, thanks to dozens more appearances on Page Three, I found myself receiving between three and four hundred letters each week.

Most of it was lovely: there were letters from teenage girls asking for advice on how they could become glamour models and asking questions about skin and hair routines. I always used to try and take the time to reply to letters like that, though as the amount of mail started to increase, it became more and more difficult.

I'd also get letters from women accusing me of stealing their boyfriends or husbands. These were people

who lived hundreds of miles away whom I had never
met in my life but, because their partner had said I was
their favourite Page Three girl, I would suddenly become
the other woman. Some of them seemed to genuinely
believe that I was responsible for the problems they were
having. Time and time again they would write and beg
me to tell their partners that I wasn't interested so they
could start rebuilding their relationships.

I'd also get letters from guys who sounded quite sweet,
even a little shy, and in the early days I often made the
mistake of taking the time to write back to them. In
their perverted minds that would be the green light they
had been waiting for and from that moment on, we
would be in a relationship. A couple of letters down the
line I would inevitably receive a picture of them, almost
always naked and sporting a great big (or not so big)
hard-on. One such picture came with a scrawled note
reading: 'This is me ready and waiting for you. How can
you resist? This is my number, call me up and we'll meet
and have mad passionate sex. You'll never have a fuck
like it.'

I'd put letters like that straight in the bin, but that
would just make things worse. The following week I'd
get another from the same guy but this time full of
insults: 'You nasty bitch, how dare you not reply to my
last letter? Who do you think you are . . .'

Occasionally I'd get it in person too. Sometimes I
would be out in a club and someone would come up
and start chatting away to me and then, after a while,
they'd start getting nasty and suggestive, assuming they
could get away with it. I'd always be happy to have a
laugh and a joke with anyone but once they crossed

that line and things became dark and sinister, I'd have to make my excuses and get out of there as soon as possible.

But for every bad experience there was always one that was so ridiculous it would put a smile on my face for weeks. Like the time Maria and I were at a nightclub and a couple of drunken rugby types appeared and asked for our autographs. The first lad unhooked his belt, dropped his trousers, turned around and mooned at me. "Ere Tracy,' he slurred. 'Sign that, will you? Make it out to Matthew.'

When I obliged, his friend decided to go one better. He too dropped his trousers, whipped out his cock and presented it to me. 'Now sign that.'

Perhaps it was a bit cold in the club, or perhaps the excessive amount of alcohol he had consumed was having some effect. Whatever the reason, his todger was no bigger than a cocktail sausage. I almost felt embarrassed for him. Almost.

'The thing is, love,' I said softly, 'unless your name's Ian or something shorter, I ain't gonna be able to do it. And there's no room for my name at all. Shall I just do my initials?'

In order to escape from the constant attention and the day-to-day pressures, not to mention the offers to sign body parts, I found myself spending more and more time at Geoff's house in Hoddesdon. Our relationship had gone from strength to strength and I remember wishing with all my heart that those blissful times would never end.

Geoff had loads of amazing qualities but I remember being particularly impressed the first time I visited his house at just how tidy he was. There wasn't so much as a fork out of place. It was almost spooky. I soon found out his secret – he had a delightful lady, Barbara, who would go round a few times a week and do all his cleaning, washing up and laundry – but even that didn't tarnish his halo in my eyes.

Geoff was a perfect gentleman, incredibly bright and with a brilliant sense of humour. He liked having a good time and living life to the full, a philosophy which suited me down to the ground. He got friendly with Maria's boyfriend, Jason, and the four of us became a regular feature of the party circuit. Spending nights on the town with my best friend and the man I adored, all the while doing a job I loved, it was difficult to know how life could possibly get any better.

Then, three months into our relationship, Geoff asked me to move in with him. There was no hesitation, I said yes straight away. I was spending more and more time there anyway and I couldn't wait to move my relationship with Geoff on to the next phase.

Geoff had a new phase in mind too. On the day I moved in, after I brought the last of my things into the house and collapsed on the sofa, something immediately struck me as being different about the place. It took a few seconds but then I realised there was washing-up in the sink and a pile of dirty clothes in the corner of the living room.

'What's happened to Barbara? Is she sick or something?'

Geoff didn't miss a beat. 'Oh, I've sacked her. I don't need her any more. I've got you now.'

For some reason – probably being so young and so

madly in love – I didn't object and instead threw myself wholeheartedly into the challenge of being the woman about the house. Having lived at home all my life with parents who happily did everything for me, I quickly realised that the workings of the modern kitchen were something of a mystery. By the time I swallowed my pride and called my mum for help, all of Geoff's white shirts had turned pink and most of his jumpers and jeans had shrunk by two sizes or more.

Cooking was an even bigger challenge. In the end I perfected a method which all but guaranteed good results – I would call my mum and get her to talk me through every stage of whatever it was, from boiling an egg to roasting a chicken, and if I came unstuck, I'd get her to come round and do it for me.

I soon came to love my new-found domestic duties and found that setting up home with Geoff had given my life some much-needed stability, a welcome contrast to the break-neck pace of our social life. During a typical week there would be at least two or three parties to attend, and I'd always try to spend at least one night going out locally so I could stay in touch with all my old friends.

Every other Saturday I'd head down to Tottenham Hotspur Football Club, where I had been appointed mascot soon after my Page Three debut. It was always enormous fun: I'd emerge from the tunnel in my special home kit with extra short shorts to the sight and sound of ten thousand fans screaming my name. I'd run into the middle of the pitch and they'd call out for me to give them a wave. When I did they would get a little more risqué, shouting, 'Tracy, Tracy, show us your tits!' I loved teasing them, lifting up my top to expose my tummy then pulling it down again. At first I used to wind up the opposing team but occasionally that would lead to fights breaking out on the terraces so I quickly dropped that part of my routine.

Most Saturday nights I'd end up clubbing with Maria and the rest of the gang at Stringfellows, Tramp, the Wag or wherever the best buzz could be found. Making the most of my minor-celebrity status, I was spending more and more time with soap-opera actors, top athletes, film stars and singers – and loving every minute of it.

Geoff loved it too and got a real buzz from being part of such an élite crowd. The one thing he didn't like was the actual work, my going out and having my photograph taken, especially if I was topless. I think he was convinced that every trip abroad was just an excuse for a massive orgy and that all the models were spending every spare moment of their days giving the photographer blow-jobs.

As I got busier and had to go abroad more often, we had more and more arguments about it. After the first newspaper stories hit the streets, it quickly got to the stage where I was going away, to Spain or Germany or some other part of Europe, for a couple of days every single week. And Geoff's suspicions about what was really going on grew to the point that he could no longer control himself.

I was out in Ibiza shooting a swimwear calendar with a girl called Colette and a delightful photographer called Colin. After two days posing in the sea and under cliffs along the beach, we had pretty much all the shots we needed and decided to take the following day off. The three of us had a late dinner at a fantastic restaurant and then made our way back to the villa where we were staying. We each had a separate bedroom but mine was the biggest and had a beautiful terrace overlooking the sea, so we decided to have a nightcap there. Colin had picked up a bottle of champagne on the way and, with three glasses in his hand, led the way.

I was just behind him when I heard a familiar voice. 'What the fuck is going on here?'

It was Geoff. Without telling me he had flown out to Ibiza, tracked down the complex where we were staying, looked into the bedroom of each villa until he sa stuff that he recognised as mine and then broken in t surprise me. When Colin had walked in with the drinks he had immediately jumped to the wrong conclusion.

The two of them started having a furious argument which almost came to blows. I was beside myself with anger, pulled Geoff to one side and started having a go at him myself. I told him that he shouldn't be there, that he couldn't just turn up where and when he wanted and that, most importantly, I was working.

Geoff's outburst almost cost me the job. Colin was all for telling the client what had happened and getting me replaced with another model, but after begging him all night, I managed to persuade him to keep quiet.

Geoff's suspicions that the three of us were planning some kind of drunken threesome couldn't have been further from the truth. Colin was as gay as it is possible for a man to be and wouldn't have been interested in a million years. In fact I think he quite fancied Geoff.

I would never have cheated on Geoff anyway, and it cut me to the quick that he didn't trust me. But at the time I didn't see it as a sign of his extreme jealousy.

Once I knew the photographer wasn't going to tell the client, I wasn't even that concerned about it. Through the rose-tinted glasses I wore whenever Geoff was around, I just saw it as a sign that he really, really loved me.

From that day on the fear that Geoff might turn up on one of my trips abroad became a constant companion. But the proliferation of drugs throughout the world of glamour modelling was a far greater concern.

One particular girl was known to have developed an extremely heavy cocaine habit and openly credited the drug with helping her stay slim. She was certainly skinny – a lot of models refused to be pictured alongside her because it made them look fat – but she also suffered from violent mood swings and quickly gained a reputation for being difficult to work with. I would be filled with dread every time I turned up at a shoot to find she was there. One minute she was as nice as pie but then the slightest thing could send her stomping off around the studio, swearing and ranting like a lunatic. She'd become totally paranoid, convinced that everyone around her was conspiring against her or planning to call in the police and have her arrested. She stood out in the early days because she was the only girl known to be doing it. But as the eighties went by the only girls that stood out were the ones who refused.

A blizzard of cocaine was sweeping into London's clubland and beyond. Suddenly every after-shoot party, particularly on trips abroad, seemed to centre round a table piled high with powder and a variety of pills. The pressure to take part was enormous: if you weren't seen to be part of the in-crowd, you were considered to be the enemy. Unless you were willing to take the same risks as everyone else, then it was impossible for them to trust you.

I'd learned the hard way that it simply wasn't my scene. The one and only time I gave in to the peer pressure I felt as though my head had been ripped apart and spent the rest of the evening in the toilets throwing up. It left me terrified and after that experience I'd always try to joke my way out of things, telling people I'd already had enough or that I had something planned for later.

But that wasn't enough for some people, who truly believed the only way to have a good time was to get off your face. I was in a club one evening during a modelling trip in Spain and a few of the girls I was with were telling me about all the different drugs they had tried and which ones they preferred. I'd already told them that I wasn't interested but when I wasn't looking, one of them decided to slip a tab of LSD into my drink.

The first I knew about it was half an hour later when someone came up to shake my hand and their fingers seemed to go straight through my palm. It totally freaked me out and I started screaming my head off. The girl who had spiked my drink was explaining what she'd done and telling me to calm down otherwise I'd have a bad trip, but that just made me panic even more. And then, as she was talking, her face seemed to start bending as if it was made of Plasticine. I ran screaming out of the club and ended up wading in a nearby pond because I thought I had heard the ducks calling out to me.

By the time I got back to England, the story had already hit the front pages of the tabloids and I actually lost a couple of jobs because some people in the industry believed I had developed a drug problem. Thankfully, within a few weeks it had all been forgotten and I headed towards the end of the year with my reputation fully intact.

The highlight of the year for girls who appear in the *Sun* is the Page Three Girl of the Year Competition. Readers are asked to ring up and register votes for their favourite and the results are announced at a lavish party attended by all the girls, dozens of celebrities and various newspaper executives.

The year I met Geoff the contest took place at Stringfellows on a chilly Tuesday night in September. For each of the previous three years, Samantha Fox had taken the top spot, but she had retired a few weeks before I made my first Page Three appearance, which meant that for the first time in years the field was wide open. As a relative newcomer, however, I knew I didn't have a hope in hell. It was just an excuse for a really good night out with Geoff and a big bunch of fun people.

To be honest it was like being back on the pageant circuit. There were a couple of cabaret acts and then some music, and then the compère got up and gave a speech about how we were all winners before reaching for the golden envelopes stacked on a table beside him.

'As is traditional,' he said, his eyes gleaming in the spotlights, 'I will announce the results in reverse order.' The lights dimmed and a drum roll erupted from offstage. 'In third place, we have Tracy Kirby.'

The crowd began clapping and the people on my table stood up and cheered. Geoff squeezed my hand then leaned over and kissed my cheek.

I did not move.

Geoff leaned in again. 'Well done Tracy, you're a star. You'd better get up there and collect your prize. It's you, you've come third.' I did nothing. This was clearly a mistake. But Geoff wouldn't leave it alone and started prodding me in the ribs, saying, 'Go on, go on.'

I turned to him slowly, a fixed smile on my face, hoping no one else was looking. Through gritted teeth I whispered to him, 'Look, I know they've called my name, but it's obviously a cock-up. He doesn't mean me, he must mean Tracy Elvik. He'll get it right in a minute, you'll see. I'm not going up there and making a fool of myself.'

Up on stage, the compère started scanning the crowd. 'I can see you there, Tracy; come on now, don't be shy. Ladies and gentlemen, let's have a big hand for Tracy Kirby.'

Geoff put an arm round me. 'No, Tracy, it's you, they're saying your name.'

'Yes, Geoff,' I replied, raising my voice and getting a little irritated, 'I know they're saying my name, but they don't mean me. They mean Tracy Elvik.'

In the end the compère got down off the stage, came across to my table and pulled me to my feet. I really couldn't believe it, it just wouldn't sink in. I was so shocked I couldn't utter a single word when I was up on stage.

I'd got 12.7 per cent of the votes. Maria Whittaker had come second with 13.7 and Linda Lusardi had won with 15.4. I'd been a Page Three girl for less than a year but somehow I'd soared ahead in the popularity stakes, beating other more established girls like Suzanne Mizzi, Jenny Blythe, Corinne Russell and Gail McKenna.

I couldn't wipe the smile off my face for the rest of the evening and Geoff and I drank and danced until closing time, stumbling out into the darkness and posing for pictures hugging, holding hands and sharing our love with the world.

We may have been the perfect fairy-tale couple as far as the tabloids were concerned but, as is so often the case, the reality was becoming very different.

The car, for example, was never quite the gift it had been made out to be. Although it was supposedly mine and mine alone, Geoff effectively banned me from driving it around unless he was with me. I could use it to pop down to the shops and pick up the week's groceries, but if I so much as dared to suggest that I use it to go for a night out with the girls, he would go bananas.

One morning Geoff went off to work and I had a bit of a lie-in. When I finally got up I threw open the curtains in the living room and almost had a heart attack. The car was gone. I was pacing around the house in my bare feet for hours, trying to build up the courage to tell Geoff. When I finally made the call he sounded far from surprised.

'Oh, yeah,' he said. 'I meant to tell you about that.'

'Tell me about what?'

'The car. I've sold it. I decided to sell it to my brother. Sorry about that, meant to tell you yesterday but I forgot. Don't worry, I'll get you another one.'

The new car never came but the feeling that I too was on my way out grew stronger and stronger. I'd begun to suspect that Geoff had had affairs during the time we had been together, but he had always denied it and I had always ended up believing him.

It was difficult not to – Geoff had bags of charisma, he could charm the knickers off a nun if he wanted to. There was also the fact that I was completely and utterly in love with him and expected us to get married and have a family at some point. I didn't want to think someone had been making a mug out of me; I wanted to believe that all the romantic dreams I'd had as a child really had come true.

There were times when it really did seem as though it was meant to be. We became especially close when Geoff fell ill. We were having a quiet night in with a bottle of wine when he suddenly collapsed in agony. I called an ambulance and he was rushed to hospital, where he was diagnosed as having a swollen pancreas. He was told to cut down on his drinking or he might die, but after a few months he was back to his old ways, which sadly for me included chasing other women.

Keeping that torch aflame meant getting my fingers burned every now and then. One time Christine Peake told me that Geoff had made a pass at her. When I asked him about it he claimed he was drunk and only messing about.

Then there were the times that Geoff would get a phone call and then rush out of the house, telling me he had some urgent business to attend to. Soon after he had gone the phone would ring again and there would be a woman's voice at the other end. The women were always different but the conversation would almost always be the same.

'Has he left yet?'

'Er yes, who's this?'

'I'm the woman he's coming round to see. He's on his way here now so we can have a fuck.'

Again and again Geoff denied everything, and again and again I told him that I trusted him. After all, I'd had enough letters from women claiming I was having affairs with their boyfriends – despite the fact that they lived hundreds of miles away and I'd never met them – to know that things weren't always as black and white as they seemed. I was prepared to give him the benefit of the doubt.

I'd also seen some of the problems first-hand. Geoff had got into terrible trouble with a teenage girl who had an enormous crush on him and, when he rejected her, started stalking him. She would follow him around, turning up at the house at all times of day and night. She got pregnant and claimed Geoff was the father. Finally, when I moved in, she switched her attention to me, threatening to kill me and my family so that she and Geoff could be together.

At times the pain Geoff caused me was more than I could bear, but I stuck it out, hoping it was nothing more than a bad patch.

The end finally came when I bumped into my friend Jules and her boyfriend Chris out in town one night and they were a bit short with me. Eventually Jules explained that she had seen Geoff and me out in his new Porsche convertible the previous day and although she had waved frantically I had just ignored her. She couldn't believe I hadn't seen her — Geoff clearly had — and wondered what she'd done to piss me off. The only problem was, I hadn't seen Geoff that day, and I hadn't been anywhere near his car.

This time when I confronted him, Geoff simply admitted it. He told me the woman was Gillian Taylforth, the blonde actress who at the time had a starring role in *EastEnders* as Kathy Beale. I knew instantly what the attraction was. Geoff had always loved the limelight — he couldn't get enough of it when he was with me and now he had found someone with an even higher profile.

I knew there and then that it was all over and my world came crashing down around my ears. I went home to my parents, lay on my bed and cried solidly for a week. I was inconsolable. Nothing anyone could say or do made the slightest difference to how bad I felt.

A few weeks later, Geoff and I agreed to meet up one last time so I could pick up some things from the house. When we got there I saw two used wineglasses on the coffee table in the living room, one of them smudged with lipstick, and fell to pieces. It was as if he had done it deliberately.

We made the drive back to my parents' house in an awkward silence. As we pulled up outside and I reached for the door handle, Geoff, desperate to fill the vacuum, started telling me all about the new kitchen he was having fitted. He was being so matter-of-fact about it all he might just as well have been talking to his mates down the pub. I tried desperately to fight back the tears.

'Why are you telling me about your kitchen?' I sobbed, 'I'm hardly going to see it now, am I?'

Geoff paused for a second. 'You don't know that. This thing with Gillian, it might not work out . . . I might want to get back with you.'

It was the last thing I wanted to hear but also the best thing he could have said: the perfect reminder of just how arrogant and bone-headed he could be. I wanted to slap his face. I wanted to tell him not to be such an arsehole. I wanted to tell him just how much he had hurt me, but I couldn't find the words. There was nothing I could have said that would have expressed even a fraction of what I was feeling.

I opened the door of the car, just as I had done a thousand times before during the days and nights we had spent together over the last two years, but this time it was different. This time was the last time. And with that in mind I got out, shut the door behind me and slowly walked away.

Chapter Three

The second I heard the main gates of Holloway Prison slamming shut behind me, a terrible unease started to grow in the pit of my stomach. Sandwiched between two burly female guards, I was escorted along a dingy passageway and into the reception area. With each step I felt increasingly unwell until the sensation that I was trapped, that I had lost my freedom for ever, became completely and utterly overwhelming.

We passed through the heavy doors that led to the main complex and the smell almost knocked me off my feet: a sickening mix of shit, vomit, rotting food, sour milk and disinfectant, halfway between a hospital and a sewer, that left me gagging. A noise like distant thunder was rolling towards us from the cell block up ahead.

'It's the inmates chanting,' explained Carol, a stocky middle-aged woman with a military-style crewcut.

'What are they saying?'

'Oh, you'll find out soon enough.'

The corridor was so brightly lit that I had to squint to stop my eyes from hurting. Cell doors painted a dull brown stretched into the distance on both sides. As well as shouting, the inmates were rattling their cups against the windows, kicking at their doors and stamping their feet. It was terrifying to be in the middle of it: there was so much tension in the air it was har believe the place wasn't about to explode in a riot.

By now I could hear their words loud and clear. The prison's bush telegraph was in full swing and the sinister message going out to the masses was that there were new faces on the block, ripe for exploitation, bullying, manipulation and sex. Over and over again, louder and louder, they were all chanting: 'Fresh fish, fresh fish, fresh fish . . .'

I was taking a tour of Holloway with two other Page Three girls as part of an event organised by the governor, who was raising money for a local leukaemia charity. That first visit was so traumatic that from that moment on, Holloway haunted me. Even driving past it would cause me to break out in a cold sweat.

The prison itself was bad enough, but what really stuck with me was the behaviour of the staff. The two guards who had been assigned to give us the grand tour clearly thought they had drawn the shortest possible straw and their frustration and bitterness quickly turned into outright hostility. Without the slightest provocation they would take every opportunity to put us down, take the mickey or make snide remarks. I remember thinking that if that was how they treated guests, their treatment of the inmates must be vicious in the extreme.

Everything shocked and horrified me, and the more disturbed I became, the more the prison officers goaded me. At one point we passed an empty cell and they asked if we wanted to sit inside with the door shut to see what it was like. I refused point blank. For as long as I can remember I've suffered from chronic claustro- It's not so much small spaces that terrify me as the thought of being trapped, not being able to come and go as I please. The officers took the piss out of me for the rest of the visit but I didn't care. One of the other girls tried the cell for a few seconds and just seeing her get locked up made my blood run cold.

The prison officers had their own bar in an annexe off the main building and we popped in for a quick drink. As I was sinking a much-needed vodka and lemonade to calm my nerves, a couple of other guards walked in and I was shocked to see that they were men – I'd expected all the guards in a women's prison to be female.

'Oh no,' explained Carol. 'You see, not all the women here are delicate little things like you. We could handle you no problem. But some of the girls, well, they're more like men than the men here are.' (Actually I'd never seen anyone more like a man than Carol. She looked like she could give the entire East German women's shot-putting team a run for their money.)

The tour continued with the gymnasium area, which comprised a large sports hall and a small swimming pool. It was all a little grubby but still not what I expected from a prison. 'Wow, is it heated?' I said, pointing at the pool.

Carol sneered at me. 'Yeah, it's heated. In fact, it's really warm. But you wouldn't be able to go in there – all that silicone in your tits would melt.'

I decided to do what I always did in awkward situations: make a joke of it.

'Listen,' I said with a half-grin, 'if I had silicone tits, they'd be a lot bigger than this.'

Carol wasn't amused. She turned towards me and pushed her face so close to mine that I could smell the stale coffee and cigarettes on her breath. 'Just you make sure you never end up in here,' she hissed. 'You wouldn't last five minutes. They'd tear you to pieces.'

After that I couldn't get out of there fast enough. I remember a sense of sheer terror that something would go wrong and I'd end up having to stay. Once we returned to the outside world I took a huge gulp of fresh air and a feeling of enormous relief spread throughout my entire body.

'Thank God that's over,' I said to one of the girls. 'I'm glad I'll never have to go there again.'

The months that followed my split with Geoff saw me plunge to an all-time emotional low. The hurt and humiliation of being dumped for another woman is bad enough for anyone to bear, but I had to deal with it in the full glare of the media spotlight.

Geoff and Gillian's relationship was anything but plain sailing: as soon as they went public dozens of women came out of the woodwork, claiming that Geoff had been having affairs with them or tried to seduce them. This led to a series of high profile rows and splits, all of which were chronicled in the daily press. And without fail, each and every time a story about them appeared, there would be a paragraph or two about the fact that Geoff had got together with Gillian after two timing me. It got to the stage where I appeared in the papers more times as an ex-girlfriend than as a Page Three girl.

I could never have got through it on my own, but thankfully it was happening at a time when I had managed to surround myself with a vast group of people who showered me with constant love and affection, never stopped telling me how fantastic I was and never got tired of my company.

They were all off their heads on drugs, of course, but it was still nice to hear.

The second summer of love had arrived, and not a moment too soon. Pay parties and outdoor raves were sweeping across Britain like an epidemic, the first time I found myself in a field at 4 a.m., surrounded by a thousand other people all doing that dance that looks like you're milking a giant invisible cow, I knew I'd become a part of something incredibly special.

The vibe was fantastic – a real sense of unity with a complete absence of tension – and I absolutely loved the music. Sometimes I'd jump up on the stage and dance for hours at a time, completely lost in the moment. People would assume I had taken ecstasy. It was so common that 'How many you had?' became the standard greeting. But I'd never take anything stronger than Pro Plus – I just knew it wouldn't agree with me.

The drugs scared me. People were chilled out and happy most of the time, but when something went wrong no one would be able to do anything. More than once I saw people collapse and had to go and call an ambulance because those around them would just carry on smiling and dancing.

Despite the drugs, the whole scene was so seductive, so nurturing, that I decided that I was going to take the summer off work and spend it in Tenerife, travelling around different clubs and helping out in bars. I had a blast and fell into a wild, crazy and passionate but short-lived relationship with a dishy MC. Back in Britain, I spent every spare minute following him around the country and dancing beside him on stage until the party shut down.

After three months of living it large, I couldn't cope. Not taking drugs meant that I simply didn't have the energy to stay up night after night the way that so many others did. My boyfriend's idea of a good time was to go from club to club to party to club, so that you never knew when one day ended and a new one began. As I started to drop out more and more, the rows began and eventually we agreed to split up.

I consoled myself with major bouts of retail therapy. I was still a leading Page Three girl with my picture in the *Sun* every ten days or so, and had more bookings than I could handle for other work. I spent ludicrous amounts of money on clothes, shoes – everything and anything I had ever wanted. And then I decided to treat myself to a nice car.

After extensive research, I settled on a metallic blue BMW 3-series convertible. It quickly became my pride and joy and, whenever the weather was good, I'd take the top down and find an excuse to drive it for as long and as far as possible.

It was soon after buying the car that I got invited to be a guest on a talk show hosted by Vanessa Feltz. The topic – essentially whether or not all models are stupid – was hardly breaking new ground, but I was happy to get a chance to put my own views across.

I gave the stock answers to the stock questions that were asked, by Vanessa herself and by members of the studio audience, and the programme quickly grew into a lively debate. I really enjoyed myself, felt incredibly comfortable in front of the camera and was actually quite sad when it was all over.

When I got a call from another talk show a few days later – the producer had seen me on *Vanessa* – asking if I would be a guest on their programme, I eagerly accepted. There was no money involved but it was great for my profile and talking on national television was a damn sight less intrusive than having my private life splashed all over the newspapers. The occasional interview became a regular and enjoyable part of my working life.

But more than anything I loved the travel. As my career developed so the destinations became ever more elaborate and exotic: Florida, Bali, Jamaica – anywhere where there was a guarantee of good weather.

The trips were always brilliant fun. All my expenses would be paid, of course, and then I would have my fee on top, but I would also get a daily allowance to spend. There would be plenty of time off and all the girls on the shoot would get together and hit the clubs, bars and shops as often as we could. It was like having a mini-holiday two or three times a month.

As a teenager I'd longed to travel and I remember being dead jealous when a few of my friends started doing courier flights which would take them all over the world. I'd tried to get involved but had never managed it because the free trips were always on a last-minute basis and I was never organised enough. But now, I was not only travelling the world for free, I was getting paid for it too. I wrote down every single trip in my diary and also noted how much I had been paid for it. Whenever I felt down or uncertain about things,

I'd just curl up on the sofa and look back at all the places I had been.

A quick look in my diary was all it took to remind me that, by anyone's measure, I was leading a pretty charmed life.

My love affair with the MC might have ended, but my love of the pay-party scene was as strong as ever. When summer came around again I started hanging out with a crowd of like-minded people close to my home in Broxbourne and we'd meet up a few times a week, usually at a wine bar, before heading to the nearest rave.

As well as the main group there would be occasional newcomers or friends of friends who would hang out with us for a time and join in the party. That was how I met Terry, a tall, black ex-boxer. I didn't know him particularly well but he was soon a regular feature of our gang and seemed nice enough, if something of a rough diamond.

After one particularly heavy night of clubbing it was too late to get home so Terry offered me and my friend Jules the chance to crash at his flat in Wood Green. I still didn't know him that well and wouldn't have agreed if I'd been on my own, but as Jules was coming as well I thought it would be fine. I'd been dancing my arse off for hours and by the time we got back I was shattered. Terry gave up his bed for Jules and me and made himself comfy on the sofa.

I was out like a light the minute I hit the pillow, so far gone that I didn't even hear Jules get up in the morning to go to work – God only knows how she managed it. I had nothing to do until later in the day and had planned a much-needed lie in. But it wasn't to be.

I woke with a start to the sound of a gruff voice booming through a megaphone from out in the street: 'Armed police. Come out with your hands up.' I looked across at the clock – it was 7.30 – groaned and tugged the pillow over my head. Some poor sod's gonna have an even worse morning than the one I'm having, I thought to myself.

Then Terry came rushing into the bedroom, panic etched in his face. 'Fuck, fuck fuck, the police are here,' he said breathlessly. 'The police are here, fuck, fuck.' I was so tired I could barely think straight. I just wanted people to stop making noise so I could get some sleep.

Terry was running backwards and forwards, practically wearing a groove into the carpet. I sat up. 'Terry, what are you doing? Where are you going to go? You'd better just go out there.'

Terry panicked a bit more then tried to make a run for it, straight into the arms of a dozen waiting officers. I could hear him fighting with the police in the corridor while I sat on the bed with my knees up against my chest, giggling, not because I thought it was funny but because I was in shock. I couldn't believe I'd got myself into such a bizarre situation.

Then the voice on the megaphone returned. 'Armed police. If there's anyone else in the building, come out with your hands up.' They couldn't mean me, could they? They'd come for Terry and now they had him. I'd been kind of hoping they'd go away.

I slipped a shirt over my shoulders and dragged my dozy self over to the bedroom window. As I pulled back the curtains, a dozen men in black boiler suits pointed their rifles at me. Jesus Christ! Suddenly I was wide awake. In fact I almost wet myself. 'You, at the window,' said a voice, 'come out of the flat right now with your hands up.' It was like something out of a film; I couldn't believe it was happening in real life.

'Don't shoot,' I yelled back. 'I'm coming down right now.'

I was so scared I could barely put my jeans on. I was desperate to get downstairs as quickly as possible before they did something rash. I couldn't do my shirt up – my hands were shaking too much – so I just rushed downstairs, pulling the material over my boobs with my hand.

I got to the front door and all the police officers trained their weapons on me once again. Curtains were twitching up and down the street and several neighbours had come out of their houses to get a better look at what was going on.

'Put your hands up.'

I looked down at my top. 'I can't.'

'Put your hands up. Do you want to get shot?'

'You don't understand. I can't.'

Just because I got them out in the papers didn't mean I was prepared to get them out in the middle of Wood Green.

They took me down to Edmonton Police Station and started firing questions at me. How long had I known Terry? What did he do for a living? What were his movements over the last twenty-four hours? I couldn't understand what they were going on about until someone explained that Terry was the chief suspect in an armed robbery on a sub-post-office in south London the previous afternoon.

Impossible, I told the officers; Terry had been with

me and the rest of the gang at a Bernie Inn in Hertfordshire the previous day. There were dozens of witnesses and the staff would be able to confirm it too. They seemed shocked and disappointed, but once they'd checked the alibi and found that it was rock solid they had to let us both go.

This traumatic morning made me glad I had a holiday coming up. A large group of the gang had decided to spend the rest of the summer in Tenerife and I had agreed to go over for a month or so to introduce them to all the people I knew over there. It had been planned for months and there were at least thirty of us going. We were all sitting around in the wine bar planning the final details when Terry walked in. We gave him a hero's welcome and when he asked if he could come along to Tenerife as well, we all agreed.

He explained that the police clearly had some kind of grudge against him and he could really do with the break. There was no reason to say no. We all knew that he'd been innocent of the robbery the police had raided him for since he'd been with us at the time. As far as we were concerned he was just an innocent victim of police harassment. He booked his ticket that same afternoon and went off to pack his gear.

The first two days in Tenerife were wonderful – a perfect mix of sunshine, sandy beaches, sea and lots and lots of sangría. We danced all night, slept all morning and sunbathed all afternoon. It was a good life.

But on the third morning a sheepish-looking Terry came skulking into my apartment with a British newspaper tucked under his arm. 'Er, I think you should look at this. It's not good.'

I unfurled the paper and a banner headline jumped out at me: PAGE 3 TRACY ON RUN WITH RAIDS CASE BOXER. The story was even worse:

Page Three beauty Tracy Kirby was last night being sought by police hunting her lover who vanished while facing serious criminal charges. Detectives said 26-year-old blonde Tracy and ex-boxer Terry Porter may be together in Britain or abroad. Porter, 28, disappeared just days before he was due in court accused of being one of a gang involved in building society burglaries which netted millions of pounds. He was last seen when police with dogs swooped on his flat last week and found him in bed with Tracy. Detectives wanted to quiz Porter – 6ft and 14 stone – about an alleged offence less than 24 hours before. Tracy told them: 'He couldn't have been involved – he was in bed with me at the time.'

I couldn't believe what I was reading. I hardly knew Terry at all but suddenly we were lovers and I had gone on the run with him. It was just lie after lie. Somehow the paper had put two and two together and made five.

Terry mumbled some kind of apology, then said he'd better make himself scarce, and vanished. We later learned that the reason the police had staged the raid on his flat the week before was because they suspected he would not turn up in court. They planned to hold him on the bogus armed-robbery charge simply so that he would be in custody. They hadn't reckoned on him having a cast-iron alibi.

I got on the phone to my parents, who were beside themselves with worry. My mum urged me to come home as soon as possible and sort things out but I really didn't want to. I hadn't done anything and I couldn't believe the police would be labouring under the same misapprehensions as the press.

Within a matter of hours the papers had learned that I was in Tenerife and dozens of journalists were sent out to the island, desperate to track Terry and me down. They believed we had set up home together in some idyllic love nest and combed the resorts, hoping to get pictures of us together. They offered huge amounts of money to bar staff and club workers to give them a tip off if they spotted us, but most of the people they asked were friends of mine and either refused outright or sent the reporters off on wild-goose chases.

Stories were circulating the island that Terry and I had been seen together here, there and everywhere, but none of it was true. By the end of the week my holiday had been completely ruined and I was fed up of playing cat-and-mouse with the paparazzi. I decided to come home.

I arrived back at Stansted Airport to be met by twenty reporters and photographers, two agents, my parents and my solicitor. I'd always hoped that one day I would be famous enough to be pictured coming through Customs, just like Joan Collins or Madonna, but this wasn't quite what I'd had in mind.

The following morning I went with my solicitor back to the police station and was immediately arrested. After two hours of questioning they finally realised that I wasn't going to be any help to them. They let me go but kept the pressure on by telling me that if they found any evidence of complicity on my part, they'd prosecute. It took three months before they dropped the threat of charges.

That just left the problem of what to do about the newspaper that had printed the story. It was a tricky situation. I was supposed to be one of their girls; they were virtually my employers. Everywhere I went and with everything I did, I was promoting the paper, yet they were writing lies about me and ruining my life and reputation as a result. I'd gone from a fun-loving Page Three model to some kind of gangster's moll who provided false alibis for people and then went on the run with them. I didn't need the press to ruin my reputation – I was doing a good enough job of that on my own.

The fall-out from the stories was horrendous. My bookings dipped dramatically: people didn't want to use me any more because they thought I was mixed up in some kind of criminal gang. The only way to prove that this wasn't the case would be to get the paper to publish an apology. And that meant taking legal action.

Yvonne was dead against me suing – she said I would be biting the hand that fed me – but I felt it was the only thing I could do. I felt pretty confident about it. The police agreed to back me up and confirm that Terry and I had not been in bed together, that I'd never given him an alibi and that I hadn't gone on the run with him.

I expected it to be straightforward but I was very much mistaken. After months and months of negotiation my solicitor finally got the paper to agree that the stories they had printed were not true and should never have been published. They offered to settle out of court, wrote me a letter of apology, offered a lump sum as compensation and agreed to pay all my legal costs. But they refused point blank to publish anything in the paper – which, at the end of the day, was the only thing I really wanted.

I urged my solicitor to keep pressing them but they refused to budge. The only option would be to proceed to trial, but he admitted that the more he pressed them, the more hostile they became, and that going to court could be a mistake. To illustrate his point, he called me into his office and put his telephone on loudspeaker while calling the paper's legal representative. When he again asked for a printed apology the reply came back that if I didn't accept what they had offered and took them to court, they would make my life a misery. Their lawyer said they'd hire the best QC around and dig up every ounce of dirt they could find. They'd drag me so far down in the mud that I would never recover.

It was a sobering thought. They had already caused chaos in my life, either by accident or design; the thought of what they might be able to achieve if they really put their minds to it was terrifying. We decided to accept the offer, partly because I really needed the money.

In the weeks before the stories about Terry and me had appeared, I'd still been appearing in the papers every week or so. Once I issued proceedings, I vanished from their pages.

At first it didn't seem to make a lot of difference to my life. The money had gone up a bit but it was still only £120 per session so I didn't miss it at all. For the first three months I was still getting plenty of bookings for calendars and catalogues as well as doing the odd personal appearance, but slowly, as my Page Three profile evaporated, so the calls started to dry up.

It took eight months to negotiate a settlement with the paper that had run the story and during that time they did not publish my picture on a single occasion. The amount of fan mail I received turned from a flood to a trickle and then just a few drops every now and then. A couple of other papers still used my pictures occasionally, but increasingly they were using old library shots rather than booking me for new ones. I couldn't hide from the truth any longer: at the age of twenty-six, after five wonderful years, my career as a Page Three girl was coming to an end.

The options for ex-glamour models who are no longer being seen in the papers but don't want to give up the lifestyle or the money are extremely limited and thoroughly unappealing.

The least horrific is to move into the world of top-shelf magazines and do the kind of fully nude, legs-akimbo pictures that would not look out of place in a gynaecology textbook. In those days there was an unwritten rule banning Page Three girls from doing any work that allowed their doormats – the favoured glamour-industry term for pubic hair – to be seen, but leaving Page Three meant the girls were free to do what they liked and there was often good money to be made. They often travelled abroad and posed for pictures on the understanding that they would never be published in Britain. (With the advent of the Internet such promises became worthless and many now bitterly regret what they once did.)

The next option, closely allied to the first, is to move into the hard-core pornographic video industry. A surprising number of girls did just that, but I never met any who enjoyed it. The only reason they went down that path was because they needed the money, and they were certainly well paid, but they were also left traumatised by the experience. I knew that wasn't for me either.

The final option is to join one of the 'modelling agencies' that basically operate as a front for high-class prostitution. Their books contain dozens of ex-glamour models, beauty queens and actresses who, because of their supposed superior looks and figures, can charge up to £5,000 a night for sexual services.

Yvonne knew which way she wanted me to go. She had received an offer from Italian *Playboy*, which wanted to pay me £25,000 for a fully nude shoot. I turned it down flat. Even when I got used to doing glamour work, I still felt uncomfortable about showing my tits. There was no way I would ever take it to the next stage, no matter how desperate I was. For Yvonne, it was the final straw. She called me into her office.

'I just don't seem to be able to do anything for you any more,' she told me.

'So what are you saying?'

'I'm saying I think you would be better off with some other form of representation. I'm letting you go. As of this moment, I'm no longer your agent.'

My work life may have been a disaster but for once my personal life was looking pretty rosy. I was seeing James, a successful first-division footballer, whom I'd met through Maria's boyfriend, who played for the same team.

Things hadn't got off to a great start. After a couple of months he started acting a bit strangely and I began to back off. He eventually confessed that his ex-girlfriend had recently had a child. His child. He said he hadn't wanted to tell me sooner because he was afraid he might lose me. Once that was out in the open the relationship quickly got a lot better. I found it hard to cope with the times when James would go off to spend time with his child – and therefore with his ex – but at least I could respect him for it. To be honest it would have been a far bigger problem if he had wanted nothing to do with the child.

By the time I'd received my settlement money from the newspaper things were going brilliantly. Even with his childcare responsibilities we were still managing to see each other three or four times a week and always had a fantastic time together. Pretty soon I was seeing so much of him that I felt I was starting to neglect a few of my old friends, so when James had to go away for a weekend I decided to have a big girlie night out and catch up with them all.

That was the night I met Alex, a male model, who had a fantastic sense of humour and was enormous fun to be with. There was no question of anything happening between us – I was more than happy with James, Alex had a girlfriend and, most importantly, he just wasn't my type – but we really hit it off. He recognised me from my Page Three days and listened carefully while I explained that I wasn't doing very much of that any more and that I was struggling to find work.

Alex mentioned that some friends of his were arranging some promotional work for a group of wealthy businessmen from Monaco and that he could put in a word for me. The job sounded like a dream assignment. I'd be flown down to Monte Carlo and board a massive yacht, which would then cruise around the Mediterranean for three weeks, stopping off at different ports. During that time I'd do a little bit of modelling and act as a hostess, greeting guests. Alex explained that there would be half a dozen girls in all and that it would be exactly like any other promotional job, only I'd be on a luxury yacht in the sun rather than some tacky exhibition centre in Birmingham.

It sounded fabulous and the money was good too – enough to cover all my outgoings for several months. The only thing that worried me was the idea of being away for that long with a bunch of people I didn't know. What if I had a personality clash with one of the other girls or one of the organisers? Then I'd be stuck on the boat. Alex nodded in agreement and said the best thing to do would be to meet his friends and make a decision then. I gave him my number and he agreed to call me nearer the time.

The more I thought about it the more excited I started to get. Even James got excited about it when I told him, though he was a bit miffed that I'd get to spend all that time on a luxury yacht and he wouldn't. Alex and I spoke several times over the next few weeks, then he told me his friends were in London and that they wanted to meet me. 'There's no pressure,' he told me. 'If you like them, join up. If you don't want to get involved, you don't have to. It's entirely up to you.

They've picked a couple of the girls already and they'll be there too so you can meet everyone.'

We met up on the Saturday night and went out for a fantastic meal, washed down with a bottle of champagne – an early celebration in case I took the job. We spent the whole time laughing and joking, swapping stories of modelling trips, before going on to Tramp, where Alex's friends were waiting.

Inside the club Alex steered me over to a corner where five Arabic men were sitting at a set of low tables piled high with bottles of spirits and mixers. There were six or seven girls too, draped over the men, running their fingers through their hair and laughing at their jokes. All the girls were stunning and all the men were repulsive. The only reason the women were there and the only reason they were acting like that was because they were being paid to. It was blindingly obvious that the trip was going to involve a lot more than just hostess work.

'God Alex, this looks really dodgy,' I whispered. 'I can tell you right now, this isn't for me.'

Alex looked over the scene. 'It doesn't look great, does it?' he said softly. I couldn't tell if he was embarrassed or disappointed. I guessed it was a little of both. 'But let's not let it spoil the evening. We're here now; we may as well stay for a drink and have a dance.'

We sat at the edge of the table, poured ourselves a couple of drinks and started chatting. Alex started telling me how he'd split up from his girlfriend a couple of weeks earlier because he couldn't handle the fact that she was bisexual. He spoke briefly to his Arab friends but spent most of the time chatting to me, which I was very glad about. I felt comfortable with him but decided that, if he left or got distracted, I'd leave straight away.

Alex said I seemed a little on edge and asked if I wanted some ecstasy. I declined, of course. We carried on chatting about this and that for a little longer and then he asked again. And again and again and again, to the point where he seemed to be the one on edge. I kept saying no but it was clear that he wouldn't accept that as an answer. In the end I said OK, took the tablet from his hand and pretended to put it in my mouth. Then when he wasn't looking I slipped it into my bag.

Once he thought I'd taken the pill Alex seemed to relax, which made me relax too. He asked if I wanted another vodka and lemonade and went off to the bar to get it. We carried on drinking and chatting as the music started to build in tempo and volume. I could feel the bass beat throbbing through my body and really wanted to get out there and strut my stuff.

Just as I finished my drink I noticed Prince was in the club. The DJ started playing a medley of Prince songs and within minutes I was right alongside the little fella himself, going wild on the dance floor and singing along at the top of my voice. I remember thinking how odd it was that I felt completely off my face when all I'd had were a couple of vodkas and a glass of champagne.

Soon after that, everything started to get weird. Alex's girlfriend came into the club, walked over to where I was dancing and began screaming and shouting at me. I didn't know what was going on and I couldn't hear what she was saying. It wasn't that the music was too loud, it was that her voice had become all distorted and slowed down, as if someone was playing a record at the wrong speed. I could see her lips moving but her words didn't make any sense.

She moved away and then I felt a sharp pain in the middle of my back. She had kicked me! I went flying across the table where all the Arabs were sitting with their girls. I crashed into all the bottles, several of which smashed, and I ended up sitting in the middle of a pile of broken glass. My hand was bleeding badly but I felt no pain. I just sat there staring at the blood dripping on to the floor, fascinated by the look of it. Time seemed to stand still. And then I remember wondering why Alex had gone to the bar to get me my last drink when there had been plenty of vodka and lemonade on the table right in front of us.

I tried to get up on my feet but I couldn't seem to move. It was such a weird feeling – my body just wouldn't respond. I felt someone grabbing me from behind, pulling me upwards, and glanced back to see that it was Alex. And then everything went black.

From that point on I remember only bits and pieces of the evening. Like a film in which lots of scenes are missing, I seem to jump from place to place in an instant, passing in and out of consciousness as the horrific events unfold around me:

I'm in the toilet of the club. Alex's girlfriend is washing my hand and pulling bits of glass from the wound. She is talking but I don't know what she is saying. Her voice is soft and low. She is forcing her hand up my skirt.

I'm in a car. Alex is beside me. We are parked by the side of the road. The door is open and my head is in the gutter. I am throwing up again and again.

I'm lying on a bed, naked. Alex is holding me down and having sex with me.

I'm being held down again. There are voices all around. One of them is a woman, Alex's girlfriend. There is laughter and music. There are hands everywhere.

Light filtering in through the window wakes me up. I feel dazed and confused, unable to speak. I see my clothes in a corner of the room and start to dress. Alex comes in. He seems sheepish. He tells me his Arab friends came back to the flat for a party. He hopes they did not disturb me, did not wake me up. I see him staring at my face, scrutinising my response. All I can manage is a weak mumble: 'I don't know.'

Alex takes me downstairs and puts me into a black cab. The driver panics when he sees the state of me. He is convinced I am going to die. I just want to go home but he pulls up outside a McDonald's and buys me an orange juice. He sits in the back with me and holds my head while I try to drink.

I get home. James is away for the weekend. I climb into the bath. The water stings. I'm covered in bruises, inside and out. I know I've had sex, violent sex, but . . . so much of it is blank. I slowly search my handbag. The tablet is gone. I have a second bath. I can't seem to get clean.

Later I call a close friend: 'I think I've been raped.'

It would be a year before I would read the first reports in newspapers about the dangers of date-rape drugs. Reading the first-hand accounts of women who had been given Rohypnol and other substances, I realised for the first time what had happened to me.

Their experiences mirrored my own to a terrifying degree. The sudden feeling of being completely drunk despite only having had a small amount to drink; the shifts in and out of consciousness during the course of the evening with no memory of the events in between; and the nightmares that followed.

I didn't go to the police – I felt I didn't have enough to tell them and that they wouldn't believe me. Sadly the experiences of the first women to report date rape bore that out. With all traces of the drug gone within twenty-four hours and the women simply unable to remember whether they had given their consent or not, there was little to no chance of a successful prosecution, and most of the early cases were abandoned.

I was still in a daze on Sunday evening when James arrived home, climbed into bed and began stroking my body.

I started crying.

'What's the matter, have I done something wrong?'

'Don't look at me.'

'What is it, love?'

'Please, don't look at me. I feel so dirty. Turn away and I'll tell you.'

I recounted some of what had happened but not everything. I was too traumatised, too humiliated to tell him everything. I felt like I'd cheated on him, like I'd let him down.

He was an absolute rock. I couldn't have got through it without him. I haven't always made the best decisions when it comes to the men in my life, but with James I really felt that I'd got it right. He was more down-to-earth and more mature than most of the men I'd been with before. And when I needed him most, he never once let me down.

The next few months were some of the worst of my life. I had an agonising wait for the results of tests: pregnancy, AIDS and dozens of other sexually transmitted diseases. I started having awful nightmares about being held down and raped. It got to the stage where I couldn't tell what was a flashback and what was just my imagination. I felt like I was cracking up.

To this day I don't know what went on that evening. Did they take pictures? Did they film me? Will I find myself on the Internet one of these days? And how many of them actually had sex with me? The whole experience was bad enough, but not knowing exactly what happened delayed the process of putting it behind me. For a long time I simply blocked it out and refused to even think about it.

A year later, James and I were still together and stronger than ever. He had been gentle, patient and understanding and slowly, gently, we had worked our way back into a sexual relationship. I loved him more deeply than ever and the fact that he had been so supportive during such a difficult time made me truly believe I had finally found the right man.

I was in for a terrible shock.

Maria and I were at my flat watching television when the phone rang. A woman's voice, with attitude, was on the other end.

'Who is this?'

'This is Tracy.'

'All right. You don't know me, my name is Nadine . . .'

'I do know you, you're James's ex.'

'What do you mean, ex? Fuck you, I'm not his ex. We've been together six years.'

'What?'

'Who the fuck are you? Your number keeps coming up on his phone. I want to know what's going on.'

'I'm James's girlfriend. We've been together two years.'

Nadine and I spoke for the next ninety minutes and at no time did we raise our voices to one another. As the details of James's grand deception began to emerge we were both horrified at the way we had been used. I had truly loved James and as far as I was concerned the relationship had been rock solid. But Nadine had felt the same.

With hindsight, the signs had been there. Whenever we were at his flat the curtains would be closed and the volume on the answering machine would be turned right down. He'd also ensure his mobile was always in another room. At the time I had thought he was just creating a romantic atmosphere and making sure we weren't disturbed. Now I saw that he was simply making sure he never had to answer his mobile in front of me. With James I was always one of the lads. I'd hang out with him and his friends but I was almost always the only female there. His friends never brought their girl-friends along – because they all knew Nadine. I had lent James my BMW while I went on holiday with my family. He had told Nadine he had borrowed it from a friend and even let her drive it. I had bought him new curtains and quilt covers for his bed. He told her they came from his mother.

I stayed on the line while Nadine started searching James's flat. She came across a drawer full of condoms. He didn't use them with her and for the last few months he hadn't been using them with me either. 'So what the fuck has he got condoms for?' she said.

She carried on searching and soon found dozens of letters from dozens of other girls. Nadine and I were obviously the two main women in his life but he seemed to have found room for a few others as well. The more I learned, the more I cried. Maria came over and sat beside me with a comforting arm around my shoulder as the tears rolled down my cheeks.

The worst thing was that James and Nadine had not had a child together: he had simply used that as an excuse to be able to go round and see her whenever he wanted. I had never felt more betrayed.

Nadine told me that James had called her earlier that day to say he was coming round that evening. Even that hurt: James had earlier promised to see me. 'OK,' said Nadine, 'if he calls you, don't say anything. I want to deal with him in person. But if he cancels me and decides to come and see you, then I won't say anything and you can sort him out.'

The second I put the phone down it rang again. It was James.

'Bloody hell, I've been trying to get through to you for an hour and a half. Who you been talking to?'

I took a deep breath. I was determined to stay digni-fied. 'Just some girl that I don't really know.'

James was incredulous. 'What, for an hour and a half?

What the hell were you talking about?'

'Just some arsehole waste of space that I thought I knew but it turns out that I don't, not at all.'

'Have you been drinking? You're not making any sense.'

Maria, her head pressed up close against mine so she could listen in on the call, squeezed my hand.

'I'm fine, I'm absolutely fine.'

'Good. Well listen, darling, I know I said we were going out but I have to go back and see my accountant. It's a bit of an emergency.'

'Yeah, that's no problem.'

'I'll see you soon then.'

'Bye, James.'

The next day, James called me early in the morning.

'Jesus Christ, why the fuck did you let me walk into that? Why didn't you warn me?'

'Excuse me, James, you think I owe you something?'

'Well . . . well you don't owe her anything, you don't even know her.'

'I don't need to know her. I sympathise with her. You've played the same dirty tricks on her as you have on me.'

'Well I don't want to be with her any more. I want to be with you.'

'Goodbye, James.'

'But, Tracy . . . I . . .'

I put the phone down. It was over.

My experience with James would have put me off men for good had it not been for Howard.

Maria and I hadn't been doing much work but we

had saved enough to get a small place together, an absolutely tiny cottage.

We were out at the Gas Club one night and I bumped into Howard, a very successful and well respected musician and close friend of the MC I had been going out with during my acid-house phase. We'd always got on well and had a right laugh together but nothing had ever happened between us. He never knew at the time but I'd always had a bit of a thing about him.

We picked up right where we left off. We got on like a house on fire and pretty soon we were seeing each other. He came round to the cottage and sorted out the garden, then he started doing the cooking and cleaning and then, before we knew it, he was actually living with us.

Maria was fine about it and so was I because Howard was a complete angel. He was a perfect gentleman and loved going out to clubs and parties, good food, good company and shopping for clothes just as much as I did. At home he couldn't do enough for me, nothing was too much trouble. He was truly wonderful and within the space of a few weeks we were virtually inseparable.

When the lease on the cottage came up for renewal, Maria and I decided to go our separate ways. We were still the very best of friends but I'd decided to move in with Howard. We'd always known that something like this might happen and it might just as easily have been her who met someone and gone off. It was going to be strange without her, but I needed to move on.

It had been four years since I'd split up with Geoff Knights, leaving him to go off and play happy families with Gillian Taylforth. In that time the couple had appeared in the papers on dozens of occasions and I had got used to ignoring the coverage. But now, completely out of the blue, the relationship we once had was coming back to haunt me.

Chapter Four

It was a balmy Wednesday evening in June, when PC Terence Talbot spotted a Range-Rover parked on the hard shoulder of the A1 near Borehamwood. Concerned that the occupants might be in need of assistance, he stopped his panda car a little way behind and got out to investigate.

Three days later PC Talbot had become the central figure in a front-page exclusive in the *Sun* which, under the headline TV KATHY'S 'SEX ROMP' FURY, said that on peering through the Range-Rover's window the policeman had seen the driver, Gillian Taylforth, giving the passenger, Geoff Knights, oral sex. 'I saw what you were doing,' he told them. 'I'll have you for gross indecency.'

After a protracted shouting match at the local police station, Geoff eventually admitted the offence and was given a formal caution. Within a week the whole thing had been all but forgotten, and that's the way it would have stayed had Gillian not made the ill-fated decision to sue the *Sun* for libel.

The original story had been little more than a tacky tabloid tale and attracted almost no interest elsewhere. In stark contrast the case at the Royal Courts of Justice a year and a half later became an absolute media circus, with representatives from all the national newspapers, television and radio stations attending en masse.

In the witness box Gillian claimed that PC Talbot had simply misread the situation. The truth, she explained, was that Geoff had suffered an attack of pancreatitis after drinking a large amount of champagne at Ascot earlier in the day. As they drove home to north London Geoff began complaining of severe stomach pains and eventually asked Gillian to stop the car so he could be sick. As they sat on the hard shoulder, he unzipped his flies to relieve the pressure on his stomach. Gillian said she leaned across and laid a comforting hand on his belly, and at that point the policeman tapped on the window.

PC Talbot, on the other hand, insisted that he had seen an erect penis. The argument raged this way and that and every last lurid detail was faithfully reproduced in the following day's papers.

From the moment the trial opened the press pack were on my doorstep, desperate for me to comment on the case. They soon made my life a living hell. 'Come on, Tracy,' they'd say. 'Play the game. All we want to know is whether you ever gave Geoff a blow-job in a car, whether it's his thing, you know.'

I had never spoken publicly about my sex life and I had no plans to start. Instead I maintained what I hoped was a dignified silence and ran the gauntlet of reporters camped outside my home as I went about my day-to-day business. It was absolutely exhausting and I quickly learned that they were not going to take no for an answer. By the second day of the trial they were also constantly on the phone, ringing my doorbell, shouting through the letterbox or holding notes up against the windows. Maria and I became too scared to leave the house.

I tried to get rid of them by suggesting a few other people they could try to talk to, but it was me they wanted and no one else. The offers became more and more outrageous: £5,000 for an interview, £10,000, £20,000, £25,000 plus a two-week holiday in Florida for me, my parents and the rest of my family to get us away from the other papers during the remainder of the trial. I had no hesitation in turning it all down but I knew I couldn't take much more – it was like living under siege.

On the third day I threw on a few old clothes, disguised myself with a mop of a brunette wig, let myself out through the gate in the back garden and hopped on a plane to Lanzarote to go and stay with some friends.

The trial rumbled on in my absence and I was shocked to discover that the wall-to-wall coverage continued, even out in the Canary Islands.

The case had been looking even until the morning of the fifth day, when George Carman QC for the *Sun* produced a video of a drunken party where Gillian could be seen simulating oral sex with a German sausage and a wine bottle.

As far as the press were concerned, it made the story bigger and juicier than ever, but for Gillian it was a disaster. Part of her defence had involved presenting herself as someone who would not indulge in 'coarse' behaviour and the video seemed to suggest the opposite. It shifted the balance and at the end of the eleven-day trial the jury found in favour of the newspaper. On hearing the news Gillian collapsed and eventually left court in an ambulance.

It was the first libel case the *Sun* had won since being

taken over by Rupert Murdoch in 1969 – a newsworthy event in itself – and it was commemorated on a grand scale. The next issue featured dozens of still photographs from the infamous video, a whole page of jokes about sex in Range-Rovers, and dozens of columns about every aspect of Geoff and Gillian's private lives – I actually felt quite sorry for her.

All the other tabloids went crazy over the story as well, and one bit of coverage which caught my eye was a column with the headline HE BRAGGED OF SECOND CAR ROMP SAYS HIS EX, with my picture. As I read the story I was horrified to see that I had been quoted talking about an incident that supposedly took place soon after Geoff and I had split up. It was nothing more than a rumour but the way it was presented in the paper made it look like it was a fact.

I couldn't believe that, after I'd made such a massive effort to avoid having anything to do with the case, the paper had just gone ahead and quoted me anyway. And the worse part would be that people would assume I had been a willing participant, that I had sold the story.

The minute I got back to London I called my solicitor and asked him to take action. Using the money I'd got from my earlier settlement, he began assembling a case, briefing barristers and so on.

As with the Terry Porter story, my motivation wasn't money, it was to get an apology out of them. I was absolutely indignant and couldn't believe that after all they had put me through during the trial they would simply make something up. I expected to reach an out-of-court settlement within weeks, but I could not have been more wrong.

The round of letters, meetings, accusations and counter-accusations rumbled on for months and then, in early September, my solicitor called me and asked me to meet him at his offices as a matter of urgency.

I could tell he had bad news for me. 'Tracy,' he said softly, 'I think you should drop the case.'

I was stunned. It was the last thing I had expected to hear. 'Why?' I gasped.

'Because you haven't got a hope in hell of winning and you can't afford to lose.' He scribbled some figures on a piece of paper. 'Look, if we stop today, it's already going to cost you this much. If you take it to trial it's going to cost you at least this much. And you might have to pay costs, even if you win.'

The first figure was more than half the money I had left in my savings account. The second was nearly five times as much. He was right: I simply couldn't afford it. I had to fight back the tears.

'But how can that be? How can they offer me all this money and holidays and things and I turn it all down, and then suddenly I turn around and say, "Actually, I'll do it for nothing". It's just not true. It's just not fair.'

But there was no sense in crying over spilled milk. I could have pressed on and taken the case to court but that would just open up another can of worms. Gillian and Geoff had made their own situation a million times worse by pursuing their case. I decided to cut my losses.

A few days after the paper learned I was no longer pursuing the case they celebrated by launching a vicious personal attack on me. One of their cartoon strips was in the middle of a storyline where a female character was about to reveal her true identity to her ex-lover.

She turned up at his home and, after being described by the butler as a 'scruffy slag' who needed a bath and told to go away, she responded by insisting: 'He'll see me. Tell him it's Tracy Kirby.' Over the next week the character was revealed to be a terrorist, accused of being on ecstasy or acid, and told she was a 'whore for the law'.

I was bitterly upset and humiliated but in some ways it made me glad we hadn't gone to court. Who knows what they would have done?

Looking on the bright side, I still had a little money in the bank and I was about to move in with my boyfriend. But things were about to get a whole lot worse.

By the time I bailed out of suing the tabloids for a second time I hadn't had so much as a sniff of modelling work for more than six months. I'd started up my own little business, selling clothes on a market stall in Notting Hill, and it was beginning to pick up quite nicely, but I was still spending money much faster than I was earning it. Thankfully I still had the safety net of the rest of the money from the newspaper settlement, and I felt optimistic about my chances of finding a new career in the near future.

The only real problem in my life was Howard. Within a few weeks of our moving in together he had quit his band and undergone a dramatic personality change. In the space of a few days he went from being sweet and attentive to being restless and edgy. He found it hard to concentrate on anything for more than a few seconds and soon it was virtually impossible to have a conversation with him.

Howard had always been a bit careless but now he became completely irresponsible. He broke everything he had – his phone, his watch, his sunglasses – and when he had nothing left he started breaking my things. He blew the engine in my BMW, leaving it a complete write-off, and when my grandfather gave me his car as a replacement, Howard borrowed it and never brought it back, claiming it too had broken down.

He became incredibly lazy around the house, turning from the man who couldn't do enough for me to the man who couldn't do anything, even for himself. Where he had once brought joy into my life, now all Howard brought were his dirty clothes and an attitude. He stopped taking baths, and would regularly stay out overnight, only to come back and be unable or unwilling to say where he had been.

My patience was exhausted within a week. I told him that we were finished and I wanted him to move out. We were soon in the midst of a furious argument. For the first time in our relationship Howard displayed an aggressive streak, shouting and swearing manically as he insisted that he would be staying put.

I knew I could no longer live with him but there was no way I was going to move out of the house. Everything was in my name, I'd paid the deposit and I'd spent ages finding the place.

Howard's absences grew to the point that he would be gone for two or three days at a time. He had got heavily into gambling but was so useless that he never won – I later learned he had actually lost my grandfather's car in a poker game – and I was forced to keep my purse with me after money started going missing from it.

It all came to a head one Sunday morning. Howard hadn't been home for four days and I'd heard nothing from him in all that time. I'd changed the sheets as soon as he'd left but the grease from his hair seemed to have soaked through to the mattress and now it was coming back on to the clean sheets. His stench was everywhere and was starting to keep me awake at night. The only thing to do was change the sheets once again and turn the mattress over.

I was still sleepy and planned to go back to bed, so I hadn't got dressed yet. I started stripping the bedclothes, pulling the cover off the duvet and stacking the fitted sheet and pillows in a pile on the floor behind me. The mattress had two plastic handles down the longest side so I locked in my fingers and took a few deep breaths. I knew it was going to be awkward to shift but I figured that if I could get it high enough, I could flip it over and then drag it back into place. As I pulled at the handles and heaved it high above my head I choked in disbelief. Sitting in the centre of the base of the bed was a large black revolver.

I don't know how long I stood there, frozen to the spot, but the moment seemed to last for eternity. I was like a rabbit caught in the headlights of a car – I just couldn't take my eyes off the gun. It seemed so out of place, so unreal. Eventually I reached over to pick it up and let the mattress flop back down into place. The gun was heavy and cold, solid like a lump of black iron. I could feel the muscles in my arm start to burn as I held it. This was no plastic toy or replica; it was the real thing.

The sound of a key moving in the front-door lock snapped me out of my trance. I said nothing when I heard my name being called. I listened to the footsteps moving across the hall, into the kitchen and living room and then on to the stairs. Howard was back and heading for the bedroom.

The closer he got the more angry I became. How dare he do this to me, how dare he betray my trust like this? He appeared in the doorway and for a split second I was distracted by what I saw. His eyes were raw and bloodshot, his hands were black with soot and dirt, his face was unwashed and his clothes were so filthy they looked like rags. He looked like he'd been sleeping on the streets.

He saw the gun and just grinned sheepishly. It was like he was a schoolboy and I'd found a copy of *Penthouse* under his bed. The anger came flooding back. 'What the fuck is this? What do you thinking you're doing bringing something like this into my house? If you want to pretend that you're some kind of fucking gangster or something then do it somewhere else, not here.'

I was as angry at myself as I was with him. I should have ended it long ago but the memory of how good things had once been had kept my false hopes alive. Now at last I knew it was over. I just wanted him to take his gun and get out of my life for ever.

From that moment everything happened in slow motion. Howard took two steps towards me and reached out for the gun, spun on his heels and walked towards the door, shaking his head and muttering to himself. He stooped and picked up a pillow, then whipped round to face me.

I saw the muzzle of the gun pointing at me for a brief moment before he placed the pillow in front of it. I looked up at his eyes. The stupid grin had gone and instead he was looking at me with pure hatred. And at that moment I knew he was going to pull the trigger.

I saw the shaft of orange flame and sea of burned feathers before I heard the sound of the shot. Even with the pillow acting as a makeshift silencer the blast still made my ears ring. There was no time to scream. Deep inside my stomach something was ripped apart. It felt like someone had shoved a white-hot poker right into my guts.

I dropped to the floor, clutching my stomach in agony. All the air had been knocked out of my lungs and I was struggling to breathe. The room was full of smoke and feathers and in the midst of it all Howard had started laughing. He was laughing harder and harder until he was almost hysterical, delighted at the sight of what he'd done to me.

The gun was hanging loosely by his side as he stepped towards me. I started kicking my heels against the carpet, trying to scramble backwards out of the way, all of which only made the burning sensation in my stomach a thousand times worse. The back of my head cracked into something solid and I realised with horror that I'd reached the base of the bed. Now there was no escape. I was trapped and convinced I was about to die. Howard stood over me, his legs straddled across my body. The hatred had returned to his face. He held the gun in both hands and moved it slowly upwards until it was pointing at my head.

'No,' I gasped. 'Please . . . no.'

I could feel myself fading but I had to do something. With all my strength I forced my left leg upwards and kicked him straight in the groin as hard as I could.

He didn't even flinch.

He reached down and locked the fingers of his left hand around my neck, lifting me up and pushing me back on to the mattress. With one hand pinning me down he tried to force the barrel of the gun into my mouth. He still hadn't said a word. I turned my face this way and that, chipping a tooth in the process.

He moved so his knees were pinning my arms down and placed the gun to one side. His right hand moved down between my legs and started ripping away at my knickers. I was screaming 'No' at the top of my voice, over and over again. I knew that Howard was probably going to kill me but there was no way in the world I was going to let him rape me. I'd promised myself that would never happen again. I started doing everything I could – biting, kicking, punching and wriggling – but he was just too strong for me. I felt the material of my knickers give way and Howard started loosening the belt of his jeans.

Suddenly my left arm worked free and I punched him in the face as hard as I could again and again. Howard swore and reached for my arm, grabbing it and roughly shoving it back under his knee. Then he leaned forward so his mouth was hovering above my face and started snorting deeply. Then he let a huge green lump of phlegm fall from his lips on to my face.

God only knows where I got the strength from but somehow I managed to shift my bodyweight and throw him to one side. I went to reach for the gun but Howard was too quick for me. A slap to the face knocked me from the bed back to the floor and left me seeing stars.

I lay in a dazed heap on the floor and watched him get off the bed and head for the bedroom door, mumbling to himself about getting a knife to finish me off. I remember thinking, Why do you need a knife? You've got a gun. For the first time I looked at the hand that had been clutching my stomach. There was no blood, though I could still feel a powerful burning sensation and it hurt like hell every time I moved. My head was spinning. Had I been shot or not? Had he been using blanks or had he just missed?

I dragged myself over to the bedside phone and dialled the number of my brother-in-law, John. I knew I couldn't ask him to come to the house because there would just be a terrible fight and I still didn't know for sure if Howard had real bullets for his gun or not. I didn't want anyone to get hurt, I just needed to get away. I asked him to meet me at a set of traffic lights at the end of my road, put the phone down and listened carefully.

I knew that if Howard was in the kitchen, I should be able to sneak out of the front door without being seen. I picked myself up, bracing myself against the wall so that I could walk, and began padding towards the doorway. I could hear the drawers in the kitchen being opened and rifled through. As long as that sound continued, I knew I'd be safe.

I reached the landing, padding my way downstairs as quietly as I could. I was halfway down when the floorboard beneath me gave a sudden creak and everything went quiet. I stopped in my tracks. Where was he? I guessed he had heard the step and was waiting to see if I was trying to escape.

The front door was less than ten feet away. I decided to go for it. I leaped down the last few steps and started running for the door. I passed the doorway to the lounge and my fingers were reaching for the lock when I suddenly felt a terrific pain in the back of my head. Howard was behind me. He'd been hiding behind the lounge door and had grabbed a handful of hair as I had run past. Now he was using it to drag me back into the kitchen.

He threw me across the room and I skidded across the lino, smashing head-first into a cupboard unit. In an instant he was back on top of me, slapping my face and kicking my body. 'Now you're gonna get it, now you're gonna fucking get it,' he hissed at me, getting up and moving away. I could taste blood in my mouth where my lip had split and my left eye was so swollen it was starting to close. The crippling pain in my stomach was worse than ever.

I couldn't bear to think about what was coming next. I just lay there. The next thing I heard was the floorboard creaking. Howard was on the stairs. I knew that if I stayed put I was going to die and that this was my final chance. I pulled myself to my feet and ran for the front door. I didn't dare to look round. I didn't need to; I knew he was right behind me.

I flicked the lock and ran down the path to the garden gate, screaming every step of the way, 'Help me, please, somebody help me.' I had just reached the pavement when I felt Howard's hands on my shoulders. A large white car was passing by and he waited until it was right on top of us before hurling me in front of it. The front bumper smashed into my hip and sent me spinning up

into the air. I crashed down on to the bonnet and spun
towards the windscreen. I managed to stop myself with
my hands and saw a middle-aged couple, sheer terror
on their faces, perched inside. Thankfully they had just
been about to turn into the road next to the house and
had slowed right down, otherwise I would have been
much more badly injured.

The car screeched to a halt and I rolled off the bonnet
and on to the road. The driver leaped out and asked if
I was OK. He was short and thin with a few delicate
wisps of grey hair barely covering his head. I could see
a second wave of shock register on his face as he took
a good look at me, half naked, bloody and bruised, lying
in front of his car.

He turned to Howard. 'What the hell do you think
you're doing?'

I desperately needed help but this man was no match
for the monster that Howard had become; I couldn't let
him get involved. 'Please, just drive away,' I gasped to
him. 'Just drive, I'm all right.' Howard stepped over my
body and answered the driver with a sickening punch
to the face. The man went down like a sack of potatoes
and his wife started screaming blue murder as Howard
started kicking at his body.

I could hear the impacts and each one made me want
to throw up. I desperately wanted to help but I knew
there was nothing I could do. I felt awful, like I was
leaving the man who had tried to help me to his death.
But I had no choice. I got up and started running.

I reached the traffic lights but I knew John wouldn't
be there yet so I carried on running, into a small patch
of woodland that lay behind the petrol station. I dropped

to my knees in the mud and tried to hide behind some bushes.

I was desperate to stay quiet but the second I stopped running I started throwing up violently. I put my hands up to my mouth and tried to stop but the hot vomit simply splashed over my face and clothes. It kept coming and coming until there was no more and I was heaving up nothing but air.

I could see the traffic lights through the leaves and was looking out for John's car when Howard suddenly appeared, pacing backwards and forwards, less than twenty feet away. I started shaking. 'I know you're out here, you bitch,' he was saying over and over again, 'and I'm gonna find you and then I'm gonna fucking kill you.' It was a miracle that he hadn't seen me but now I was trapped. As long as he stayed there I couldn't leave, even when John turned up. As he came past I ducked down further, my eyes fixed on the mud in front of me, praying that somehow I'd make it through.

The sound of twigs snapping behind me almost made me scream. I spun round as fast as I could to see a man walking his dog along the path a few feet behind me. He was huge, a shaven-headed nightclub-bouncer type, and his dog was a fierce-looking Dobermann. I instantly felt safe.

His eyes fell on me. 'Oh my God,' he said and started to walk away.

I reached out to him. 'Please, please help me.'

'Sorry, love, I don't want to get involved. I just don't want to get involved.' And with that he was gone.

There was still no sign of John but I could see Howard continuing to look for me. There was another rustle behind me, as a large Alsatian walked past accompanied by a middle-aged woman and her teenage daughter.

'Oh God, have you been raped?'

All I could think about was how easily Howard would be able to hurt them.

'Please, leave me alone,' I wept. 'Just go away. If he comes back and sees you then he'll attack you.'

The woman stepped through the undergrowth and knelt down in the mud beside me. 'We're not going anywhere.'

No matter how much I pleaded, they refused to go. Howard walked past a few more times and they just held me tight until he was out of sight. After about ten minutes I saw John's car pull up at the traffic lights. Howard was out of sight but I was too scared to leave the safety of my hiding place. Instead, the woman sent her daughter to go and fetch him.

My sister Sarah had come along even though she was heavily pregnant. John had also fetched a friend – he suspected there might have been some kind of trouble and wanted some back-up.

Whey they saw the state of me they were hell-bent on revenge. My sister managed to talk some sense into them and they bundled me into the car to take me back to their place. We had to stop three times on the way so that I could get out and throw up.

There was no way I could call the police. I knew that if I did, the press would get hold of the story and I'd be all over the front pages again. And it wouldn't be a one-off either. There would be the court case and that would mean they would drag up Terry Porter and everything else that I'd been involved in. I'd never live it down.

It was a week before I felt brave enough to go back to the flat to collect all my things. I arranged for a mutual friend to take Howard away somewhere so I would be free to get my stuff. His sister and his cousin helped me because they felt so bad about what had happened. It was through them that I learned what had been responsible for Howard's dramatic change.

Soon after I'd met him, Howard had become addicted to crack cocaine. His wild mood swings, unpredictable behaviour and lack of personal hygiene are all symptomatic of abuse of the powerful drug. As he slipped further and further into addiction, so he would spend more time trying to find new supplies, selling whatever he had to pay for his next fix.

We arrived at the flat along with my dad and Maria and went inside. It was virtually empty. Howard had gone, and taken all his things; he had also taken most of mine. He stole all my jewellery, two music centres and other bits and bobs. I'd bought thousands of pounds' worth of stock for my clothes stall – that had all gone as well. The following day I found that he had emptied the £15,000 savings I had in our joint account. The bank said there was nothing I could do – technically speaking it was his money too.

I explained the situation to the letting agency and called up the electric, phone and gas companies to take all the services out of my name. During the last months of our relationship Howard had started seeing a girl who worked as a prostitute, mainly because she had a regular source of income with which to buy drugs. He now got her to phone all the companies pretending to be me and then had all the amenities reconnected under my name. They moved back into the flat and proceeded to run up huge bills, some of which I was eventually forced to pay.

But my immediate concern was the pain in my stomach, which, after three days, was as bad as ever. After a series of tests and assessments my doctor explained that the shock of thinking I had been shot had sent a powerful spasm through my lower intestine, which had virtually twisted itself into a knot. Although it eventually uncoiled, it gave rise to a case of irritable bowel syndrome (IBS), which I have suffered with ever since.

IBS is caused by an abnormality in the way the intestinal muscles contract. Some sufferers experience crippling constipation, others diarrhoea, but most get a combination of the two – unable to go one day, having to go all the time the next. There is also a near-constant bloated feeling in the abdomen and severe cramps, which at times have brought me close to passing out.

There is no cure, but by having a supply of Imodium to control the diarrhoea, watching my diet and doing my best to avoid certain situations, I can keep most of the symptoms under control.

It's made all the worse by stress – especially the stress of not knowing where the nearest toilet is – so my first priority at any social event, restaurant or club is to find the ladies. Only then can I start to relax. It also links in with my claustrophobia: being trapped in a small space becomes even more terrifying because I know I won't be able to get to the loo. I have no choice but to tell anyone I work with about the condition; that way they understand when I have to run off suddenly and don't return for absolutely ages. People try to be kind, but that doesn't make it any less humiliating.

Howard not only took all my money, he also robbed me of my dignity.

Chapter Five

After only a week back at Broxbourne, I knew I had to get away as soon as possible. Although I loved them dearly, living with my parents again was rapidly destroying what little self-esteem I had left. With the passing of each day I felt increasingly worthless.

No matter what they said or how much support they tried to give, I couldn't help thinking that I had become the running joke of the family: the little girl who had to come crawling home every time the big bad world got to be too much for her.

I took a job as a barmaid in a small family pub and moved into a tiny flat on the outskirts of Cheshunt. I could barely afford the rent and, with no modelling work and no savings to fall back on, I found it increasingly hard to make ends meet.

When the pub changed hands a couple of months later the new manager decided to let me go and I was forced to sign on the dole. There were vague promises of other jobs in the near future but in the mean time I cut back my spending as far as humanly possible. Despite that, I found myself falling more and more deeply into debt.

Once my dole cheque was late coming through and I had nothing in the house to eat apart from two old cans of baked beans. The phone had long since been cut off and I was living without hot water and lighting because I had no money to charge the electricity meter, fitted after I'd fallen behind with the bill one time too many. With no way of heating the beans, I had to eat them cold: I opened the first tin, swallowed three large spoonfuls and then replaced the lid. That was my lunch; I'd save the rest for dinner.

Of course, I knew that all I had to do was get in touch with my parents and they would have been round in a matter of minutes, but I was too proud. They would have insisted that I move back home so they could look after me, and I would have ended up feeling worse than ever.

The dole cheque failed to materialise the next morning but I was too scared to leave the house just in case the postman was late. I had a few mouthfuls from the second tin of beans, but by late afternoon I was almost delirious with hunger. Evening came and I just sat there in the dark like a zombie. When the doorbell rang I was so disorientated that I thought it was the post and jumped up to answer it.

It turned out to be my friend Jules. She had dropped by to find out why my phone wasn't working and why she hadn't heard from me for a few days. I was so ashamed that I begged her not to come in. She insisted, and when she saw how I'd been living she started crying. More than anything, she was really upset that I hadn't felt able to turn to her for help.

Ignoring my feeble protests, she went out and charged up my electricity key meter, bought masses of food and took a copy of my phone bill so she could get me reconnected.

'And next week, you're coming out with me and Chris.'

'I can't,' I insisted. 'I don't feel like going anywhere. I don't have any money to go out.'

'Stop it, Tracy, I'm not listening. There's a testimonial for some Arsenal player and Chris has got a spare ticket. I know you haven't had a proper night out for months – it's just what you need.'

The Westbourne Suite of the Royal Lancaster Hotel in Bayswater was an endless sea of extravagantly decorated circular tables. The men wore black tie and the women glided around the room in a dazzling array of glamorous evening dresses. The air was heavy with the sound of clinking glasses, popping champagne corks and the half-hearted laughs that accompany small talk as the guests waited for the main event to begin. I'd been to dozens of testimonial dinners in my time but I hadn't been out for so long that at first I felt like a fish out of water.

It took only a few drinks for me to be able to relax, forget my troubles for the night and get into the swing of things. The food was absolutely beautiful – my first meal out in months – and after a series of hilarious speeches and presentations, the evening descended into a kind of good-natured free-for-all. Our table, which was getting more drunken and boisterous by the minute, challenged those sitting behind us to a game of table football. We emerged triumphant but along the way the two tables seemed to gel. A few of us swapped seats and set about making new friends.

I found myself sitting next to a short blonde woman who was wearing the most amazing necklace I have ever seen. It was a diamond-studded gold cross about two inches long which caught the light and sparkled beautifully in her ample cleavage. For a moment I was hypnotised; when I looked up, she was staring at me with a smile.

'Blinding necklace.'

'Thanks. I don't get the chance to wear it that often but I thought it wouldn't look out of place here. I'm Lynn.'

'I'm Tracy.'

She wore a black dress covered in gold safety pins with a plunging neckline. Her shiny blonde hair was piled high on top of her head and her bright blue-grey eyes sparkled with mischief. We got on like a house on fire and were soon knocking back the drinks and chatting away like old friends.

'So what do you do then, Lynn?'

'I spend money.'

'Nice work if you can get it.'

'Too right. I've got two boys but my mum looks after them most of the time, so I just spend money. My husband and I own some property and a few businesses. We do quite well out of them so it leaves me free to shop.'

She then proceeded to go through each item of clothing and jewellery, telling me where she had bought it and how much it had cost. Everything had a label. Even her hairpins were designer.

I didn't see it as showing off – it was exactly the sort of conversation I used to have when I sat down with another Page Three girl. For a while, it was like I was back there again. It made me realise how much I missed buying and wearing lovely outfits and accessories. I hadn't bought anything new for months and I was starting to go through cold turkey.

Just then I felt a tap on my shoulder and turned to see a slightly spotty teenage boy standing beside me. I recognised him as the son of a football manager I had spotted in the crowd earlier. 'Sorry to bother you, Tracy,' he said softly, 'but do you think I could have your autograph?'

I was cringing with embarrassment as I scrawled away in his book. When I turned back to Lynn her eyes had grown to the size of dinner plates and her jaw was hanging open. 'What's going on, who are you? Are you famous? I feel embarrassed for not knowing. I hope I haven't insulted you.'

'Not at all. I used to be a Page Three girl, that's all.'

'Page Three. What, topless in the *Sun* and all that?'

'That's right, but I don't do it any more; it feels like it all happened a long time ago.'

'Wow. That's absolutely fantastic. What a brilliant thing to have done.'

Lynn immediately wanted to know absolutely everything about it. Well, in truth she only really wanted to know whether I'd slept with anyone famous, but we managed to cover a few other aspects of glamour modelling along the way. She asked what I'd been doing since and seemed genuinely interested in my efforts to break into television.

Twenty minutes later she declared that I was her new best friend and she insisted on taking my phone number so she could arrange for the two of us to go shopping together.

When Lynn was called away by another of her friends, I found myself chatting to her husband. Michael was of Greek extraction, tall and stocky with dark, slightly greying, wavy hair. I'd noticed him earlier in the evening because he'd insisted on buying champagne for everyone on both tables. It was clear that he was a man who had a lot of money and liked to throw it around.

Lynn had mentioned that, as well as running a string of health clubs, Michael had recently set up his own bureau de change on the Edgware Road and I had made the mistake of asking how the business worked.

'It's all about the spot rate, you see,' said Michael, frantically scribbling figures on a napkin. 'That's how you make your money. You buy for this, you sell for that and this figure here is your profit.'

From there Michael was off, ranting and raving about the pros and cons of dealing in guilders, dinars and kroner, about the deregulation of this, limitations of that and the statutes of whatever. It was clear that this new business was his pet project and something he felt passionate about. At one point he even offered me some part-time work with the bureau, making deliveries around London and the south-east. Even though I knew he was drunk and therefore not to be taken seriously, I couldn't help being interested – I thought the job might come with a car, or at least a little van, and I hadn't had any transport of my own since Howard had destroyed my last two vehicles.

When Michael realised I didn't have a car of my own he went back to talking about currencies until, fearful that my brain was starting to harden, I managed to steer the conversation round to a new topic.

The more we chatted, the more I liked him. Michael had a very dry sense of humour and, away from the world of international money markets, was quite entertaining. In our drunken state it seemed to take me for ever to understand that his full name was actually Michael Michael ('No relation to George – I'm much better-looking'). At the time it seemed like the funniest thing in the world.

Michael was typical of the men that I'd met on the Page Three circuit: arrogant, flashy businessmen who had made a lot of money and liked to hang out with celebrities and wannabe gangsters. He reminded me of so many people I'd met before that a couple of times I found myself laughing out loud at some of the things he said, not because they were funny but because of the memories they brought back. Luckily Michael assumed I was laughing with him, not at him.

Just as I was running out of things to say I was rescued by Jules and spent the rest of the evening talking to her and Chris until the DJ came on. At that point, I went wild on the dance floor and stayed there with a small band of hard-core party-goers until the hotel management threw us out in the early hours of the following morning.

It was one of the best nights out I'd had in years.

Early the next afternoon I was recovering at home when my phone exploded into life. Wearily I reached over and pulled the receiver to my ear.

'Tracy darling, it's Steve. Clench your buttocks, I've got great news for you.'

Steve was the funniest, campest man I had ever met.

He was also my new agent. It had all happened after Jules had come round and rescued me from the edge of despair: she had been so kind and so encouraging, it really made me get off my arse and try to sort my life out. I didn't want to squander the opportunity that she had given me.

A few days before the testimonial dinner I'd gone to see Steve and somehow managed to get myself on to his books. We had hit it off instantly and it soon became obvious that, as well as being my agent, Steve, along with his equally camp gay entourage, was destined to become a close friend as well.

I had no interest in going back to Page Three – not that they would have had me anyway – but had little idea what else I might be able to do. After a hilarious brainstorming session in Steve's office we came up with the perfect career: I was going to be a TV presenter.

We set aside some time for later in the month to try and come up with programme ideas that we could pitch to various networks, but the first step was to raise my public profile. Since that first meeting, Steve had been working double-time to get the ball rolling, setting up interviews with any local newspaper or magazine that could be persuaded to run a feature about 'life after Page Three'. I guessed his news was something to do with that.

I tried to sound cheery but with my hangover all I could manage was a low groan.

'Tracy, you sound terrible. What's wrong?'

'Nothing, I was just out on the town last night.'

'Without me! You cow! You had me feeling sorry for you. And the whole time it was self-inflicted. Well, you'll get no sympathy from me, you big sissy. You better toughen up, girl. You'd never survive a proper night out with me. I won't tell you what I got up to last night then. Your mind is too fragile, it would haunt you.'

'Were you just calling up to show off?'

'Do you mind? I have my professional hat on. Can't you tell from my superior telephone manner? Don't answer that. The point is that I, being absolutely fabulous in every possible way, have got you a spot as a guest on a top television chat show.'

'Wow, that's great.'

'Yes, it is great. It's going to do wonders for your profile and it will be something recent to add to your showreel . . .'

'What's the programme?'

'. . . and that's what it's all about at the moment, building up your showreel . . .'

'Yeah, what's the show?'

'. . . because without that, you haven't got anything.'

Eventually Steve admitted that the programme was *The Sex Show*, a late-night slot on L!veTV, a struggling cable channel headed up by the former editor of the *Sun*. It wasn't exactly a big break, but it was still better than nothing. It had been years since I'd done any telly and starting off small was the perfect way to build my confidence.

Steve liked to accompany me to anything I did, and so it was that just over a week later I found myself sitting in his car along with his secretary, Abs, as he gave me a pep talk on the way to record the programme. At one point I casually looked out of the window and saw someone who looked familiar walking past. It took me a second to realise it was Michael Michael and by then he had disappeared into a shop called Travel 2000, which had a glowing neon sign in the window advertising a bureau de change. We were on the Edgware Road and I realised this must be the business Michael had been telling me about. I wondered if I'd ever hear from Lynn, or whether her declarations of friendship were just the booze talking.

Steve saw me looking wistfully out of the window and snapped his fingers to get my attention. 'Come on now, Tracy, you've got to start concentrating. I know it's only a cable show, but you've got to think about how it's going to look on your showreel.'

By the time we arrived at the studio he had me repeating, 'I am a calm blue ocean. I am nature's greatest miracle,' out loud over and over again. I felt like a complete idiot but he insisted it would help my performance. 'If it's good enough for Madonna, it's good enough for you.'

Appearing on *The Sex Show* turned out to be the most enormous fun. The whole thing went out live and as I was ushered to the sofa in front of the cameras I was absolutely terrified, even with Steve's calming mantra running through my head. But the presenter, Helen, was a glamorous, giggly brunette around my age and she did a wonderful job of putting me at my ease.

It turned out to be less of an interview and more of a gossipy, girlie chat as we swapped stories and laughed at each other's jokes. We talked about how I'd got into modelling, tricks of the trade to make your boobs look bigger and whether all the different girls got on together.

When she asked me what I had planned for the future, I rather cheekily told her that I fancied having a job like hers. 'You should go for it,' she said, touching my knee. 'I think you'd be great on TV.'

Out of the corner of my eye I could see Steve behind the cameras giving me a big thumbs-up and I knew then that it was going really well. Afterwards the producer came over and introduced himself. I chatted and flirted to the best of my ability – I wanted to be sure that if he ever moved on or launched another show he'd keep me in mind.

In the weeks that followed, Steve's efforts to get me back in demand started to pay real dividends. Although I was trying to move away from straight modelling work, a few offers started to trickle in as a result of my rising profile. Although none of the jobs came to anything, it was still very encouraging.

I realised that a big part of the problem was that my portfolio was badly out of date. The pictures were so old that it was embarrassing to show them to anyone – it looked as though I was trying to lie about my age. And while I had a few videos of my old television appearances, I needed to get them professionally edited on to a single tape if I wanted anyone to take me seriously. But I couldn't afford it.

I knew Steve would have lent me the money in an instant, but I didn't want to compromise our professional relationship. There was also the fact that he was already investing loads of time and energy into my career, none of which he was being paid for. He was already going beyond the call of duty; I couldn't ask for more.

Instead I found some more part-time bar work. First

I had to pay back Jules which was going to take a few weeks, but once I'd done that I was determined to start saving, confident that it would only be a matter of time before everything fell into place and I'd be able to take pride in knowing that I'd made it on my own.

It was more than a month after we'd first met that Lynn called. I was pleased to find that she was just as chatty and bubbly sober as she had been at the party, and she soon had me in fits of giggles as we caught up on each other's news – she told me about her most recent shopping trips and I told her all about my appearance on *The Sex Show*.

Then, out of the blue, she started talking about the job that Michael had mentioned. 'The thing is, I know you don't have a car so you couldn't work here, but the business has expanded and we're now making some deliveries abroad, mostly to Ireland. You get on a plane and then come straight back, but it's always at very short notice, so we're trying to put together a small team; that way there's always going to be someone who is free.'

I'd only wanted the first job because I thought it came with a car, and my lack of enthusiasm for what Lynn was talking about clearly came across in my voice.

'I'll tell you what,' she said, 'just come over to the house tomorrow, say about midday. I'd love you to see the place anyway and Michael's working from home so he can tell you all about it. Just jump in a cab – don't worry about the cost, I'll pay the driver when you get here.'

The following morning my cab pulled up outside an

enormous white rustic-style farmhouse in the Hertfordshire village of Radlett and I couldn't help but gasp in admiration. Set well back from the road and surrounded by impressive gardens with a large pair of wooden gates at the end of the drive, it was less a home and more a small country hotel.

Lynn rushed out to greet me and, after paying the cabbie, insisted on giving me the big tour straight away. The house just seemed to go on and on and on. The amount of space and the number of rooms they had was just incredible. Not only that but the interior was every bit as impressive as the exterior and it struck me that almost every room had been decorated just the way I would have done it myself. Every fitting was of the highest possible quality and there were dozens of original paintings and antiques dotted around.

Lynn wouldn't tell me what they had paid for the place, but she said it had recently been valued at just over £1 million. She loved the house, she told me, but she'd be even happier if she had one just like it somewhere where the weather was better.

The centrepiece of the back garden was a large swimming pool that would not have looked out of place in an upmarket health spa. The tour continued into a conservatory area overlooking the garden. It was here that Michael had his office. He was sitting at a high table surrounded by three televisions, each suspended from the ceiling by a metal bracket. Each screen showed a different teletext page displaying currency rates from around the world.

As we walked in, Michael was tapping the keypad of one of those calculators that prints on to a roll of paper, and scribbling down numbers into an accounts book. He got up and greeted me warmly, and then the three of us made our way to the main living room, dominated by a large electric-blue sofa with dozens of soft cushions, and sat down to talk.

After exchanging pleasantries, Michael got right down to business and asked if I was interested in working for the bureau. 'My mum's been doing some but she's getting on a bit now. My brother and Lynn's sister help out too but we need a few more. Also, there's a limit on the amount one person can take out of the country, so sometimes we have to send two people together. I know you're not working full-time so I thought it might suit you.'

The mention of limits intrigued me. 'What would I be delivering?' I asked.

'Just currency,' he replied.

'Oh, but isn't that all done by computer these days?'

Michael nodded and leaned forward. I felt myself dreading another lecture on high finance. 'A lot of it is, but at the end of the day, if you're going to France and you want to spend French francs, then someone needs to bring the physical notes from one country to another. It doesn't matter how much money it says you've got on the computer screen, without the hard currency it's useless.

'When we get busier I'll start sending it by Securicor, but at the moment the amounts are so small that it's just not cost-effective. It also takes longer – the money has to sit in a warehouse for a couple of days waiting to clear Customs. If I send my mum or someone, they can go through Customs there and then.

'It's like courier flights, you know, when people get those cheap flights abroad so the company can use their baggage allowance. The companies who send stuff don't just do it because it's cheaper but because it's much quicker too.'

'Do I have to bring anything back?' I asked.

'Oh God no. Just hand over the money and come straight back. It couldn't be simpler,' Lynn pitched in. 'You might even have time for a bit of shopping, especially on the overnight trips.'

It all seemed to make sense, but I still wasn't sure if I was really interested. It took only one more sentence from Michael to convince me that I was. 'The money's pretty good. It sounds like a lot but it's a fraction of what we'd have to pay to hire Securicor or someone like that. Basically it's £400 for the day trips and £800 if you have to stay overnight.'

Michael was explaining about the hotels they used and how my expenses would be paid, but I was no longer really listening. All I could think about was the money, about how this could be a new start for me: the chance to get a new portfolio and finish my showreel. It was just the break I'd been hoping for.

I eagerly agreed to travel to Dublin that same afternoon. As Lynn phoned the airline and booked me on the next flight, Michael unlocked a steel cabinet close to his desk and took out two slim bundles of £50 notes, each held together with a paper band with '£2,500' printed on it.

'Is that it?' Somehow I'd been expecting there to be a lot more.

Michael grinned. 'Yeah. That's what I'm saying, the

amounts are so small it's not worth using a security company.' He slipped the money into a small brown envelope, which I then put in my bag. He handed me a few more notes to cover cab fare and I set off for the airport.

I arrived in Dublin late in the afternoon and jumped in a taxi, asking the driver to take me to a nearby hotel as I'd been instructed. As soon as I walked into the lobby a middle-aged man in a leather jacket and blue jeans got up and headed towards me. 'You must be Tracy. I'm Don. Michael said it would be easy to spot you. He told me to look out for someone who looked like a Page Three girl.'

We made our way to a sweet little café in an annexe of the hotel, where I handed over the money and Don ordered tea and cakes for two. Over the course of the next twenty minutes we chatted about how he and Michael had met, life in Ireland and the joys and perils of flying. The conversation had just started to dry up when Don finished his second slice of chocolate fudge cake and offered me a lift back to the airport.

Michael had told me to drop in on my way home so that he could pay me there and then. It was dark by the time I finally got back to my place and I was so exhausted that I just flopped down on the floor in front of the sofa.

I must have been there ten minutes before I remembered the money. I pulled the wad of forty £20 notes out of my bag, spreading them out on the floor in front of me. Even after I'd paid off my remaining bills and given Jules back the money she had lent me, there would still be plenty left. I felt like I'd won the lottery.

The following day I took Jules out to lunch and then went shopping, thrilled just to know that I was about to buy something for the first time in months. I wasn't going to spend it *all* on clothes, but I felt I deserved a little treat. After several blissful hours of trying on dozens of items, I settled on a fantastic pair of boots and, eager to try them out with some of my favourite trousers, I rushed home.

As I put the key in my front door, I heard the phone start to ring. By the time I reached it, the answering machine had picked up the call and Steve's voice was pleading with me to pick up if I was there.

'I can't believe you're screening your calls, who are you hiding from?'

'I've just got in, honestly.'

'And I'm the Queen of Sheba. Actually I might well be. I once had this session with this hypnotist who took me back into past lives and discovered—'

'Steve, is there a point to this call? I'm busy, I've got new boots to try on.'

'That's great. You can wear them next week: the producer of *The Sex Show* wants you to go back as a guest presenter.'

I was so stunned I couldn't think of a single thing to say. I just sat there with the phone against my ear, replaying Steve's words over and over again in my head.

'Tracy? Tracy, are you there? Oh my God. Quick, Abs, get me an ambulance. Tracy's had a heart attack. Then get me Linda Lusardi, see if she's free to do a presenting job next week.'

'Hey!'

'Just kidding. It's great news. It's your first proper

presenting job and it's going to look fabulous on your showreel.'

'What does it pay?'

'Oh, there's no pay, and it's strictly a one-off, but it means that all the hard work you've been doing is really starting to pay off. You're on your way, Tracy, you're on your way.'

Chapter Six

Working on the time-honoured principle that it is best to stick with what you know, I decided to devote my episode of *The Sex Show* to the world of the Page Three girl.

The whole show was going to be transmitted live and the last thing I wanted was to end up looking like an idiot: at least if the theme was a subject I knew well then I'd be less likely to dry up. The producer was more than happy with the idea, particularly as the transmission date almost coincided with the twenty-fifth anniversary of Page Three.

The fact that it was L!veTV meant that the audience would only amount to a couple of thousand people at best, but it was such a golden opportunity to show what I could do that I wanted to make sure it went as smoothly as possible.

Maria agreed to be a guest – I only had to twist her arm a little bit – and I set about tracking down Flannagan, one of the very first women to pose topless in the *Sun*. As well as chat, the show would include a live phone-in and reviews of some soft-porn videos.

Just as I was getting into my stride preparing the programme, Lynn called and asked if I'd be free to go to Spain the following day. This time I'd be travelling with her younger sister, Karen, and staying overnight in a five-star hotel. I couldn't say yes fast enough.

I got to Radlett just after midday and sat drinking tea and making small talk with Lynn and Michael as we waited for Karen to arrive. I'm always a bit nervous meeting new people – I worry what preconceptions they might have about me – and when the doorbell rang I took a deep breath and desperately tried to think of a witty and interesting way to introduce myself.

But instead of Karen I found myself saying hello to a stout Arabic man who told me his name was Sam ('It's short for Housam') and explained that he was the manager of the Edgware Road bureau de change. He and Michael started talking business and Lynn and I started talking designer shoes and before long the doorbell rang once more. The minute I set eyes on Karen I knew that everything was going to be just fine. She looked incredibly friendly, and had a really dirty laugh and a fantastic sense of humour. By the time our taxi to the airport arrived, we were more or less ignoring the others and nattering away like long-lost chums.

Just as we were leaving, Sam asked Michael whether he'd given us the authorisation notes. When Michael admitted that he hadn't, Sam was furious. Rolling his eyes and swearing under his breath, he started hunting through his briefcase, pulled out a few forms and began filling them in. The authorisation notes, he explained, showed that Karen and I were working for a legitimate bureau de change. If we didn't have them with us, Customs officers could take the money and keep hold of it until we could produce them. Sam had experienced that situation in the past and said it could take weeks to get the money back. Michael apologised softly as Sam slipped the notes into an envelope and handed it to Karen.

It didn't take Karen and me long to get on to the subject of men. In the back of the car on the way to Stansted, sitting in the departure lounge waiting for our flight and in between a shocking number of vodka-and-lemonades on the plane itself, we learned that we'd both had more than our fair share of losers, abusers and heartache. Although our lives had been very different, we had a huge amount in common and by the time we arrived in Spain we were great mates.

Karen had made the trip dozens of times before and knew the routine like the back of her hand. We arrived just after 4 p.m., took a taxi down to Marbella and booked into a hotel called the El Fuerte.

Sitting at the end of a beautiful palm-shaded road, the El Fuerte was a bright pink four-storey building right on the beach. I followed Karen inside the cool marble foyer, glad to get out of the afternoon heat, and slowly drank in my surroundings. To my right was a mini-shopping-mall, where tiny boutiques sold designer clothes and elegant jewellery; to my left was the main bar, its dark wicker chairs, squashy leather sofas, heavy tables and brass lanterns making it look like an old English gentlemen's club. The narrow part of the bar opened out on to a large garden, filled with more palm trees, tables, chairs and sun loungers, all of which surrounded a crystal-blue swimming pool. On a small stage tucked into a corner, a pianist played instrumental versions of popular ballads.

We still had a couple of hours before our meeting

with Michael's business partner, so we dumped our things in our room and rushed down to catch the last of the sun's rays while sipping cocktails beside the pool. I sighed deeply. It was just the kind of place I had stayed in during my many modelling trips abroad. If I shut my eyes, it was like nothing in my life had changed.

Just after eight, Karen and I made our way to a little Chinese restaurant just opposite the hotel. There we met Michael's contact, a Moroccan guy called Mohammed, and his girlfriend Aisha. Karen handed over the currency, then we had a beautiful meal. After bidding the couple goodbye an hour or so later, Karen and I donned our glad rags and took a trip to a local nightclub, where we spent our time dancing and drinking until the small hours.

On the plane back to England we continued to get to know one another. Lynn had told Karen all about my Page Three past and she wanted to know all the juicy details. After that it was my turn to find out all about her life. I was in for a bit of a shock.

Karen had been talking about her two-year-old daughter, Paige, and how hard it was to balance looking after her with earning a living, especially as her relationship with Paige's father was far from ideal. And then, quite casually, she said something about having worked as a receptionist in a brothel that Lynn and Michael owned.

She saw my confused expression as my badly hungover brain took in what she had said. She paused mid-sentence. 'You do know about the saunas and massage parlours, don't you? I thought everyone did.'

I shook my head slowly. I wasn't at all sure that I wanted to hear what was coming next.

And that was when she started to tell me how Lynn and Michael had got together and the incredible story of how they had made their fortune.

Karen and Lynn were never close as children. The five-year age gap meant that when Lynn got to the stage of staying out all night partying, Karen was still getting a thrill out of sneaking into her bedroom and trying on her make-up and clothes. As an eighteen-year-old woman, Lynn had no interest in hanging around with a thirteen-year-old kid and even less in Jill, the youngest in the family, who was just eleven.

For as long as anyone could remember, Lynn had always loved money and always lived life in the fast lane. She would spend her nights at clubs like Tramp and Browns, being chatted up by rich men before deciding who would be the most likely to bankroll her increasingly extravagant lifestyle until she got bored and moved on to a new victim. It didn't take her long to make the jump from exchanging sex for gifts to cutting out the pretence and simply offering sex in return for money. Working both the club circuit and also briefly in a local sauna, it was a career in which she quickly excelled. By the age of twenty-two, Lynn was driving a flashy sports car and dripping with fur coats, diamonds and pearls.

Her first truly steady relationship was with Jason, the owner of a chain of clothing shops, who drove around in a large white Bentley with gold trim. He believed it was true love, but for Lynn he was just another meal ticket. After six months the relationship began to founder. Only too well aware of just how mercenary Lynn was, Jason offered her £20,000 to stay with him.

He badly underestimated her: she took the money and left him anyway.

For once, rather than going out on a massive spending spree and blowing the lot in a few weeks, Lynn figured it would be far better to invest the cash in a business where she knew she would be guaranteed to get a good return. So she decided to buy a sauna.

After exploring various options, she ended up going into business with a woman called Ruth, who had run the saunas that Lynn had briefly worked in. A good fifteen years older, Ruth had been in the vice business for decades and knew everything there was to know about how to make a success of it. They settled on a property in the middle of Highgate and sat back to watch the money roll in.

By the time Karen was in her early twenties she envied the lifestyle of her older sister. Although she had no desire to work as a prostitute herself, she accepted an offer to work as a receptionist at the sauna. By then Lynn had given up 'working' and settled into a managerial position. Although they were getting close, the relationship between the two remained strained: Lynn made a point of not offering Karen the job herself and got Ruth to do it instead.

'Most days I'd get there at eleven in the morning and work a twelve-hour shift,' Karen told me. 'There would be two girls working and my job would be to answer the phone and describe the girls for the customers: "Today we have Tina; she's twenty-five, brunette, slim, busty and gives a very good massage." A lot of the time the calls would be from regulars wanting to know if their favourite was doing a shift that day. When people turned up, I would take £20 from them – the cost of a straight massage. Anything else they negotiated with the girls. That's how you get round the law, that and not mentioning anything sexual over the phone.'

Under the current legislation, Karen explained, prostitution itself is not illegal unless you advertise your services. That's why girls walking the streets and then going up to men and offering sex can be arrested – they are soliciting. But if a woman advertises herself as an escort and at the end of the evening the man offers money for sex, no law is broken. The same regulations mean that a house only becomes a brothel if there are more than two prostitutes working there. As long as the saunas only ever had two girls at any one time, they were pretty much safe.

'I really liked the work. Every day was different and some of the things that happened were so fascinating, it was worth being there just to see them for myself. There was one guy who used to bring his own dog lead. He'd pay his money and then go to see one of the girls. Then after about fifteen minutes, the door would open and the girl dealing with him would check that the coast was clear and say, "I'm just going to bring him out now."

'The bloke would be on all fours with the lead around his neck and be led around the reception area barking like a dog. It was hard to keep a straight face. There were even a couple of well known celebrities and television personalities.' My eyes widened as Karen told me their names and what they used to get up to. 'I never got bored of it. I loved talking to the girls during the quiet times and listening to their stories. Each one of them was different: some of them really liked it, some of them hated it. Some had pimps, others had husbands and kids. It was fascinating.'

One woman, Tina, had been married but her husband used to go off to the sauna on a regular basis in order to have sex with Ruth. Then, when they got into trouble with bills at home, he had suggested that Tina might earn some extra cash by working in the sauna too. Before too long, Tina had started a relationship with Ruth, and not long after that kicked the husband out of the love triangle.

Ruth had long employed Michael Michael as her accountant and when she and Lynn bought the new business, Michael got the job of looking after the books. Ruth had told the two of them that she thought they would be perfect for each other, and when they were finally introduced they hit it off right away. As their relationship developed, so Michael became more and more involved with the running of the sauna. He would pop in every now and then to see how things were coming along and appointed his younger brother, Sonny, as the company odd-job man.

'I got to know Michael quite well during those early days and really liked him,' said Karen. 'There was never anything deep, just general chit chat, but he seemed like a nice guy. He had a lot of money and that meant he was just the type of bloke that Lynn went for. I thought he was just another boyfriend and that before too long it would all be over – she'd never been serious about anyone in her life. But there was obviously something much more to the relationship because it lasted and lasted and then before I knew it he and Lynn had started living together.'

The couple also started expanding their business operations. Pooling their resources, they bought a sauna in Neasden, another in West Hampstead and another in Hornsey. The money began to roll in.

'In the Highgate sauna, on a good day I would take in at least £300. Because the girls were getting paid separately, the only overheads were a bit of advertising in the local papers; the rent, which was always dirt cheap; and a bit of electricity. And on the top of each premises there would always be a flat or set of bedsits which they would rent out. Now Lynn and Michael are up to six or seven saunas. They must easily be making £5,000 a week, all of it in cash. That's how they bought the house in Radlett and how they live the life they do. But now Michael wants to do other things so he's started up this bureau de change.' Karen smiled at me. 'And just like before, here I am working for him again.'

We'd moved on to other topics by the time we landed back at Stansted, but I couldn't help looking at Lynn and Michael very differently when we arrived back at Radlett to collect our wages.

When I got home, I sat down and thought about it all. So far as I could see, Lynn and Michael were not doing anything illegal and my contact with them had nothing to do with that side of their business. Although the thought of it still made me uncomfortable, I hoped the feeling would fade. More than anything, I really needed the money: I decided that, for the time being at least, I'd carry on.

I took out my diary and filled in the details of the last two trips abroad, writing the amount I had been paid for each alongside, just the way I used to when I had been modelling. For the first time in a very, very long time I had money in the bank, I could buy drinks in the pub for my friends and I didn't have to worry about how I was going to pay my next set of bills. More than that, I was going to be presenting a live television show in a couple of weeks' time. Having felt like a nobody for such a long time, I now felt like a somebody again.

The next two weeks flew by in the blink of an eye and I found myself sitting on the opposite side of *The Sex Show* sofa, facing a line of cameramen, floor managers and technicians who expected me to know what I was doing. I was absolutely terrified.

Flannagan was on almost straight away and was utterly amazing. She was in her fifties but still drop-dead gorgeous and with the most incredible figure. I started by telling the viewers that she was famous for two things in particular and asked if she would show them off. Then she stood, hitched up her dress and displayed her smooth, firm and very, very long legs.

We chatted a little about the early days of Page Three and how the then editor, Sir Larry Lamb, did not like girls with big boobs and was more of a leg man, and how times had changed. That was the cue for Maria to join us and for the conversation to shift to hairstyles, dance competitions and her new career as a singer.

After a short commercial break it was time for the naughty-video view. The show's resident reviewer joined me and we settled back to watch three clips of the latest releases. The first, *Screen Test*, set the tone for what was to follow. Shot on the cheap in a set that looked like the director's house, it was about a bunch of girls trying to get parts in porn films. I hadn't seen any of the films in advance and I suddenly felt really self-conscious and embarrassed. I could feel myself starting to blush as my companion went through details of the plots – if you could call them that.

Finally it was time for the last item – the phone-in. Earlier in the show both Maria and Flannagan had lamented their lack of boyfriends and I asked any eligible young men to call in and ask them out. Big mistake.

The first caller was pretty normal but then Tony from Enfield came on asking to speak to Maria and wanting to know what sort of chat-up lines had been used on her in the past and which had been most successful. The hairs on the back of my neck stood on end. My body's nutcase alarm was ringing loud and clear. 'For example,' said Tony, 'if I came up to you in a club and said, "Get your coat, love, you've pulled," would that work for me?' You could hear the smugness in his voice: he genuinely seemed to expect Maria to be impressed. We looked at one another and shook our heads. 'Actually, Tony, I think you'd get a punch in the mouth with that one,' I replied.

Undeterred, Tony pressed on, his true motivation becoming clear. It turned out that he had met Maria a few years earlier. 'I worked a chat-up line on you then but I didn't get anywhere. So what advice would you give me if I was going to try again?'

'Tony, just be yourself, just stay as you are,' said Maria, single-handedly ensuring that future generations of women would be safe from his slimy clutches.

Soon it was over and Steve assured me it had gone

really well. The whole experience put me on a high for days. Although I'd been nervous throughout, I'd loved every single minute of it: it was the most fun I'd had in years. It felt like I was finally doing something that was right and to be honest a damn sight more natural than taking my clothes off in front of a camera.

As we walked to his car, Steve turned to me.

'Tracy, you were really great tonight and I have an idea of something we should do together.'

I was intrigued but had no idea what he was talking about so I decided to respond with mock horror. 'But Steve, I'm a woman: it would never work.'

He rolled his eyes. 'Honestly, Tracy, you wouldn't have the first idea what to do with my body. What I'm talking is clubbing. I've been chatting to a friend who owns a bar that's a bit quiet on Sundays. I think we should take it over and run a gay club there, together. With your profile and my fantastic contacts, I think we'd do really well.'

And so it was that 'Tracy's Lunchbox' was born. The club was a success right from the start. We opened up at 11 a.m. on Sunday mornings and ran through until midnight, appealing to clubbers who were in no mood to stop partying just because it was the middle of the afternoon. Steve and I worked well together – he organised the publicity and I was the main host – and we kept the seemingly endless stream of punters busy with drinking, dancing and live cabaret acts.

Sundays soon became my favourite day of the week and it all started getting so popular that Steve and I began looking for a bigger venue so we wouldn't have to turn people away. My fears about life after Page Three proved to be unfounded: things couldn't have been much better.

At least once a month I'd get a call from Lynn or Michael asking me to make a trip. As the weeks went by I made day trips to Paris, Dublin and Amsterdam, which was nice as far as the money was concerned but pretty dull in every other way. What I loved most was going to Spain, especially if I went with Karen.

By the time we made our fourth trip to Marbella together, we had a routine all worked out. We would book into the El Fuerte and then head straight to Sinatra's, a tiny bar overlooking the marina at Puerto Banus. It was the place that everyone went to be seen and the view – a sea of enormous yachts from around the world – was always absolutely breathtaking.

A few doors along sat the Azul Marino restaurant, which became our favourite place to eat. The attentive young staff in their fake naval uniforms soon got used to us because our meal would always be the same. To start we would have the oyster mushrooms served with Serrano ham, garlic and parsley; and then bass *a la sal* – the sea bass in rock salt – which had a beautiful, delicate flavour.

From there we would head out to Trader Vic's, a smoky bar full of dark African wood, totem poles and log boats overlooking a swimming pool. We had plenty of time because, following a few panics when the flights had been delayed, the handover of the money had been switched from the evening to the following morning. It meant Karen and I could treat our time in Spain as one big all-expenses-paid holiday almost right up until the moment that it was time to go back.

The only time I didn't enjoy going to Spain was when Michael asked me to go with Sonny, his younger brother. It was only after I'd already made the commitment and allocated which bills I was going to pay off with the money that I learned that, for reasons unknown, Sonny intended to drive to Marbella rather than fly.

As I sat in Michael's living room waiting for Sonny to turn up, my biggest worry was how I was going to cope with being cooped up in a cramped car for such a long time. What if I had to go to the toilet? The more I thought about it, the more stressed I felt. I desperately needed something to take my mind off it. Michael was sitting at the table, straightening piles of notes and running them through a counting machine. The pile sitting nearest me was completely ragged. 'Do you want me to straighten those out for you?' I asked. Michael was so focused on what he was doing that he didn't even make eye contact. 'Please,' he replied.

Sonny stepped into the room a few seconds later and I pushed the straightened pile of notes towards Michael, then stood up to introduce myself. There was little family resemblance: Sonny was taller and slimmer with a slightly wasted look and a pronounced nervous manner, which I put down to him being a little shy. I'd guessed that he was probably scared of flying, but as a member of the family was keen to earn money whenever he could.

The awkwardness continued as we climbed into Sonny's spacious jeep and headed towards Dover, where we would board a train to take us through the Channel Tunnel. And then Sonny finally worked up the courage to say what was on his mind: he explained that he suffered from Crohn's disease, a condition that causes inflammation of the intestines with pain and diarrhoea. Like IBS, the condition is made worse by stress and can lead to the sufferer having to get to a toilet urgently.

With a huge grin on my face that I'm sure Sonny initially found quite disturbing, I explained about my IBS and the fact that effectively we were in the same boat. 'So basically,' Sonny said, 'we're just a pair of big shits.'

After that we both relaxed and got on with the task in hand. Or rather, Sonny did. I thought I was going to be sharing the driving to stop me from getting bored as much as anything else, but Sonny seemed to want to do it all himself. As our conversation started to dry up I began to wonder why Michael had bothered to get me to go along at all.

It seemed to take for ever. At the end of the first day, having travelled for almost twelve hours straight, we were still in France and had hundreds of miles to go. When we finally got to Marbella a day and a half later, we booked straight into the El Fuerte and I collapsed into my room. Sonny took the car off to a local garage – he wanted to make sure it was OK for the journey back – and said that he'd take care of delivering the money too.

I was too tired to go out that night and could barely face the idea of making the drive all the way back. Michael had said that because the journey took a little longer than flying, he'd pay me £1,000 rather than £800, but it had taken so much longer than I'd expected that it just wasn't worth it. The only good thing about it was that all my expenses were paid during the whole trip so for four days I didn't have to worry about food or other bills. But by the time we set off on the journey back – during which Sonny seemed much more relaxed – I'd already made up my mind that I'd never drive to Spain again, only fly. A week or so later I spoke to Karen and learned that she too had done the drive with Sonny, and had quickly come to the same conclusion.

It was a lavish affair, even by the extravagant standards of the Dorchester Hotel. In fact, the surprise party that Lynn threw Michael for his fortieth birthday was a wonder to behold.

The highlight was the unveiling of a cake made to reflect Michael's lifestyle: alongside a bright red '40' were icing-sugar copies of the three mobile phones he always carried, his silver Porsche, the stacks of £50 notes that bulged in his wallet and the Silk Cut cigarettes he constantly smoked.

The whole event was like a miniature version of the testimonial where I'd first met Lynn and Michael. In a large private room about 60 of us were split on to separate tables and enjoyed a sumptuous four-course meal washed down with gallons of champagne, fine wine and liqueurs.

I hardly knew anyone there but by the end of the evening I'd met dozens of wonderful people. I found myself sitting at a table with an incredibly funny guy called Richard Jones who worked as a lorry driver. He didn't seem to have a care in the world and, when he wasn't keeping us all in stitches, spent his time being all lovey-dovey with his wife.

I also met Jill, Lynn and Karen's incredibly beautiful younger sister, whose high cheekbones, long blond hair and perfect skin could easily have led to a career in modelling. She was lovely and, because she and Karen were only eighteen months apart in age, the two of them were clearly much closer to one another than they were to Lynn.

As I moved around the room, meeting more and more of Michael's friends, cousins and family, I got the distinct feeling that this kind of event took place quite regularly and that a fringe benefit of working for Michael was becoming part of a glamorous social circle.

I'd been part of a similar scene during my Page Three days but back then, I'd been too young to appreciate it properly and I'd taken it for granted. Now I was older, I was ready. I could get used to this, I thought to myself.

A week or so after the party, Michael left a message on my mobile asking if I'd be free to make a trip. I rang back and greeted him with a cheery hello.

His voice immediately became soft and low, almost breathless.

'Hello, darling,' he said. 'I'm a bit busy right now, babe, but why don't we meet up later?'

My jaw fell open in shock. 'Michael! It's me, Tracy.'

There was no reply, just an embarrassed silence.

'Who did you think it was?' I continued.

'Oh, erm, I knew it was you,' Michael stuttered. 'I was just er, you know, being funny.'

'No you weren't. You thought that was someone else. Who did you think it was?'

Another silence.

'Well, you sounded like Lynn.'

I could hardly speak for giggling now; it was a joy listening to Michael squirm. 'You don't talk to Lynn like that either. You've never called her "babe" in your life.'

My mind started to work overtime. It was pretty clear that Michael was having some kind of affair, but who with?

My questions were destined to remain unanswered as Michael swiftly switched the subject back to work. He had a large quantity of cash to take to Spain and had arranged for a bunch of girls to travel out together. There would be myself; Karen; Debbie, who was married to one of Michael's cousins; and Jan, who was a long-standing friend of Lynn's.

As far as the four of us were concerned, it was just an excuse to party. We spent the night at Trader Vic's, cackling away like a coven of witches and praying that there would be an air-traffic controllers' strike or something so we'd be stranded there for a few days.

It was while we were on our fifth round of vodkas that Debbie bumped into someone she vaguely knew. Freddie was about sixty and so fat his breasts were bigger than mine. He had a mop of greasy thinning hair and produced a steady stream of white goo from the corners of his mouth whenever he spoke.

Eager to impress, he bought us all drinks and, in between puffs on a fat cigar, began feeding us his well-worn lines about how he had become a multi-millionaire by importing soft drinks from Russia and how he knew this and that celebrity. I guess we weren't acting impressed enough because pretty soon he was promising to prove his claims by taking us to an exclusive club, the sort of place that wouldn't let you in unless you were on the guest list.

The club turned out to be fantastic and we were really enjoying ourselves, taking turns on the dance floor and propping up the bar. It was while I was doing the latter that, without warning, Freddie grabbed me by the shoulders and stuck his tongue down my throat. It was just like the scene in *Alien* where that horrible-looking creature jumps on someone's face and tries to suck the life out of them. I couldn't move, I couldn't breathe. It was disgusting.

When Karen saw what was going on she didn't hesitate: she lashed out and gave Freddie a right-hander to the back of the head. 'You dirty old bastard,' she said. 'What the hell do you think you're playing at?'

Freddie began to protest that he'd bought us drinks and taken us to a club so he had every right to get a little something in return.

After putting him straight on those points in no uncertain terms, we left. It took more than an hour for me to get the taste of his cigar and spittle out of my mouth, but only a few minutes before I could laugh about the whole experience.

Back in Radlett the following day Karen and I were recounting the story to Michael and Lynn when Michael suddenly went pale. He asked us to describe how Freddie looked in more detail and when we'd finished he got up and started pacing around the room. He seemed to be genuinely distressed.

'Jesus Christ, Tracy,' he said, 'you're so naïve. You've got to be careful. That man Freddie, he's a drug dealer. A big fucking drug dealer. You've got to avoid him – don't have anything to do with him. He's really bad news. He didn't ask you to do anything for him, did he?'

I shook my head.

'Well thank God for that. Listen, I really mean this, you've got to keep away from that guy. He's really dangerous.'

It was as if Karen and I were a couple of teenagers and Michael was our father, lecturing us on the evils of drugs. But he was so passionate, so adamant about protecting us that we couldn't help but be moved by his level of concern. We both assured him we would never speak to Freddie again.

As I made my way home I thought about the lucky escape I'd had. In the past I'd often made bad decisions, ended up hanging about with the wrong people and suffering as a result. It was nice to know that Michael Michael was watching out for me.

The advertisement in *The Stage*, the weekly newspaper for the entertainment profession, caught my eye straight away. A production company was looking for reporters for *Show Talk*, a new programme destined for Channel Four. There would be two people in the studio interviewing guests and introducing film clips and one roving reporter out at gigs, clubs and premieres.

I knew Steve must have seen the ad too because he read the paper cover to cover every week. When he didn't call to suggest I applied I knew it could mean only one thing – that I didn't have a chance. But I decided to go for it anyway.

It was an open audition, which meant you could just turn up, and as soon as I arrived, I realised why Steve hadn't said anything. There were at least two hundred people there, many of whom I recognised from other

TV shows and all of whom seemed to have far more experience than me. Having spent months building up my confidence, I felt it crash back down to ground level.

But there was no way I was just going to walk out. I took my place in the line and, after waiting for an hour and a half, stepped into the main room, where the producers sat at a long table. They took a Polaroid of me, asked me to say a few lines into a video camera and then sent me on my way. The interview had lasted less than a minute. I was annoyed at myself for having wasted so much time and energy but I consoled myself that I'd learned a valuable lesson. Two days later I got a call from the production company asking me to go back for a second interview at the end of the month. I was so convinced it was just a friend winding me up that I almost blew it.

I told Steve right away and he was really excited and set about getting me ready as best he could. The second audition was going to be identical to the first but with fewer people around and slightly more time in front of the camera. Steve took me through a few sample questions and shot some video of me doing some mock introductions so I could see what mistakes I was making.

I didn't have many nerves on the day – partly because Steve had done such a good job preparing me and partly because I didn't think I had a hope in hell so I had nothing to lose. As soon as I'd finished, the producer told me that he wanted me to come back for a third time.

I still didn't think I had much hope of landing the job but I was so chuffed about getting through the first couple of rounds that I felt it was worth celebrating. Maria was also in the mood to party, having fallen madly in love with a musician who had been riding high in the charts. Having not spent any quality time together for months, we decided to have a good old girls' night out.

We got ourselves all dolled up and headed for the Ministry of Sound. We were soon in the midst of a large group of friends and friends of friends and I found myself talking to a bloke called Chris whom I vaguely remembered meeting at a party a couple of years earlier.

We were sitting at a table in a corner of the club, our heads close together so we could hear each other above the sound of the music, when in walked Alex, surrounded by a group of Arabic men, and sat at another table. I was lost for words. All I could do was stare. I'd almost convinced myself that the rape had been nothing but a bad dream. Seeing him again made it only too real.

Chris followed my gaze. 'Aw fuck, not him. That guy's bad news. You don't know him, do you?'

I hardly knew Chris. I had no desire to confide in him, but somehow I couldn't stop the words from coming out of my mouth. 'I don't know what happened,' I mumbled. 'I went out with him. I don't really remember much after that.'

Chris leaned forward on the table and rested his forehead on the heels of his hands. 'Shit,' he said softly. 'Shit. Listen Tracy, you know I'm a drug dealer, right?'

I moved back a little. 'Actually no, I didn't know that at all . . .'

'Well, it's not really important. The thing is that guy, Alex, he's a pimp—'

'No, he's a model.'

Chris shook his head again. 'No no, that's his line. He's a pimp. Those Arabs you see him with, they're his clients.' Chris took a deep breath. His next words were barely a whisper. 'Did you have sex with him?'

'I . . . I don't know.' Tears were starting to roll down my cheeks.

'If you don't know it means he drugged you. There are these tablets called Rohypnol, it's a tranquilliser; I used to supply him with them until I found out what he was using them for. If his clients see a girl they like but she won't go along with them, he uses the drugs. He doesn't always need to – the girls earn good money and a lot of them do it just for that. But if you weren't having any of it, then he wouldn't want to take any chances. He would have been paid a lot of money for bringing them someone like you so it's worth his while.'

Maria came over to where I was sitting. 'What the hell's going on here?' she said. I tried to stand but my legs were shaking. I tried to speak but my throat was drying up. I felt like I was about to faint. I could hear the concern in Maria's voice. 'What's wrong, Tracy? You're scaring me. What's the matter?' She was holding me now, keeping me upright. I managed to lift an arm and extend a finger in the direction of the tall man in the leather coat at the other end of the room.

'That's him, that's the one.'

'What do you mean?'

'That's him. That's the rapist.'

In a split second Maria was standing in front of Alex. She slapped her hands against his chest, knocking the wind out of him and pushing him back against the bar.

'You fucking pervert, you nonce, you fucking rapist!' she screamed at the top of her voice.

Alex had been taken completely by surprise. 'I don't know what you're talking about,' he said calmly. He was desperately trying to be cool, trying not to draw attention to himself in front of his Arab friends. He was smiling smugly at those around him as if to say, 'Who is this weirdo?'

It just made Maria even angrier. 'That's what I'm talking about,' she said, pointing at me. 'You raped her.'

Alex's face fell. I could see the fear in his eyes and it made me feel strong. I stood up and walked over to him.

'You're a sick, sick man.'

'I . . . I didn't do anything. I . . .'

He was trying to calm me down, using his hands to signal for me to keep my voice down. I wasn't having any of it. 'Yes you did. You raped me, you and your friends raped me.'

By now a crowd was starting to gather round and an angry buzz began to develop within it as the details of what was happening were explained. Behind me, I could catch snatches of angry conversation: 'He did what?'; 'Fucking animal'; 'That's one sick motherfucker.'

I stood back and pointed at Alex. 'This man raped me. He drugged me and then he raped me, and then his friends raped me.' Then I grabbed Maria's arm. 'Come on,' I said, 'we're leaving.'

Behind me the crowd closed in. The Arabs scattered and I could hear Alex's increasingly desperate pleas as the mob surrounded him. 'No . . . it wasn't like that . . . she wanted . . . no, I never . . .' Then I heard his cries of pain as the first blows began to rain down on him.

Running into Alex had been horrendous but having the chance to stand up to him and tell him what he had done to me was incredibly liberating. I felt as though my life was once again under my control.

Maria and I kept walking until we were out of the club. I did not look back.

Chapter Seven

When I'd first started working for Michael Michael, the money was all that mattered. The fine detail of the bureau de change business, the distinctions between the different currencies, the prevailing rates of exchange – none of it was of any interest to me at all. But as the weeks went by and the number of entries in my diary started to increase, so did my feeling of unease.

I'd been so busy there had been no time to take stock, so I made myself sit down and look over my records: I'd made my first trip for him back in mid-August and by the following March I'd been away more than 25 times. In the early days, I'd made deliveries maybe once or twice per month. Now I found myself going away two or three times in the same week.

The money was still nice but far from essential. Thanks to Steve I was getting bits and pieces of modelling and advertising work, some of it quite well paid, and the Lunchbox club was also turning a tidy profit. I was so busy that it was getting more and more difficult to make deliveries at short notice. I'd turned down a couple of trips and Michael had been quite pissed off about it, which troubled me. Ever since the beginning of the year his mood had become increasingly surly and he was becoming difficult to deal with. I knew that he and Lynn were no longer getting on that well and I guessed the strain of having an affair behind her back was starting to get to him.

But there was also the work itself. Although travelling to Málaga with Karen was still great fun, the other trips had lost their novelty and now held little appeal. After thinking it over long and hard, I decided the best thing all round would be for me to quit.

I spent almost a month trying to find the right time to tell Michael that I no longer wanted to work for him, but I could never catch him on his own. I knew that if both of them were there, it would be much harder to turn them down. When another trip to Spain came up I agreed, partly because it was another chance to go shopping with Karen, but also because I knew Lynn was away with the boys and that I'd get a chance to chat to Michael alone.

I put on my best smile and rang the doorbell, hoping to soften the blow with a healthy dose of glamour-model charm, but as soon as Michael answered I knew I was wasting my time – he looked completely exhausted, as if he'd been up all night, and was clearly in no mood for bad news.

He took me through to the conservatory and explained that Sam was on his way over with currency so I'd have to wait awhile. I tried to start a conversation, asking how the building work was going, but Michael just shrugged his shoulders. He just sat in a chair, staring intently at a spot on the floor in front of him.

Gently, slowly, he started rocking back and forth. His breathing became heavier until I could hear the air hissing in and out of his nostrils. He started wringing his hands and then began mumbling something under his breath. I leaned forward, desperately trying to make out what he was saying, but the words were all jumbled together.

Then he turned to face me. He was looking straight at me but his eyes were so cold that it felt as though he were looking right through me. And then he spoke. 'I told her not to do it.'

There was something about the tone of his voice that sent a shiver down my spine. My throat got so dry I had to swallow three times before I could reply, 'Do what, Michael?'

'I told her not to fucking do it, but she did it anyway.'

I leaned back in the seat, trying to put as much distance between the two of us as possible.

Michael pulled himself to his feet and began pacing around the room, his words rattling out of his mouth like machine-gun fire. 'I ain't gonna put up with it any more. I'll teach the fucking cow. I'll fucking kill her. I'll make sure she sees it coming. I'll shoot her in the head. I'll do it myself. I ain't afraid.'

He stopped directly in front of me. I glanced over to the door. It might just as well have been a mile away. My limbs were stiff and leaden with fear. I was cold all over and I could feel myself starting to shake. When I tried to speak I found that I'd developed a stutter. 'M-Michael, what's going on? Wha . . . what has Lynn done?'

Michael's voice grew louder with each new word until it hurt my ears to listen. 'It's not what she's done,' he spat back, pacing the room once more, 'it's what she's gonna fucking do. She'll grass me up, anything happens and she'll grass me up straight away, the fucking bitch. You'll see.'

My mind was racing. I so wanted to get out of there.

I just wanted to be anywhere else in the world apart from there in that room with Michael but I was rooted to the spot with terror. Grass him up? Grass him up over what? What the hell was he talking about?

My instincts took over: I had to calm him down. I said the first thing that came into my head, keeping my voice as soft and low as I could: 'She wouldn't do that, Michael, I'm sure she'd never do that—'

His whole body whipped round and his fat fingers pointed at me. 'Yes she fucking would,' he hissed. 'And you fucking would as well. You'd do the same.' Michael took a step towards me. His face was red and sweaty; his fists were clenched so tightly that his knuckles had turned white. I wanted to tell him that I didn't know anything, that I couldn't grass him up, but I couldn't form the words. I couldn't even scream.

He took another step forward and I closed my eyes, unable to watch whatever was going to happen next. I expected to feel his fingers around my throat; instead I felt the cushions of the sofa shift as Michael sat down beside me.

As quickly as it had come, his rage dissipated, though the atmosphere remained thick with tension. I was still terrified, and we just sat there in silence for several minutes until the doorbell rang and Michael got up to answer it.

It was Sam. With another man in the house Michael seemed to calm down completely and pretty soon it was as if nothing untoward had ever happened. But I wasn't taking any chances. Stuffing the bundles of cash into my bag, I left the house so quickly that I'm sure Sam thought I was trying to avoid him.

⋆　⋆　⋆

I arrived at Málaga Airport, rushed through Customs and took a taxi straight to the El Fuerte, where Karen was staying, having arrived on an earlier flight. I was still a bundle of nerves as I stepped into the room and collapsed on the bed. As I recounted the details of what Michael had been saying her eyes widened with horror. She too had been growing increasingly concerned about the frequency of the trips she was making; now we were both convinced that something incredibly dodgy was going on. But what?

We tried to list the facts as we knew them, but we quickly ran out of things we could be absolutely certain of. The only thing we knew for sure was that Michael and Lynn were making vast amounts of money from their chain of saunas and massage parlours.

The bureau de change seemed genuine enough – I'd seen the offices myself – and there was no doubt that Michael was obsessed with the rates of exchange for foreign currency, but the trips we'd been making didn't seem quite right. Why deliver the money at a hotel or restaurant? Why not simply go to the bureau de change itself? Suddenly all the questions we'd never thought to ask were at the forefront of our minds. Top of the list: what was the money for?

We talked through the various options: bootlegging, international prostitution, drugs, VAT fraud, even terrorism and arms-smuggling – there was no evidence to support any of it. Then Karen leaned forward, her fingertips resting gently on her upper lip. 'I've just thought of something. On the very first trip I went on, Michael told me that if we got stopped and asked about the money, we should say we were buying a property in

Spain. Maybe that's what he's doing.'

Somewhere in the back of my mind I recalled Lynn talking about wanting to live abroad. At the same time, Karen remembered a drunken conversation about a Spanish villa that Michael was trying to buy.

It all seemed to fall into place. Michael was taking the profits from his saunas and massage parlours and investing it in property all over Europe. We didn't know what the exact scam was – whether he was trying to evade VAT or whatever – but it had to be something like that for him to be worried about Lynn grassing him up. Whatever it was, I knew I couldn't afford to get caught up in a new scandal at a time when my career was back on the up. I had to end it.

As for the threats Michael had made, Karen had heard them a thousand times before and told me to ignore them. 'It's all bollocks,' she said. 'He just likes to think he's a bit of a hard nut. But you've seen him, you know him. He's not a gangster, he's just a chubby Greek bloke.'

Two days later I was back in Cheshunt and Michael phoned me, full of apologies for his outburst, and asked me to fly to Amsterdam. I took a deep breath and told him that I didn't want to go. I knew there was no point in lying and saying I was too busy – he'd only call me the following day and ask again.

It was as if I'd unleashed a caged animal. After a second or two of silence, he began screaming at me.

'What do you mean, you can't go? Don't give me that shit. If I say you're going then you're fucking well going, you bitch. You ain't gonna let me down. You can't just fucking walk away from this.'

I was totally unprepared for such an onslaught. My heart was pounding and I could feel painful spasms in my stomach. I thought I was going to be sick. The more I tried to get out of it, the angrier he became. In the end he simply put his foot down. He wouldn't have it any other way. 'Don't fuck about with me, Tracy. You've got to go. End of story.'

After that, there was no way I was going to risk meeting him at home, especially as Lynn was still away. I started to feel quite anxious because I could tell that he knew I was scared of him and I suspected he liked it. I hated being in such a weak position. He kept insisting that I go to his house but I was determined to stand my ground. Finally we arranged to meet up at the Hilton Hotel at Watford.

I arrived to find the hotel lobby buzzing with people, but Michael stood out like a sore thumb. He was sitting at a table in the corner wearing a full-length black leather coat and had three mobile phones spread out in front of him. Instead of an earpiece he had a full headset – the kind of thing pop stars wear when they dance about on stage. He could not have looked more conspicuous if he'd tried. I was overcome with a sudden urge to back out of the lobby and run away but it was too late: he had already seen me.

He beckoned me over, standing up to kiss both my cheeks and smiling warmly as he introduced me to his companion. 'Tracy, lovely to see you. This is André. Sit down, sit down. What are you drinking?' All I could think was, Just give me the money and let me get the hell out of here, but Michael insisted on making me suffer. 'I don't think I've got time,' I said weakly. 'I should probably get going . . .'

Michael glanced at his watch. 'Nonsense, nonsense, there's loads of time. I'll get André to call you a cab a bit later. Sit down, relax. I'll get you a vodka-lemonade, that's your drink isn't it?'

Michael and André were doing their best to make small talk but I just wasn't in the mood. I had a few sips of my drink then told them that I'd heard there had been an accident on the M11 and that unless I left immediately I might not make it to the airport. Reluctantly, Michael let me go.

I sighed with relief as I settled into the back seat of the cab. I hadn't quite worked out how I was going to break the news to him, but I knew for certain that this was going to be the last trip I'd ever make for Michael. I tried not to think about how uncomfortable he'd made me feel or the way he had threatened me; I just wanted to be alone with my thoughts and prepare myself for the next audition for *Show Talk*.

Sadly, my taxi driver had other ideas. He was one of those really annoying types who feel some uncontrollable urge to fill any silence with a string of inane chit-chat: 'You off on your hols then, love? Where you off to, then? What's the weather like there? How long you going for? Nice seafood, they say. Been there before, have you?' I could have cheerfully throttled him but then I would have missed my flight. Instead I told him that I had a headache and the remainder of the journey to the airport passed in a blissful silence.

I arrived in Amsterdam, handed over the money and dashed back to the airport, desperate to get home as quickly as possible. I was devastated to learn that I'd missed the last flight, and had to find a hotel to stay in.

I finally got back to Cheshunt late the following morning. I called Michael and asked him to give my money to Karen as I knew I was due to meet up with her the following week. I put the phone down and realised that I'd been shaking throughout the entire call. The man who had once amused and entertained me now absolutely terrified me. Nothing on earth would ever make me set foot inside his house again. Somehow I had to find the strength to tell him it was all over.

My third call-back for the job on *Show Talk* was one of the most nerve-racking experiences of my entire life. Two days before, I had learned that the producers wanted to see how the candidates would perform in a live situation, and had brought in an actor to play the part of a pop star whom we each had to interview.

As well as trying out the presenters, the producers were also using the auditions as a way of rehearsing the crew. There were dozens of people milling about, manning cameras, shouting into walkie-talkies, swinging lights this way and that and touching up people's make up right up until the last second.

The introduction had to be read off an autocue but the rest of the time I was on my own. Steve had given me a good talking-to and said there was no point in trying to be something I was not – the only way to handle it was to be myself. So I did what I always do in slightly awkward situations: I took the piss.

I'd gone from not caring one way or another to working myself into a complete state. I wanted the job so badly, but I was convinced that I was going to blow all my chances, that I'd freeze up and fall at the last hurdle.

They promised to let Steve know by the end of the week and I spent the next two days trying my absolute hardest not to think about it – which meant that I spent every single second thinking about it. The hardest part was knowing that I'd got that far, that I'd managed to outperform literally hundreds of others, some of whom had far more experience than I did. The more I thought about it the more convinced I became that I was going to fail.

I knew that Steve would be calling whatever the decision, and when his name came up on my mobile phone I immediately felt sick. I couldn't help but notice that his voice lacked any excitement. I started to fear the worst. I knew I'd get over it pretty quickly – I'd never expected to get the job anyway – but I just needed to know the worst and move on.

And I was so convinced that Steve was trying to break the bad news as gently as possible that when he told me that I'd got the job, I didn't believe him. He told me again and again and I was waiting for him to burst out laughing or shout out, 'April fool!' or something but it never happened. And then it struck me: he was being serious. I felt a hot flush spreading across my face and a knot of excitement growing in the pit of my stomach.

'You mean it, Steve, do you really mean it?'

'Honest to God, Tracy, you've got the job. I'm so proud of you. Congratulations.'

All I can remember is dropping the phone and running around the house, screaming and screaming at the top of my voice. Steve managed to calm me down for long enough to fill me in on all the important details. Rehearsals were just ten days away and the first episode would go out live a few days later. He was going to send them a set of draft contracts that same afternoon and that's when the negotiations for payment would come in. He promised to ensure he got me the best possible deal but I would have done it for peanuts. Tears of joy were running down my cheeks.

When Steve had finished I called my parents, my sisters, my brother, Karen – everyone I knew – and told them all about it. I was thrilled to bits. For the first time in years I was going to be able to hold my head up high, do a job that I loved and make my parents proud.

It also meant I wouldn't have to work for Michael any more, and that the next time he got heavy with me I could tell him where to stick it. I could hardly wait for him to call.

I took off all my clothes, stood in front of the mirror and had a good long look at myself. The initial excitement of getting the job was being replaced with a fear of not being up to it. It was all very well messing around during an audition, but how would I perform when it came to doing it for real?

I turned this way and that and watched my reflection copy my movements. I wasn't fat by any means but at the same time I wasn't quite as slim as I would have liked. Given a couple of months, I would have watched what I was eating, stepped up my exercise programme and ended up looking just the way I wanted in time for the rehearsal. But I didn't have a couple of months – I had just ten days.

Following in Lynn and Karen's footsteps, I decided to have liposuction. It wasn't ideal, but this was my big break and the more comfortable I felt with myself, the better I would come across.

The basic cost for liposuction on my lower stomach was £2,200 – about as much as I'd saved since working for Michael – but the clinic offered a special deal where, for an extra £200, you could have a further body part done at the same time, up to a maximum of four body parts. I opted to have work done on my upper and lower stomach, my upper arms and waist.

The idea of going under the knife absolutely terrified me and brought back horrific memories. At the age of fourteen I went into hospital to have my tonsils taken out. It was a fairly routine operation and I should have been back home the following day, but I was allergic to the anaesthetic. My heart rate dropped dramatically and when they tried to revive me I just didn't wake up. It took almost three days before I started to come round. Back home I continued to feel groggy for the next two weeks and had to stay off school. During the whole time I didn't know where I was or what was going on. I'd fall asleep at the drop of a hat and felt like I was trapped in a nightmare that was never going to end.

I told the doctors at the liposuction clinic about the problem but they were confident they would still be able to carry out the operation. Of course, they wanted me to sign all sorts of forms and disclaimers in case anything went wrong, and as I filled out the documents it really hit me about just how big a risk I was taking.

Even without my problems with anaesthetic, liposuction is still an extremely dangerous procedure, responsible for a handful of fatalities each year. The key problem comes if too much fat is removed in one go – it upsets the fluid balance of the body and the patient can go into shock and die.

Fat is very hard to break up so initially a cold salt solution, which also contains adrenaline and a local anaesthetic, is injected into the areas being operated on. Next, a large, hollow needle, about three millimetres in diameter, is attached to a powerful suction machine and then inserted into the pockets of fat through several small cuts in the skin. The needle is then rammed back and forth with considerable force, sucking up the fat as it goes. The procedure is so physically demanding that surgeons have been known to have to stop midway through an operation to get their breath back.

The violent movements rupture blood vessels so, whilst the hole in the skin is very small, a mixture of blood and saline leaks out of the body for some time afterwards. The areas that are operated on are left bruised and tender, and the skin becomes loose as there is now a gap between it and the rest of the body where the fat used to be. In order to help the skin form a new bond, liposuction patients have to wear skin-tight outfits for the first few days after the operation.

I managed to stay calm as the nurses carried out a blood test to see what my type was, just in case I needed a transfusion during the operation, but as the doctor stopped my trolley on the way to the theatre and drew black circles on my body where the incisions would be made, I felt a wave of panic starting to rise within me.

I'd wanted to tell my mum but I knew that she would be sick with worry if she knew in advance. Ever the drama queen, I had left a letter for her on top of the dresser in the bedroom at my flat: 'Dear Mum, if you are reading this then I am dead and I'm well pissed off. But at least I've died skinny . . .'

As they took me into the operating theatre, I remember looking upwards at the ceiling as the lights flashed past. 'Please don't let me die, God, please don't let me die,' I murmured. The doctors and nurses surrounded me with reassuring smiles. I didn't feel the needle go into my arm but slowly my eyelids became heavy and I felt myself slipping away.

I woke with a start and tried to breathe but nothing happened. It was as if my lungs weren't working. I felt like I was underwater, drowning. I started to panic. I managed to lift my head a little and all I could see was that the sheets were soaked red. It was only the saline solution flushing through my body but I was convinced I was bleeding to death. I tried to scream but no sound came out. I tried to move but I couldn't seem to control my limbs. All I managed to do was knock a glass of water from my bedside table and it smashed on to the floor.

A nurse rushed in, took one look at me and immediately called for the doctor. I couldn't make out what she was saying but I could tell from the look on her face that I was in big trouble. Other members of staff came running in, a couple of them hauling banks of monitors and other equipment. It was getting dark outside and I was sure I wasn't going to make it through the night. I tried to tell them to call my mother but my words made no sense. The last thing I remember was someone fitting an oxygen mask over my face, then I passed out again.

I woke the next morning utterly amazed that I was still alive. I would later learn that during the operation my heart had slowed down so much that the surgeon had been convinced it was about to stop. I had been slipping in and out of consciousness all through the night and towards the end the nurses had been forbidden to talk to me because anything they said simply sent me into a panic attack and made everything worse.

Although I still felt incredibly groggy, the anaesthetic was starting to wear off, which meant that I was just starting to feel the first twinges of pain. I'd been warned to expect some discomfort and friends who had had liposuction in the past had tried to prepare me, but none of them had had anything like the number of procedures in one go that I'd had. I began to realise that even though I was alive, my ordeal was far from over.

Within a few hours the pain had become more intense than anything I'd ever known. With every tiny movement I felt as though my skin was ripping and tearing and as the hours went by it just got worse and worse. The nurses gave me extra-strong painkillers but they barely dulled the worst of it. They kept telling me that I'd recover rapidly over the coming days but it was hard to believe I'd ever feel normal again.

The operation had taken place on Wednesday morning and by Thursday night I'd been discharged. My sister Claire came to take me home, which was just as well as I could barely walk. Not realising quite how bad things were going to be, I'd let Steve book me for an advertising job on the Monday. I had to get him to call up and cancel – I couldn't even go to the toilet unaided, let alone make my way to a studio.

My mum came round as soon as she heard – she was furious that she hadn't known about the operation but also relieved that it was all over. I explained that I couldn't have told her before because I knew she would have talked me out of it and I really needed to have it done.

I showed her the 'If you are reading this' letter, but she had a hard time finding it funny, particularly when she saw the state of me. My entire lower body was covered in the most horrendous black bruises – I looked as though I'd gone twenty rounds with Mike Tyson.

Maria volunteered to come round and stay for a few days. It wasn't an entirely unselfish act – she'd had an argument with her boyfriend and wanted to spend some time apart from him – but I was glad of her company.

The blood/saline mix was still pouring out of me so I got Maria to put some plastic bags under the sheets and just lay in bed. Over time the liquid congealed and hardened and each time Maria helped me to the toilet she literally had to peel me off the mattress.

By Saturday afternoon I had started to feel a little more normal, but only so long as I stayed in bed and didn't try to do anything rash like moving around. I still felt pretty groggy and found it hard to concentrate on anything for more than a few seconds, but I knew I had come through the worst of it.

Maria was doing a fantastic job of looking after me and having her around made it feel just like old times. Most importantly, I could already see that the liposuction had done the trick. It was all going to be worthwhile.

With a smile on my face and thoughts of a brilliant new future as a top television presenter running through my head, I drifted off into a deep, blissful sleep.

Chapter Eight

The sound of four sharp knocks on my bedroom door pulled me out of my slumbers and into the twilight zone between sleep and wakefulness. Even in my groggy, drugged-up state of mind I knew it didn't make any sense. 'Maria,' I called out weakly, 'what you playing at? Just come in, will you.'

There was a short pause, followed by three more knocks, this time a little louder than before. I tried to pull myself up into a sitting position but as soon as I moved I felt as though white-hot flames were dancing across my stomach and down my back. As I collapsed back on to the bed, tears of pain and frustration rolling down my cheeks, my bedroom door swung open and Maria appeared.

'Are you all right?' she asked. 'I heard you knocking.'

'I thought that was you.'

Maria leaned back a little so her head was in the hallway. 'Actually, I think it's coming from the front door.'

That was a bad sign. Each flat in the block had an intercom connected to the front door and visitors would usually call up to be buzzed in. Occasionally dodgy salesmen or Jehovah's Witnesses would use the fact that they had got into one flat to try all the others. 'Oh bollocks. Do us a favour, Maria – can you try and find out who it is without letting them know I'm in? I'm not moving a muscle unless it's an emergency.'

I was OK walking around, just so long as I took things slowly, but the bruising made it impossible for me to get out of bed or go from a sitting to a standing position without help. The muscles around my stomach and back were simply too tender to put any strain on.

Maria sneaked along the hallway and pressed her ear up against the door. It was clear that there were several people outside the flat, but she had no way of knowing who they were. Then she heard Mr Carter, my neighbour from the flat opposite, open his door and talk to them. 'I don't think she's in. What's all this about?' he asked.

'Don't you worry yourself, mate,' replied a man with a gruff voice. 'You can read all about it in the papers tomorrow.'

Maria came scuttling back to the bedroom, her face flushed with a mixture of fear and excitement. 'Bloody hell, I think it's the press.'

'The press! Shit. What do they want? What have you done?'

'Me? I ain't done nothing. What have *you* done?'

'Nothing. I mean, it can't be the liposuction. You can't tell me that anyone cares about that, not these days.'

The knocking gave way to a furious pounding as the group at the door ran out of patience. A deep male voice came booming through the letterbox: 'We know you're in there and if you don't open this door in the next five seconds we're gonna break it down.'

Maria and I looked at each other open-mouthed. Whoever it was, they weren't going to take no for an answer. 'That ain't the press,' I said. 'You'd better let them in before they wreck the place.'

She vanished back into the hallway and I heard the front door open followed by shouts, grunts and heavy footfalls echoing through the flat.

It took a few seconds before they found the bedroom and came piling in, one after the other, six men and two women, all dressed in casual clothes, followed by a baffled-looking Maria. A tall man with sandy hair and a blue checked shirt moved up the side of the bed and waved an open wallet in my face. 'My name is Richard Hartwell. I'm an officer of Her Majesty's Customs and Excise. I am placing you under arrest for conspiracy to import Class A drugs, conspiracy to import Class B drugs . . .'

As soon as he mentioned drugs I burst out laughing – I just couldn't help it. I was laughing so hard that it hurt all over, but I didn't care. It was hilarious. All I could think was, You prat, you've gone and raided the wrong bloody house, you're gonna be so humiliated when you realise what you've done. The other officers looked at me as if I was completely mad while their colleague carried on with the list of charges.

I was still giggling like a schoolgirl but managed to compose myself for long enough to force a few words out in between chuckles. 'Class A drugs. What, like cocaine? You've got to be kidding. I get a rush if I take an aspirin. What are you on about?'

He ignored my questions and started reading me my rights, telling me that I did not have to say anything but anything I did say could be used against me in court. 'We need to search your flat. I take it you've no objections.'

Of course I didn't. I knew they weren't going to find anything, just as I knew that I didn't have anything to do with smuggling drugs. And I'd always been careful to make sure no one was slipping anything into my bags when I came back from all those trips I'd made to carry money for Michael . . .

And then, all of a sudden, it wasn't funny any more. What if Sonny had brought something back in his car during that long drive from Spain? I knew I had done nothing wrong and that Michael's bureau de change was legitimate, but I couldn't help thinking that Customs were about to jump to the wrong conclusion, just the way the police had over my trip to Tenerife with Terry all those years earlier.

The thoughts were racing through my fuzzy mind so fast I barely heard the sandy-haired man asking me to get up and accompany him to the living room so they could start the search. It was only when he repeated himself for the third time that I managed to mumble something about not being able to get off the bed and called Maria over to give me a hand.

A female Customs officer came over to help, making me wince with pain as she clamped her hands around the bruises on my back. 'Leave her alone,' yelled Maria. 'She's just come out of hospital, she's had an operation.'

The woman apologised profusely as I explained about the liposuction, the super-strong painkillers and the after-effects of the anaesthetic. For some stupid reason I was hoping I might be able to convince them to go away and come back in a few days. Instead they agreed that I could stay in bed and that Maria could supervise the search. There was no hurry for me to get up – it would take at least a couple of hours.

They started going through absolutely everything: all

my shelves, papers, portfolios and photo albums. They looked behind radiators, underneath rugs and carpets and inside the toilet cistern, and even took out all my drawers to make sure there was nothing stuck underneath.

As they moved from room to room under Maria's watchful eye, I sat on the bed, guarded by a single female Customs officer, just in case I made a sudden miraculous recovery and found the energy to do a runner out of the window. Twenty minutes into the search the silence was broken by the ringing of my mobile phone, which was in my handbag on the bedside table.

I just ignored it – whoever it was, I couldn't face talking to them.

Then it went off again. After a few minutes it burst into life yet again. This time I reached into the bag and switched it off.

'Can you leave that on, love,' said the woman.

'Actually, the battery's dead,' I lied.

I'd barely finished the sentence when my home phone started ringing out in the hallway. I bit my lip. It was obviously the same person who had been trying my mobile, and I knew that after six rings the answering machine would pick it up. As the machine kicked into life, all movement in the flat came to a halt as everyone stopped to listen. The voice on the other end of the line sounded absolutely desperate.

'Tracy, Tracy, it's Karen. Pick up the phone.'

Please don't say anything, and for God's sake don't mention going to Spain with Sonny.

'Tracy, it's urgent. I need to speak to you. Something terrible has happened.'

I know, Karen, I know. They're here now, they're right here.

'Tracy, I need to speak to you really urgently. Call me when you get this message, as soon as you get this message.' Then she rang off.

'Who was that?' asked the woman, a tiny hint of a smirk on her face.

I lied again. This was becoming a habit. 'Oh, it's just a friend of mine who had some cosmetic surgery as well. She's just had her boobs done and maybe they've gone wrong. They've probably exploded or something.'

I was doing my best to make light of the situation but inside I was cringing. It was obvious why she was calling and everyone in the flat knew it. I was also getting a bit scared. I obviously wasn't the only one getting a visit from Customs.

I had wondered before if Karen was somehow involved in drugs, but I'd dismissed the thought almost immediately – I felt certain I knew her well enough to know that she'd never get involved in anything like that – and the tone of her voice told me she was every bit as confused and terrified as I was.

I could tell that Maria desperately wanted to ask me what was going on, but there was no way for us to be alone together. Instead we communicated our shock and surprise with a series of raised eyebrows and open mouths whenever the others weren't looking.

The search continued. They found my old cuttings books and, after a series of naff jokes and comments about working on Page Three, one officer sat down and started looking through everything I'd done in my career, paying careful attention to the cuttings about me supposedly going on the run to Tenerife. I was thankful that the letter from the same newspaper agreeing that none of it was true was also in the scrapbook.

I wasn't worried when they found an old plane ticket to Málaga, even though they treated it as some kind of triumph. I was equally relaxed when they found some Spanish currency and a few receipts from some of my shopping expeditions. But then they started searching my wardrobe.

If I could have found the energy to leap out of bed and stop them, I would have done it. It was where I kept my stash. My stash of vibrators, that is. I wasn't worried about the ordinary ones; my concern was the pride of my collection, a little something I had picked up a few years earlier while doing a promotion at the Erotica Show. Two feet long, as thick as a tree branch and made of super-realistic flesh-tone rubber with a huge glans at one end and a suction cup at the other, it was my special party piece. The only thing it's any good for is bashing people over the head – it's simply too big for anything else – and it always raised a laugh when it made an appearance during drunken nights in with my mates.

The officer searching the wardrobe got to the bag containing the item in question and I could feel my cheeks start to flush bright red.

'I don't know who's going to be more embarrassed, you or me.'

'Don't worry, love,' he said, 'I'm sure it's nothing I haven't seen before.'

'I wouldn't be so sure.'

He opened the bag and gasped. 'Jesus H. Christ. Oi, lads, come and have a look at this. I can't believe it. Look at the size of it.'

All work on the search was put on hold as the massive

dildo was passed around and examined while they laughed and made comments. Everything that had happened since the officers had arrived had been embarrassing enough; this was a further humiliation that I simply didn't need.

After two hours the eight complete strangers had laid bare virtually every aspect of my private life and filled several clear plastic bags with papers and other items. That was when Hartwell decided it was time to take me away to their offices at City Airport for a formal interview.

'How long will that take?'

He gave a half-shrug. 'Couple of hours.'

'OK, so I don't need to take anything with me then.'

'No, not at all . . . well, you might want to take a toothbrush, just in case.'

Even with the toothbrush remark, he was being so casual about things that I felt sure this was something that was going to get sorted out pretty soon. They would ask a few questions, realise I had nothing to do with drug-trafficking and let me go. I grabbed a couple of essentials – my Imodium, some cleanser and the super-strength painkillers they had given me at the clinic – then started to lever myself across to the edge of the bed. When Hartwell took a step towards me I assumed he was planning to help me up. Instead he snapped a pair of handcuffs on my wrists.

'What do you think I'm going to do? I can hardly walk, let alone make a run for it.' He said nothing as he and two colleagues lifted me to my feet and led me downstairs.

It was just getting dark but all along the street curtains were twitching away like crazy as they loaded me into the back seat of an unmarked car.

'Is this really necessary? I mean, what the hell am I supposed to have done?'

'I'm sorry, Tracy,' said Hartwell as he squeezed his bulk into the seat beside me. 'We can have a general chat if you like, but we can't discuss anything that's to do with the case, not until it's on tape.' We made the remainder of the journey in complete silence.

The airport was all but deserted and we made our way to the Customs unit through a side door adjacent to the main check-in area. At a reception desk they told me to empty my purse and pockets and then logged each item before sealing everything into a plastic bag. I protested and told them that I desperately needed the painkillers and the Imodium but they said I couldn't be allowed any kind of medication until I'd been seen by a doctor.

They took me along the corridor and put me into a holding cell. At first I was relieved to see it was far bigger than I'd expected, but the second they shut the heavy door, my claustrophobia started to kick in and the panic started to rise within me. The cell was a bare, white-walled rectangle with a slim wooden bench against the longest wall, on top of which sat a dark blue solid-rubber mattress. The two officers that took me inside had helped me to lie down, but within a few minutes I realised I desperately needed to use the toilet.

I tried to call out but my body was so bruised that speaking in anything more than a whisper was agony. There was a call button you could use to alert the staff but I couldn't reach it from where I was. I could feel myself getting into a state and the more stressed I became, the worse I felt. It was hopeless. As the minutes ticked by I knew that I simply had no choice: I was going to have to get up on my own.

I laid my hands flat by my sides and then dug my fingernails into the mattress beneath. When I was sure I had a good grip, I began pulling and lifting my head. The pain was horrific – it felt as though my skin was being ripped off my bones, strip by strip. I could feel myself slipping back and gritted my teeth as I made one last-ditch effort to sit up.

Suddenly my left hand lost contact with the mattress and I ended up rolling off the bed and crashing to the floor below. I landed painfully, my knees smacking into the hard concrete floor. I stayed in that position for a few minutes, sobbing and waiting for the pain to subside. Then, with my forearms and elbows pressing down on the bed, I pulled myself up, reached out and pressed the alarm.

Help came almost immediately in the shape of a tall, skinny woman called Pam. Getting me to the toilet turned out to be a major operation as I was still wearing the skin-tight cat suit, and I couldn't lift my arms more than a few inches. I had to get Pam to undress me, which apart from being humiliating was also incredibly painful as she was anything but gentle. It was obvious that I was in a bad way but she didn't seem to care and I couldn't help feeling that in her mind I had already been judged guilty.

Pam lowered me down on to the toilet and then stood right outside the cubicle. I shut my eyes, pretended I was back at home and desperately tried to relax so that I'd be able to go but it was no good. I could hear Pam breathing, pacing up and down and shifting from foot to foot as her impatience grew.

'I don't mean to be rude, but can you please go away, just for a few minutes?'

'No.'

'But you're making me really stressed. I can't go. I've got IBS, and you're making it worse.'

'So?'

'So if you go away, it will really help.'

There was a brief pause while she considered my request. 'I'm not going anywhere. Just get on with it,' she replied firmly.

Half an agonising hour later, I'd finally finished. There was more pain and humiliation as Pam helped me to dress and then escorted me back to my cell. I made the mistake of trying to lift my spirits with a touch of humour: 'One day,' I told Pam as she lowered me back on to the mattress, 'we're both going to look back at this and laugh.'

Pam walked to the cell door then turned to look at me. I had never in my life seen a face less capable of smiling than hers at that moment. It sent a chill down my spine. 'Yeah, right,' she said, and shut the door.

I'd been in the cell for an hour or so when the duty solicitor came in to see me. With none of the Customs officers able to tell me anything about what was going on, I was desperate to get as much information out of him as I could. He told me all he knew – a large consignment of drugs, including several tonnes of cannabis and dozens of kilos of cocaine, had been recovered from a warehouse in St Albans. A total of seventeen people had been arrested, but he didn't know their names. The Customs officers had told him that I was known to have made a number of trips abroad and that I had been observed meeting up with a key player in the conspiracy on at least one occasion.

The solicitor seemed like a nice enough guy but I really didn't know whether I could trust him – I didn't know whether I could trust anyone. The idea that I'd been under observation made my head spin. I'd been thinking that Sonny might have had something to do with it – why else drive to Spain unless you have a car load of drugs? – but I couldn't imagine him being a key player in a game of solitaire, let alone a drugs gang. Then there was Freddie, the drug dealer that I'd met in Spain, the one Michael had warned me to keep away from. That would almost make sense, but I'd only spent a couple of hours with him.

Then, of course, there was Michael himself but I couldn't believe that he would have been involved in something like that, *and* put members of his own family at risk. I mean, even his eighty-year-old mother had been taking some of the money abroad! Karen and I had become really close over the previous months and we'd even discussed our concerns about where the money was coming from. I knew her well enough to know that if she had even the slightest suspicion that something was wrong, she wouldn't have carried on and she would have made sure I got out too.

I was a mass of mixed emotions. I felt angry and let down but I didn't know who to blame. Someone among my group of new friends, the people I had come to trust and like, had let me down. One of them was laughing at me. I was certain I'd been made some kind of scapegoat.

Knowing so little about what was going on meant I was in an incredibly difficult position. I didn't want to drop myself in it, but at the same time I didn't want to say something that would get someone else in trouble. Ever since I was a little girl I've always believed it was wrong to tell tales on people, that it only ends up backfiring on the teller. I'd never done it in the past and I certainly wasn't going to start now.

I explained to the solicitor that I planned to make no comment during my interviews with Customs. I'd barely finished the sentence before he started shaking his head vigorously. 'I've got to warn you, Tracy, that if you give a no-comment interview it's going to reflect very badly,' he said. 'It will look as though you're hiding something, as though you're trying to buy time in order to think up an alibi. I strongly advise you not to go down that path.'

We were still talking over my options when there was a knock at my cell door and Pam announced that the doctor had arrived to examine me. What a relief – I hadn't had any painkillers for nearly four hours and as the drugs wore off, even lying perfectly still on my back was starting to get painful. The doctor – middle-aged and floppy-haired with garlic breath – poked and prodded, asked a couple of questions and then announced that I was perfectly healthy and did not need any medication.

I was so taken aback I could hardly speak. How could that possibly be true? I couldn't even undress myself without wincing in pain. The doctor ignored my protests and, instead of the prescribed painkillers, reached into his bag and gave me two paracetamol. 'Oh wow, that's great.

You have to start somewhere!

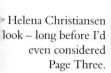

Helena Christiansen look – long before I'd even considered Page Three.

My first time on the *Sun's* Page Three. Despite the helmet, I was later recognised and asked for my autograph – another first.

Maria Whitaker and me, with our agent Yvonne Paul.

The Page Three football team: I'm in the top row, on the left, with our goalie and Christine Peake; Jenny Blythe, Tracey Elvik and Debbie Ashley are below. The other teams couldn't get past our hair to score a goal!

Tits out, bum out, breathe in, smile and hold. And they call it glamour modelling.

Tasteful nudity, and lots of baby oil! Where Page Three meets
Herb Ritts.

The best of friends: me and Maria during the good times.

Lyn and Michael – the drugs baron who went on to become Britain's most notorious supergrass. Their faces are obscured for legal reasons.

Me and Karen, long before we knew what horrors lay ahead.

Just some of the hundreds of kilos of cannabis and cocaine that police found after raiding Michael's warehouse.

Drugs hidden in barrels: one of the many methods used to smuggle them into Britain.

Michael made hundreds of lists detailing the huge amounts of money going in and out of his drug business. It was only when I saw them that I realised the true scale of what I'd been involved in.

Prison pals: me, Eileen and Amanda. The bonds we formed inside will never be broken.

My first birthday after leaving Holloway. I shared it, in Cannes, with the friends who had stuck by me: Suzanne, Joanne and Tracey.

It took sixteen years, two of
them in prison, but I finally
made it to the catwalks.
Here I am doing a show for
Marks & Spencer.

These would be just what I needed if I had a headache, but unfortunately I haven't. I've just come out of a major bloody operation.' I was still ranting as he walked out of my cell, ignoring my words every step of the way.

A few minutes later Pam returned and told me that, even though the doctor had pronounced me fit, Hartwell and the other Customs officers had decided it was too late to interview me there and then. I would have to stay overnight and wait until the morning. So much for only being gone a couple of hours.

Once I realised I wasn't going to be able to go home, I knew I couldn't keep my arrest a secret any longer. If there was one thing I'd learned from all those nights in watching *L.A. Law* and *The Bill*, it was that I had the right to a phone call. Another torturous reach for the alarm bell brought a pissed-off Pam back to the door. I heard her muttering under her breath as she went off to fetch a phone card and then took me out into the corridor, standing over me as I dialled Sarah's number. She answered on the second ring.

'It's me. I've been arrested.'

'Jesus Christ! What on earth for?'

'I don't know, Sarah. I really don't know. They say it's something to do with drugs, cocaine.'

'What! What the hell have you been doing?'

'Nothing, nothing to do with drugs.'

Even though the situation was looking increasingly desperate, the mere sound of a sympathetic voice instantly made me feel a million times better and I felt my favourite defence mechanism – my sense of humour – starting to return. 'You know, I've tried telling them that, but they still won't let me go.'

I told Sarah as much as I could, made her promise not to tell our parents – I hoped I might be released after I'd been interviewed – and asked her to get me a solicitor as I didn't really trust the one Customs had provided. We'd been talking for barely two minutes when Pam indicated that my time was up and I said a hurried goodbye.

I didn't sleep a wink that night. I lay awake trying to make sense of everything, but when the morning came I was as confused as ever. I was desperate to get out and find out more about what was going on. I needed to buy some time, let the anaesthetic clear out of my head and get hold of Karen and the others. Then a cunning plan popped into my head and I started picking at the scabs on my stomach and side. Within a few minutes, fresh blood was seeping out of my wounds. Surely now they'd have to let me go.

When Pam brought me in an inedible breakfast, I told her I needed to see the doctor again. Half an hour later the same floppy-haired man was back in my cell, poking, prodding and asking questions about how I was feeling. Then for the second time he announced that there was nothing wrong with me and that I was fit to be interviewed. I couldn't believe it – everything was conspiring against me.

My first interview didn't take place until just after 2 p.m. I'd spent the morning alternately sitting on the toilet and consulting with David, the solicitor my sister had arranged, who also advised me that giving a no-comment interview would be a huge mistake.

I didn't know what to do, I felt completely paranoid. Even though David had been recommended to me, I still didn't feel able to open up to him fully. All I knew for certain was that somewhere along the line I'd been tricked into bringing drugs into the country and, until I knew who had been responsible, I didn't want to trust anyone.

I tried to sort it out in my head but the combination of exhaustion and anaesthetic made it hard to concentrate. If Sonny or Freddie were somehow involved in drug smuggling, there wasn't really anything to implicate me, even if I had been seen with them. So long as I could make it clear to Customs that I'd never brought any cocaine or cannabis into the country, they would surely have to let me go.

By the time we sat down in the interview room I felt so weak and dizzy that I had to lay my head down on the table. My solicitor was by my side while Hartwell and another officer sat opposite. They switched on the tape and began.

The questions came thick and fast: had I ever been to the warehouse in Hatfield? What was my involvement in concealing the cocaine in the French cars? How many times had I been to Paris, to Spain, to Amsterdam? What was the purpose of my visit? Who paid for my tickets? Who did I meet while I was there? What role did I play in loading or unloading the cannabis in the tankers?

They went on and on, covering the same ground two, three, four times, as if they were trying to catch me out. When the tapes ran out after forty-five minutes, Hartwell gave me a much-needed toilet break and the chance to talk to David before the second interview began. That finished some forty minutes later and I thought it was all over. Instead I was taken back to my cell with a warning that they would probably want to speak to me again.

At 7 p.m. they called me out for yet another interview. This time they went through list after list of names. Most of them I'd never heard of and the more they went on about them, the more confident I was that they'd made some kind of mistake. They continued with yet more names – Michael Michael, Lynn, Jan, Karen and Jill. By the time they'd finished they'd covered virtually every person that I'd met in the previous two years but I was no closer to knowing exactly who was supposed to be involved in the drugs gang of which I was accused of being a key member.

I don't know what I expected at the end of that third interview. Somewhere at the back of my mind was the hope that they might just let me go, that I might have managed to convince them that I didn't have anything to do with the things they were talking about.

When he had finished asking questions Hartwell leaned back on his chair, pressed the tips of his fingers together and stared at me for a few moments. I held his gaze for as long as I could – I wasn't going to let him psych me out – but the silence was deafening and in the end I had to turn away. It seemed a lifetime before he finally spoke.

'OK, Tracy. We've given you the opportunity to tell us your version of events and I've listened very carefully to everything you've had to say. But basically, I don't believe a word of it. It is my opinion and that of my colleagues that you are fully involved in this drug-trafficking enterprise. What's going to happen now is that we are going to speak to our superiors and find out where we go from here. In the meantime, you're going back to your cell.'

If I'd been able to move around I would have spent the next two hours anxiously pacing back and forth. Instead I just lay on the bed, staring up at the ceiling and wondering what was going to happen next, when this nightmare was going to end.

I heard a key in the lock and then my cell door swung open. A young female officer helped me to my feet and explained that I had to go and sign out my things as I was leaving. A huge wave of relief swept over my body. At last I was going home. But then Hartwell appeared and explained that I was being taken to Bethnal Green Police Station where I would be formally charged with conspiracy to import cocaine. After that, I would remain in custody overnight and be taken to court in the morning.

I just stared at him open mouthed. 'This can't be happening,' I gasped. 'This just can't be happening.'

It was dark by the time we arrived at the station. I was taken through to the custody suite and told to wait while they got the paperwork ready. I heard a couple of Customs guys saying that someone linked to the same operation named Mark Hooper was on his way in.

The name rang a bell as someone who Michael had talked about every now and then. I knew he'd been at some of the same parties that I'd been to but I couldn't remember if we'd actually met, much less recall what he looked like.

About ten minutes later three men came in and stood by the desk. The first looked incredibly familiar and smiled as he saw me. I smiled back and started to wonder if I had met Mark before, after all.

'How are you doing?' I asked, trying to sound as cheery as possible.

'Can't complain,' he replied. 'How about you?'

Just then the man behind him threw me a harsh look and interrupted. 'Don't fucking talk to him.'

I was indignant. I hated the way some of these Customs officers were such bullies and tried to control you all the time. 'I'll talk to who I like.'

'Tracy, don't deal with them. He's from Customs.'

'Eh? Who the hell are you?'

He lifted up his wrists and I realised he was wearing handcuffs. 'I'm Mark.'

Now I was really confused. If that was Mark, then how come I recognised the first one, a Customs officer? I stared at him again, lines forming across my brow as I tried to imagine where I might have seen him before. A silly grin spread across his face.

'You remember me, don't you? I gave you a lift to the airport a couple of weeks ago.'

It was as if a bottomless pit had opened up in the centre of my stomach. Oh my God! It was the cab driver who had taken me from the Watford Hilton to the airport after I'd met Michael and André. I'd mostly been staring at the back of his head but I caught a glimpse of him when he dropped me off and I paid him. It all came flooding back and launched a new wave of terror. That was the time I'd met Michael and André. That must be what they meant when they said they had seen me meeting with senior members of the gang. I started to throw up but I was so dehydrated I was just dry-heaving.

Mark, his face twisted with concern, tried to come over and comfort me but the officers held him back. My mind was racing. This was unbelievable. How long had they been watching me? Who had they seen me meeting?

I came out of my trance to hear Mark talking to me gently. 'Are you all right, babe, are you all right? You're much better-looking in real life, you know. Oi, mate,' he called out to the nearest police officer. 'Can't you put us in a cell together? Promise I'll be good.'

Mark kept talking, making jokes and silly comments. He was funny and confident and that soon rubbed off on me. He didn't seem at all worried about having been arrested or being at the police station and I started to believe that things really would be all right. 'You've got nothing to worry about,' he said softly. 'In court tomorrow you'll get bail, no problem. You'll be home before lunchtime.'

The custody officer didn't want the two of us talking so he moved us into cells. The only good thing was that the cell had a toilet in it – one less thing I had to worry about.

Just after midnight my sister arrived at the station with some fresh clothes and a few bits and pieces, but they wouldn't let her see me. I'd been counting on getting more emotional support from her and knowing she was so near but out of reach pushed me into a deep depression. By now I was in a pretty appalling state. I hadn't had any painkillers for nearly eight hours, I hadn't had a bath or washed my hair for almost a week and I was still suffering from the effects of the anaesthetic. I just wanted it all to be over.

Everyone had been taking the piss about my modelling career at every opportunity. I knew that at some point I'd have to have my photograph taken and I was determined to at least try and look my best, even under such difficult circumstances. They took my fingerprints at 1 a.m. then put me back in the cell. I just sat there on the edge of the bed, waiting and thinking.

Two hours later nothing had happened and I decided I couldn't keep my make-up on any longer. I needed to get some sleep. I leaned over the little steel sink in the corner of the cell and started washing my face. Within a few seconds of my finishing, the jailer came to my cell and told me I was being taken out for photographing. I swore repeatedly under my breath.

The policeman operating the camera was a good-looking young guy. He was trying to laugh and joke but I wasn't in the mood for it at all. 'I don't know whether I should ask you to sign these for me or not,' he said, grinning.

I gave him the filthiest look I could manage. 'You're not funny, mate. Can I go back to my cell now, please?'

The combination of nerves, pain and distress meant that for the second night in a row I hadn't managed to get any sleep. I was in a terrible state by the time they put me in a car to go to Thames Magistrates Court the following morning, but I still believed that now, at last, things would start to be sorted out.

Flanked by two officers, I was escorted into the basement through a series of gates and into a short corridor with three cells on either side. The doors were solid metal apart from a small hatch. Sitting on the bed, wondering when this was all going to get sorted out, I heard the jailer close the main gate and then heard two vaguely familiar voices.

'Who's that, who's just come in?' It was Jan and Debbie, the women I had travelled to Spain with along with Karen. Sylvie, another friend of Lynn's whom I'd met briefly a few weeks earlier, was there too and within seconds we were all shouting across at one another through the hatches.

'Does anyone know what the hell is going on?' yelled Sylvie.

'Buggered if I do,' said Debbie. 'Haven't got a clue.'

'Don't worry,' said Jan. 'It's all going to be all right.'

'How can you say that?' I replied. 'How can you possibly say that? We don't know what's going on. I'm amazed it's gone as far as it has.'

'You're right, Tracy,' she replied. 'This should never have happened.'

I wanted to ask Jan exactly what she meant, but there was no time. Two jailers appeared and began pacing up and down the small corridor between the cells, telling us it was almost time to go before the magistrate. We all fell silent, petrified of saying anything in front of anyone outside our little group.

They took us up into court two at a time. As Debbie and I sat in the dock the solicitor representing Customs and Excise, a short woman with small round glasses perched on the end of her nose and her hair pulled back into a tight bun, began outlining the case against us.

None of the words that came out of her mouth seemed to make any sense: she said we were key figures in one of the largest drugs gangs ever apprehended in the UK, that we were linked to French and Dutch drug traffickers and that we had helped bring tens of millions of pounds' worth of cocaine and cannabis into the country. It just wasn't true. It was like she was talking about someone else. I leaned over to Debbie: 'Can they do this? Are they allowed? Can they just stand there and tell lies about us?'

When the woman had finished, David, my solicitor, stood up and started telling the court about all the charity work I had done during my Page Three heyday and what a good person I was until I felt myself turn bright red with embarrassment. 'On that basis,' David said, 'and taking into account the fact that she is a person of previous good character, I urge you to grant bail.'

Dozens of journalists were sitting on the press bench, scribbling the details into their notebooks, and up in the public gallery I could see my sister looking down at me. As our eyes met she mouthed: 'I love you, it's going to be all right.'

But it wasn't. The Customs woman stood up again and started rubbishing everything David had said. She said there was a wealth of evidence to show that I was intimately involved with the senior figures at the head of the drug-smuggling syndicate. I had been kept under close surveillance for weeks and had been observed acting suspiciously on a number of occasions.

I wanted to stand up and shout at the top of my voice that they were talking a load of old nonsense but David had already warned me that any outburst would only cause more trouble. Best leave it to him to sort out, he told me.

The magistrate flicked through a few papers and then

asked me to stand up. He told me that he would not grant bail because there was a substantial risk that I would not appear in court. I'd seen the same scene played out in a thousand films and television dramas but, as they took me back to the cells, I still didn't really understand what was happening.

After twenty minutes or so, David came to see me, sitting next to me on the bed in my cell.

'I must say Tracy, you're handling this very well.'

'You think so? Well the only reason I'm not freaking out is because I still don't know what is going on.'

He smiled. 'I don't know much more than you do. The only thing that's certain is that we're going to try for bail again.'

'OK, that's good,' I said, lifting his wrist and glancing at his watch. 'What time are you doing that?'

'Er, next week.'

His words cut through me like a knife. What the hell was he talking about? Why wasn't he up in court there and then trying for it straight away?

'Next week, what do you mean next week? What am I supposed to do until then?'

David was clearly much more used to dealing with persistent offenders, people who knew exactly how the legal system worked and what to expect at each step of the way. I could feel the hesitation in his voice as he spoke, uncertain as to how I'd react to what he was going to tell me. 'Well, Tracy,' he said, speaking slowly and deliberately, 'in the next hour or so you're going to be taken to prison, to Holloway Prison.'

My heart jumped up into my stomach. The memories of the awful time I'd had during the charity visit came flooding back, as did the screw's ominous warning: 'Just make sure you don't end up in here, they'll eat you alive.' The panic was starting to rise within me. This was all of my worst nightmares rolled into one.

'No, no, I can't go to Holloway. I just can't . . .'

'Now come on, Tracy, just keep calm and it will be all right.'

Being told to keep calm at a time like that was the last thing I wanted to hear. I reached across the cell and grabbed David by the shoulders, shaking him furiously. 'Calm down! Don't tell me to calm down. If you think it's going to be so easy, you go to fucking Holloway then.'

Then I caught myself, took a few deep breaths and apologised. I knew it wasn't his fault, I was just feeling ill, angry and frustrated and didn't know what was going on. I just wanted to get back home and put all this behind me. David nodded and placed a sympathetic hand on my shoulder. It was obvious he had more bad news for me.

'Look Tracy, you've got to understand. They've arrested loads of people, and they've picked up millions of pounds' worth of drugs, guns, hundreds of thousands of pounds in cash. As far as they're concerned, they've busted a major international drug-smuggling ring and the evidence they have says you're a key part of it.'

'But I haven't done anything . . .'

'I know that, but you can't prove it and that means they're not going to give you bail because they don't think you'll turn up for trial if they do. I have to be honest Tracy, they rarely give bail first time around to people who are potentially facing long sentences. But I'm certain we'll get it next time.'

Up until that point it hadn't really occurred to me just how serious a situation I was in. I'd been charged with all these offences and now I was going to prison to await trial. I was already losing all my faith in the judicial system; I wondered how much worse it could possibly get.

'When you say "long sentence", what exactly do you mean? How long?'

David bit his lip. I could tell this was going to be almost as painful for him to say as it was for me to hear. 'I won't lie to you, Tracy. These charges are just about as serious as anything I've ever dealt with. If you get found guilty, you're looking at eighteen years.'

Chapter Nine

From the outside it looked like an ordinary prison van.

It was only when the officers escorting me out of the courthouse opened the rear doors that I realised the next stage of my ordeal wasn't going to begin in prison, but rather on the journey there.

I'd expected the inside of the prison van to be one large space; instead I found myself looking at a narrow corridor separating two identical rows of cubicles. It looked like a mobile toilet from my days on the festival circuit, only this time the doors were made of solid metal with heavy locks.

The officers opened the first cubicle and ushered me towards it. It was tiny. I quickly realised that I would have to go in backwards as there was only barely enough room to move my elbows and, once inside, I wouldn't be able to turn around. I sat on the rough wooden bench at the end and was shocked to discover that when they closed the door it practically touched my knees.

As soon as the lock snapped shut, I was in trouble. The air inside the cubicle was hot and dry and hardly any light was managing to get through the heavily tinted window. I shut my eyes and tried not to panic, but it was no good. I felt as though the walls, the floor and the ceiling were all closing in on me. I couldn't focus. Everything became a blur. My heart started beating faster and faster – I was sure it was going to explode. My throat started closing up so tight that I struggled to breathe. My hands started sweating and I got so dizzy that even though I was sitting down I had to hold on to the walls to stop myself falling. I knew I had to get out of there.

My claustrophobia has never been about small spaces. I don't get panic attacks when I'm trying on clothes in a changing room because I know I can open the door and walk out whenever I want. But if someone bolted the door from the outside, I'd fall to pieces.

Like the vast majority of claustrophobics, I've never bothered to try to get help, I just live my life avoiding situations that make it worse. Most of the time that's easy to do – I take the stairs rather than the lift, I choose the table nearest the door and so on. Being locked in that cubicle and knowing that I was on my way to prison, it was like descending into my own personal circle of hell.

There was music blaring out from the stereo and I could hear the muffled conversation of the prison officers in the front of the van. I banged my fist on the door a few times, even though the sudden movement tore at my scabs and made me wince with pain. The only response I got was being told to shut up.

'But I can't breathe,' I gasped.

'Yeah, right. Never heard that one before. Do you think we're stupid or something? Put a sock in it, we're almost there anyway.' And they turned the music up, drowning out my protests.

I couldn't move to see out of the window but I knew we'd pulled up outside the prison when we were stationary for at least twenty minutes. Then I heard an ominous grinding and groaning of gears that told me the heavy gate at the front of the prison was slowly sliding open. The van crept forward about twenty feet then stopped again and I heard the gate closing behind us.

I kept my breathing under control for as long as I could, trying to convince myself I could open the door at any time. But it was all taking much too long and I knew I couldn't hold on for ever. Come on, Tracy, I told myself. You can get through this. It's only for a week. No matter how awful it is, you're only going to be there for a week. You've got to remember that.

Just then a strange noise broke in above the sound of the music. A woman in one of the other cubicles was starting to lose it. It began with a few sobs and groans but before long had turned into a full-scale tantrum. She was screaming and shouting, pounding her fists and feet against the floor and walls and demanding to be let out. Her panic was infectious; within a few seconds it had spread to all the prisoners and the whole van was alive with the sound of it.

In a bid to stop us hurting ourselves or, more importantly, damaging the van, one of the officers finally opened the doors to the cubicles, which instantly made things a lot more bearable. That was when I realised that Sylvie had been in the cubicle opposite me and that it was her panic attack that had started the rest of us off.

She looked terrible. Her blond hair was plastered to her face with sweat. Her make-up had begun to run. She was breathing hard, her head down between her knees. When she looked up we managed to exchange weak smiles. The guards warned us not to speak or they would close the cubicles again.

After what seemed like an eternity the back of the van was opened up and we were taken through to the holding room of the reception centre, a grubby square room with a large two-way mirror all along one wall, bars over the windows and a few benches and chairs. Debbie and Janice had been in the van too, along with a couple of women we didn't know, and we sat next to one another, trying to put as much distance between us and the other girls as possible.

The holding room was already half full when we arrived and the other inmates looked really hard and street-wise. Some of them smoked, or huddled together in conspiratorial groups. Others just sat and stared at us, wide-eyed and dazed. Janice spoke for us all: 'I don't fucking believe this is happening,' she whispered. 'It's not right, it's not right at all.'

It was almost an hour before my name was called and I was taken through to an adjacent room and made to stand in front of a desk. Behind it was a prison officer with thinning grey hair and leathery grey skin. Remaining sour-faced and miserable throughout the entire procedure, she barked out a series of questions in a nasal monotone: date of birth, nationality, religion, dietary requirements and so on, scribbling my mumbled answers into a large book. Everything I had on me was spread out on the desk in front of her and she counted out the money in my purse – £3 – and wrote that down too.

She sorted my property into two piles – the stuff I'd

be allowed to take into my cell and the stuff that would have to be stored in the prison vaults. I had a bottle of cleanser, a really expensive brand that I'd sworn by for years. She held it up to the light, shook her head and put it in the pile of things to be taken away.

'What are you doing?'

'You can't have that.'

'Why not?'

'Because I can't see what's inside the bottle. You might be using it to conceal drugs. There could be anything in there.'

'But it's Clarins.'

'Well now it's gone. Get over it.'

She then flipped open the tiny plastic case that held my foundation powder, shut it and put it down next to the cleanser. 'You can't have this either.'

'Why on earth not?'

She sighed. 'It's got a mirror in it. You might use the glass as a weapon against someone else or try and cut yourself with it.'

I snatched the case off the desk, put it on the floor and stamped my heel on it until the mirror fell out.

'Can I have it now?'

She made a big show of opening and carefully inspecting it once more before putting it down in the other pile. 'OK.'

I then had my photograph taken and was issued with my prison number – CF6539. At the end she summarised everything she had done up until that point.

While I recognised most of the individual words she was using, the way she was using them made so little sense she might just as well have been speaking a foreign language. There was no allowance for the fact that I hadn't been to prison before. 'OK, there's three quid in your purse so that's your spends for the week. You've got your "thirty-nine" right here in your IP and the rest of your prop goes downstairs. If you want to change, just make an app. I'll finish your F-eleven-fifty and you can go back in the holding room. We're pretty full so you might end up down on the Ones tonight and be split from your co-d's, OK. Any queries, just find an SO.'

Then she asked me to undress so she could search me.

'I . . . I can't,' I said softly, unsure whether I was allowed to speak or whether I should call her 'sir' or 'madam' or 'officer' or whatever.

She sighed again, this time deeply, and then rolled her eyes. 'Look, love, I've had a shitty day, right. And I've still got two hours in this hellhole before I come off shift and I'd really like it to go smoothly, right? Don't give me any shit. Don't fucking mess me about, just go over there and strip off.'

I could feel my bottom lip start to quiver. 'I can't. I've just had an operation. I can't lift my arms and I can't bend over. I'm gonna need someone to help me.'

She smacked her pen down on the desk and stood up, swearing under her breath. She manhandled me into a small space behind a curtain and began roughly removing my clothes. As soon as she lifted up my top she recoiled in horror. My entire back, both of my sides, the whole of my stomach and the tops of my arms were covered in black, red and purple bruises. I'd been wearing the same bandages for two days and they were encrusted with dry blood and starting to stink.

'Jesus Christ! What happened to you?'

I jumped at the chance to lighten the mood. 'Well, you know what those Customs officers are like, gave me a good beating didn't they? At least they had the decency to give me some bandages though.'

When she failed to laugh or even crack a smile, I told her the truth. She said nothing but at least she treated me a little more gently during the remainder of the search.

I was sent back to the holding room and told that I'd have to go and see the doctor. It wasn't special treatment – every new inmate has a health inspection before they are taken to the cells, mainly to see if they have any infectious diseases or conditions like diabetes requiring regular medication. It's also a chance for the prison staff to assess the mental health of the new arrival, so that those thought likely to attempt suicide can be placed under special supervision.

The doctor, who had a thick foreign accent I found impossible to place, went through a list of questions – had I ever had this or that? did I have any plans to kill or mutilate myself? – then asked about the last time I was in hospital. I told him I had just had liposuction.

Deep furrows appeared on his brow. He looked at the nurse next to him, then back at me, then at the nurse again, then back at me. 'Liposuction? What is this liposuction?'

I looked into his eyes, waiting for some sign that he was making a joke. It never came. 'You've got to be kidding me,' I said, half giggling with shock. 'I mean, you're having a laugh, aren't you? Please tell me you're having a laugh.'

The doctor shook his head. 'I have never heard of this

liposuction.' He turned to his nurse. 'What about you?'

She shrugged her shoulders. 'I have no idea what she is talking about.'

This did not bode well. Any confidence I might have had in the medical staff was fading fast. I tried to explain the procedure – 'Well, they make a little hole in your body, stick a tube inside you and suck out all the fat' – but in that context it sounded more like something out of a medieval torture chamber than modern medicine. By the time I'd finished, both their jaws were hanging open in shock. The doctor turned to his nurse: 'Why would someone do such a thing?'

My painkillers had been put into storage and because he did not know what liposuction was, the doctor refused to give them to me or prescribe anything stronger than paracetamol there and then, but said he would look into it and get me something else for later. He also refused to give me any Imodium.

After that it was back to the holding room one last time before the moment I dreaded more than anything – being taken to my cell. We'd missed dinner so one of the staff dished out a few ready meals that had been heated up in the microwave. It was completely inedible. The different bits of meat and vegetable were either horribly burned or sickeningly raw and the whole thing smelled of hot plastic. I pushed it all to one side – I wasn't hungry anyway. I had a cigarette instead.

Two new prison officers arrived, called my name and the names of two others and said they would be escorting us to our cells. 'The place is jam-packed,' one of them told me, 'so all you new girls are going to spend tonight on the medical wing.'

What a touch! For the first time in days I had something to be thankful for. Everything I'd seen up until that point confirmed my belief that Holloway was a real shithole, but at least the medical wing would be nice and clean, even if the staff were a bit clueless.

Our little group started making its way through a series of passageways and corridors on our way to the ground-floor cells, or the 'Ones' as I would later learn they were called. By the time we stopped off at a room marked LAUNDRY I was getting flashbacks of the time I had made the charity visit to the prison, and the smell that had haunted me was becoming stronger. We were issued with one blanket and two sheets. 'Sorry, we're out of pillows,' said one of the officers, not actually sounding sorry at all. 'We'll try and sort you out tomorrow.'

We continued our journey and as we descended a flight of stairs I felt a tap on my shoulder and turned around to see another inmate, a tall slim woman wearing a denim jacket and jeans, who was close behind me. 'Do yourself a favour, love,' she said in a soft Scottish accent, pointing to the packet of cigarettes in my hand. 'I can see it's your first time. Don't walk around with a whole packet of fags. You're just asking for trouble. Stick one behind your ear and crotch the rest.'

'Right, thanks,' I said. I was just about to ask her to explain what she meant when my attention was distracted by the sound of a woman's desperate screaming. It was horrific: she was pleading for her life, begging for help and as we descended the stairs it got louder and louder. It was such a horrible sound that it made me want to rush to her aid.

I looked around me: the Scottish woman, the guards

and the other inmates, none of them seemed to have heard the noise at all. Then, as suddenly as it had started, it stopped. It crossed my mind that I had imagined it, that I might be the only one who could hear it.

Then, as we reached the bottom of the stairs and passed through a couple of double doors it started up again, along with the noise of other women screaming. It was as if we were descending into hell.

'I'm going to kill myself, I'm going to kill myself.'

'The devil made me do it, the devil made me do it.'

'Aaaaaaaaaghhhhhhh!'

'Help me, help me, for God's sake somebody help me.'

'Aaaaaaaaaaghhhhhhh!'

The Scottish woman caught my eye.

'Is this the medical wing?' I gasped.

She grinned. 'Fucking loony bin, more like. There's no one sick here, not physically anyway. Don't worry, you'll get used to it.'

But I didn't want to get used to it. I just wanted to go home. Far from being a safe haven, I was about to discover that the medical wing was one of the worst places in the entire prison. It was hard to believe people like that were being locked up at all. They were clearly in need of serious help.

I shut my eyes again: Come on, Tracy, you can handle this. Just hold on for a week and then you'll be out of here. Don't panic, just make people laugh and you'll be fine. You've always got on with people. It's going to be OK.

Halfway along the corridor the warden leading our little group took out a bunch of keys, unlocked a large heavy door with a thin glass slit at eye level and stood to one side to let me go in.

Then the door was locked behind me and I was alone in my cell. And it was worse than anything I could have imagined. To my left was the bed: a metal bench with a mattress made from a piece of solid rubber foam about five inches thick. The surface of the mattress was covered in hard plastic rivets, each of which sat in a tiny pool of sticky black gunk. Behind me, on the left of the door, there was a stainless steel toilet and a tin sink. The toilet had no seat and no lid. It was caked with filth, as if someone had taken handfuls of shit and smeared them on the inside and outside of the bowl as well as up the wall behind. The sink was just as bad, with years of grime covering its entire surface. The bed was the only piece of furniture – apart from that the cell was empty.

To the right of the bed was a window. It was made up of vertical slats and went from waist height to over my head. Three of the slats were slightly open, letting in an icy breeze. I tried to close them but quickly discovered they were faulty: I could open them wider but it was impossible to shut them completely. There was no way to stop the draught.

Outside the window was a small yard of grass and concrete, flanked on all sides by other cell blocks. Looking upwards I could see only a tiny patch of sky which looked grimly grey in the fading light. I tried to push my head out to see more but the slats were too narrow. I could get my hand through but that was all. Below me, just a few feet away, were piles of rotting food, sanitary towels, old newspaper and bits of rolled-up toilet paper, old Pot Noodle cartons and other stuff. Some of the rubbish was moving. I saw a flash of brown and realised there were rats and mice amongst the rubbish.

Finally I looked back at the main door. The side facing the corridor had been covered in a mock-wood veneer but inside it was just painted metal. Just below eye level was a long Perspex strip which served as a peephole. To the right, directly above the toilet, was a small hatch which opened outwards and allowed prison officers to inspect the cell more thoroughly without having to come in.

When I'd examined every corner I stood in the centre of the room and turned round and round four or five times, taking everything in, until I felt giddy. I went and sat on the edge of the bed. And then I cried for the first time.

I cried and I cried and I cried, then I started talking out loud. 'This can't be right. What the hell am I doing here? If this is the medical wing, what's it going to be like when I move upstairs? I can't stay here, I just can't stay here.'

I sobbed my heart out. I was still wailing like a banshee when I suddenly realised that people would be able to hear me. I didn't want anyone to know how I felt, that they had got to me already. Everything I had seen was a thousand times worse than I had imagined, but, no matter how awful it was, I was determined to get through a week of it. As I quietened down I heard someone calling my name.

Sylvie had been put in the cell next to mine and had heard me sobbing. I didn't really know her, but she seemed kind and was close to my mother's age, which

I found particularly comforting at a time when I really could have done with my family being around. I walked over to the window and we started talking, even though we couldn't see one another. She had managed to keep hold of her matches and lit a cigarette, which we shared. If I reached through the bars, stretching my arm as far as it would go and she did the same, we could just about touch fingers and swap cigarettes.

I couldn't sleep because I was freezing. It was the last week in April but spring was starting late and it had been unseasonably cold. There had even been snow in the north of England. I tried undressing but I was too uncomfortable so I had to put all of my clothes back on. The one blanket was incredibly thin, with holes in it, and stank to high heaven. The sheets had dark stains on them – blood, shit, possibly both. I found it hard to get comfortable without a pillow.

The voices of the inmates echoed around the yard, then suddenly they were joined by a new voice, stronger, closer. From along the corridor a woman was calling out: 'Medication, medication?' in a thick Jamaican accent. It was the nurse, doing her rounds for the night. Thank goodness. Now I'd be able to get some painkillers and some Imodium to take me through the night.

I went to the hatch and called out to her as she approached. 'Hello? Yes, I'm on medication. The doctor said he was going to get me some painkillers.' She had a broad, round face and her dark skin shone under the harsh lighting. She glanced at the name by the side of my cell and then vanished.

I went back to the bed and sat down, relieved that she was going off to get my drugs. My bottom had barely touched the mattress when her face appeared back at the hatch and she started screaming at me.

'Who the fuck do you think you are?' she yelled. I didn't know what to say, I had no idea what I had done to make her suddenly so hostile. 'You've got to learn to show some respect. You don't make me wait for you. You stand by the fucking hatch and you wait for *me*. You hear me? It don't matter what you were on the outside, in here you're just a criminal. You play by our rules.'

The mistake I had made was assuming she had to go off and get the drugs. In fact she had a trolley with her. I was so emotionally raw that anything would have made me cry at that point. As she carried on screaming at me, tears began to roll down my face, but that just made her even angrier.

'Don't start all that fucking nonsense. You're wasting your time. You think I care about your tears?'

'Please,' I sobbed, 'I just want my medication.'

'What medication?'

'Painkillers . . . and Imodium.'

'Well there's nothing on the list.'

'But the doctor—'

'Are you fucking deaf? Are you stupid? I said there's nothing on the list. Don't make me tell you again.' And she moved on, pushing her trolley in front of her.

I couldn't sleep and neither could Sylvie. We got up and spoke to each other a couple of times during the night, and in between I just lay on my bed staring up at the ceiling and listening to the shouts and screams of the women around me. The night seemed to last for ever.

*   *   *

I could hear the wardens working their way down the corridor, unlocking the cells and rousing the inmates from their slumbers. I had no idea what the time was. The sound of the key in my own door told me it was my turn to go and get breakfast.

The pain from the operation was starting to fade but I still wasn't moving as quickly as the officers would have liked. 'Oi, get a move on, we ain't got all day,' I was told as I slowly made my way towards the breakfast room.

The dining area was like a small version of a school canteen. There was a long queue at a small hatch with white Formica panels. Behind this was a serving table piled high with tin trays full of bread, boiled eggs, beans and other items. In an annexe there was a toaster and bowls of cereal.

I was still feeling pretty rough and none of the things swimming in grease in the metal trays looked like they were going to make me feel any better. The queue was quite long and getting boisterous as people chatted and argued away. I didn't fancy joining in so I decided to make do with some toast and tea. As I placed a slice of bread in one of the slots, a stocky Indian girl in black leather trousers and a sweatshirt appeared beside me and did the same.

Something about her told me she didn't speak English so we just stood there in silence, watching the machine. The two slices popped up and the Indian took one and went to reach for the other. 'No, no, that's mine,' I said. She turned, slowly looked me up and down, and then grabbed the second slice. I didn't stop to think, I just acted on instinct. My hand flicked out and slapped hers out of the way.

She looked at me again. There was fire in her eyes and her nostrils flared slightly as she started to breathe hard. If looks could kill I would have dropped dead on the spot. I tried to hold her gaze but I just couldn't and turned away.

'Big mistake,' she hissed. I just stood there alone, shaking. I really was going to be torn apart. I'd honestly thought I'd be able to survive for a week but now I was having serious doubts about whether I'd be able to make it through breakfast. It seemed like everyone had it in for me – the guards, the medical staff, the inmates, the lot of them.

I stayed in the annexe until I'd regained my composure and produced a new slice of toast, then I skulked around the corner to an empty table, waiting for Sylvie to join me. Out of the corner of my eye I could see the Indian girl sitting at a corner table with two other women. She was pointing at me and saying something to them. By the time Sylvie joined me I was as white as a sheet. I told her what had happened.

'I was talking to one of the other girls on the way to my cell,' she told me. 'She said that new arrivals are targets for all the bullies. They try to suss out how hard you are in the first few days. After that you either get to join them or you're their victim and they take everything off you.'

'God, it's like being back in the playground.'

After breakfast I was told to gather my things because I was being moved. The prison authorities felt it was dangerous to have so many defendants from the same trial on the same wing and had decided to split us up. Carrying my bundle of blankets and the paper bags of my possessions, I was taken to wing B3.

My escort was the same officer who had taken my details and strip-searched me at the reception area the previous day. As I walked alongside her, clutching my things to my chest, I saw her in profile for the first time. Her skin and eyes were grey and pallid and sunken, and her nose was long and bent slightly downwards at its tip, forming a small hook. She looked a little like a vulture.

On the way to my cell, she told me that I had missed the canteen – the name given to the prison shop – for that week but that as a concession I'd be allowed to order some items, which would then be brought to my cell. She reminded me that I had £3 in my 'spends' – my weekly spending allowance. 'So, what do you want?'

'Well, what is there?'

The prison officer let out a bored sigh. 'There's loads of stuff, I haven't got time to go through it all. Just tell me what you want.'

'But how can I tell you what I want if you won't tell me what there is? I don't even known how much the things cost.'

The officer glared at me for a long time. It had seemed like a perfectly reasonable thing to say but somehow I had managed to rub her up the wrong way. Answering back was obviously not a good thing.

Finally she asked, 'Do you smoke?'

I nodded weakly. 'Right so you'll need some ciga-rettes. The prices are exactly the same as they are on the outside. What else? Tampons? Toothpaste?'

In the end I got four cigarettes and a bottle of cheap shampoo, because I knew I'd be able to wash with it. But that was it — all my money was used up.

New inmates are supposed to get an induction so that they can get to grips with the prison regime and the jargon; but nine times out of ten, due to staff shortages and inmates arriving after the cut-off time, this does not happen. It means they haven't got a clue what is going on.

My new cell was a huge improvement on the first, but that's not saying much. Whereas the cell downstairs had been bare, this had a small two-drawer cabinet and a cupboard for hanging clothes with a few shelves. There was also a table and chair.

The mattress looked slightly more comfortable than the foam-rubber brick I had slept on the night before but, as I quickly learned, appearances can be deceptive. I pushed my hand down on the mattress to feel how soft it was and my hand sunk into it. When I took it away, the mattress didn't even try to spring back into place. I could see I was in for another sleepless night.

Again there was no toilet seat so the previous occupant had made her own makeshift one out of sanitary towels. They seemed to have been in place for some time. They were stained with drops of urine and had pubic hairs sticking to them. I wrapped some toilet paper around my fingers and gingerly peeled them off, depositing them in the nearby bin.

When I could see the toilet bowl clearly I almost threw up. The rim and inside were caked with streaks of shit which had become as hard as concrete. The stench was appalling.

I sat on the bed and stared at the wall. Almost immediately the door of my cell swung open and a girl came in. She was in her mid-twenties, dressed in tatty dungarees and with fuzzy mousy hair sticking out in all directions. She smiled at me and I saw she had only one or two teeth in her entire mouth. She looked like she'd spent years living on the streets.

We were in the midst of 'association', a time when prisoners are allowed to wander throughout their wings and in and out of each other's cells with a large degree of freedom.

She walked in, her eyes darting about my cell, and plonked herself down on the bed beside me. 'Watcha. I'm Ruth.'

'Er, hello. I'm Tracy.'

'Yeah, right. How long you in for? What you done? Got any fags?'

I didn't know which question to answer first. Before I could get a response out a female prison officer who was walking along the corridor peered through the hatch. 'Everything all right?' Ruth and I both nodded and she moved on.

'Fucking screws,' hissed Ruth. 'They put a uniform on and they fucking think they're God.' She turned back to me. 'You're quiet, ain't ya? What have you got then? 'Ave you been to the canteen yet? I need some fags. You must have something.'

I'd been waiting for her to take a breath so I could get a word in edgeways. Now I seized my chance. 'I'm sorry, I don't have anything.'

As the words left my mouth, it was as if someone had flicked a switch in Ruth's head. Until then she had seemed nice enough, if a little eccentric. She turned in an instant.

'Don't give me any of that fucking crap. I know you've got stuff. You come in here all la-di-dah like you're Lady fucking Muck with your nice dress and your fancy boots.'

I was already feeling about an inch tall and wishing the ground would swallow me up when the door swung open again and a second girl came in. Taller and broader than Ruth but every bit as rough, she joined her friend in taunting me, also calling out the names of their friends. Within seconds there were seven of them inside my cell, all looking through my stuff, asking me when I was going to the canteen and telling me how many cigarettes I should get for them. I was absolutely terrified and soon felt a familiar urge bubbling away inside.

'Oh God,' I gasped. 'I really need to use the toilet.'

'Well go on then,' replied Ruth. 'We ain't fucking stopping you.'

The very thought of using the toilet in front of this group of harpies sent shivers down my spine. 'No, look, can you please all go outside?'

Ruth looked at me like I was mad. 'Oh I forgot,' she said cynically, 'you're a lady ain't ya? Not used to having people around you all the time. I'll be outside and keep watch.'

I sat on the toilet and tried to relax. After thirty seconds Ruth poked her head around the door. 'You all right? Just checking.'

'Please,' I gasped. 'Please, just give me ten minutes. I'll talk to you later. Just give me ten minutes.'

*   *   *

Later that morning, after I'd managed to get rid of Ruth and her mates by giving them all but one of my precious cigarettes, I was sitting on my bed when I heard a knock at the door. I looked up and saw a grinning male face at my hatch.

'Are you Tracy?'

I nodded slowly. He moved from the hatch and walked in through the half-open door. He had wavy black hair plastered to his scalp with its own grease. His pock-marked face was chubby but affable. His thin lips broke into a smile and he held out his hand. 'I'm Mr . . . actually, that's much too formal. Just call me Matt.'

'Hello,' I said weakly, wiping the tears from my face with the back of my hand before shaking his. He sat down on the bed beside me and put a comforting arm around my shoulders, pulling me towards him. His voice became soft and low.

'Listen mate, I heard you were coming in and I wanted to get to see you as soon as possible. I know you're not the usual type we get in here and because of that you might end up having a hard time. Most of the time we just deal with scum but I know you're a decent girl. I remember you from Page Three. Actually, you were always my favourite, I had your pictures up all over the place.'

I managed a weak smile as it crossed my mind that he was about to ask for my autograph. 'So what I want to say,' he continued, moving his arm from my shoulders and taking my hand gently in his, 'is that if there's anything you need, or if you ever have a problem, just come to me and I'll look after you. And always remember, it's not as bad as it seems. You'll do fine.' He squeezed my hand then got up and left, pausing at the door of my cell to smile and wink at me as I thanked him, then he turned and vanished.

As soon as he was gone I started crying again. I was overcome with emotion. It was the first time that someone had been nice to me since I'd arrived in prison.

Chapter Ten

It had been more than three days since I'd last spoken to my mum. Normally after a gap like that I'd be suffering withdrawal symptoms and getting desperate to catch up with her. Instead, the mere thought of talking to her, let alone seeing her again, was so stressful it made me want to throw up.

Our last meeting had been far from ideal – she'd been furious after learning that I'd had liposuction without telling her. Since then Customs had raided my home, I'd been arrested and taken away in handcuffs, spent two nights locked up in cells, been charged with drug-trafficking, appeared at court, had bail refused and finally been sent to Holloway – all of which had been kept from her. There was no way I'd be around to do eighteen years – my mum was going to kill me.

Apart from Maria, the only person who knew anything about my predicament was my sister, and I'd sworn her to secrecy. During those first three days I'd been so certain that things were going to get sorted out, so convinced that Customs would soon realise they had made some silly mistake, that I saw little point in making my parents worry unnecessarily. But once I found myself in that van and on my way to prison, I knew I was all out of options.

My mother finally learned what had gone on behind

her back in a late-afternoon phone call from my sister. Once the initial hysterics had subsided, she and my father set about trying to find out as much as possible about my situation, speaking to my solicitor, and to Holloway to find out when they would be able to come and see me.

They soon learned that, as I was on remand and therefore technically considered to be innocent until proven guilty, I'd be allowed a visit every day (convicted prisoners get only one visit every two weeks). Just before lunch, a gruff screw with a skinhead haircut informed me that I had visitors coming in to see me at 1330 hours and I knew the time had come to face the music.

Visits take place in a large room filled with around twenty numbered tables, each of which is surrounded by three blue chairs (visitors) and one red chair (prisoner) so the screws can tell at a glance where the inmates are. There is a small canteen area where visitors (but not inmates) can purchase things like coffee and cups of soup. At the back there is a small play area for children filled with brightly coloured toys. The whole thing is overseen by a group of screws, some patrol around the tables while the others sit at a desk and keep a watchful eye.

Before prisoners can enter the visiting room they are searched, and then made to wait in a small room charmingly referred to as 'Cunts' Corner' until their name and the number of the table they have been assigned is called out. As this was my first ever visit, I was told I would be sitting at table 1, which was directly in front of the desk where the screws sat. That way they'd be able to keep an eye on me and ensure that no one in my family tried to smuggle any contraband. When my name was finally called, I came out of the room to find my mum, my dad and my brother sitting and waiting for me.

They all looked absolutely awful, as if they had been up all night fretting and worrying – which, of course, they had. As soon as they saw me, an expression of sheer horror fell across their faces: they had never seen me in such an appalling state. I'd tried to make myself look as presentable as possible but that was no easy task with no mirror and no make-up. Worse still, since I couldn't raise my hands above my head, I hadn't washed my hair for five days and I couldn't even brush it properly. It felt as if I had a gigantic greasy peroxide mop sitting on my head.

As soon as I sat down, my mum exploded with rage. 'What the hell have you done, Tracy? What the hell have you been doing?' I tried to explain that I hadn't done anything but I couldn't get a word in edgeways: every question, every dark thought that she'd been holding inside her came bursting out. 'They said you've been smuggling drugs. Drugs! For God's sake! What have you been playing at? How could you do this to us? How could you be so bloody stupid? Don't you think we've got enough to worry about? And what else have you been doing? What other nasty surprises are lurking around the corner? I can't take this, Tracy, I just can't take it any more.'

Again I tried to explain that I hadn't had anything to do with drugs, but my words just bounced off her as if she was wearing armour. Nothing was getting through. Deep down inside I knew the real reason she was so angry was because she was scared and didn't know what was going to happen to me, but it was still heartbreaking to see her like that. My dad and my brother just sat there, shaking their heads. I felt so small, like a child who'd been caught stealing sweets from the corner shop. I started to cry, then my mum started to cry, and for the rest of the visit we just sat at the table holding hands, sobbing and wailing our hearts out.

The sound of a ringing bell signalled the end of visiting time and the screws busied themselves rushing around and telling people it was time to leave. Until then the atmosphere had been bearable and my family had been so focused on me that they hadn't taken in their surroundings. But as the screws became more determined, so the atmosphere became more aggressive.

When two of them tried to usher a visitor towards the door, things suddenly turned nasty. 'Don't you fucking touch him,' screamed one girl as a screw placed a guiding hand on her boyfriend's shoulder. 'He's not in here, he hasn't done anything wrong. You've got no fucking right to touch him.'

At that moment a visitor on the other side of the room tried to take advantage of the commotion to pass over a small packet of heroin that she'd been hiding under her tongue. One of the screws spotted her, shouted out a warning and all hell broke loose. Screws ran in from all directions, leaping over chairs and tables, wrestled the inmate to the ground and tried to make her spit out the drugs before she had a chance to swallow them.

As I was herded back into Cunts' Corner, I caught

a glimpse of the startled faces of my mum, brother and father as the mayhem exploded around them. I knew exactly what they were thinking because the same question had been playing on my mind ever since I arrived: would I be able to survive such a hostile, violent environment for a whole week? I was glad they'd never asked me: I was beginning to have serious doubts that I'd make it through the weekend.

It had been another bitterly cold night and I had ended up wearing all my clothes before I finally got warm enough to fall asleep. It made me so dozy that it took me ages to get up in the morning and I found myself well towards the back of the queue that stretched out of the dining room and along the corridor. I was starving and starting to get anxious: you have only a limited time to collect and eat your breakfast. If you don't make it for whatever reason, you simply go hungry.

After ten minutes, I'd moved forward only a few paces and the people behind me were getting tense and restless. I kept my eyes to the floor and tried to concentrate on my breathing to prevent myself going into a panic attack. As I finally moved around the corner into the entrance to the dining room, I was knocked sideways by a muscular, shaven-headed black woman in a cut-off T-shirt who pushed her way in front of me.

I was stunned. Without thinking, I reached up and jabbed her in the back of the shoulder. 'Oi, what do you think you're doing?' She spun around to face me and immediately went off on one, letting loose a tirade of insults in a thick patois that I could barely decipher. The only words I understood, mainly because they were repeated again and again, were 'motherfucker', 'bitch' and 'blood clot'. Tiny flecks of spittle leaped out of her mouth and splashed on my face as she started poking my chest, forcing me backwards. Then her eyes landed on my feet and she finally calmed down.

'I'm 'aving dem boots,' she hissed after a long pause. Acting on instructions passed on by my sister, my parents had sent in a package of clothing to the prison including a pair of trendy but comfortable Dr Marten-style boots that I had bought a few months earlier and knew that, far more than anything else in my wardrobe, would be well suited to life inside. Having only just got them, I wasn't prepared to give them up for anyone.

'I don't think so.'

'I am. I'm 'aving dem boots.'

'Over my dead body.'

I'd barely finished the sentence before I started regretting it. Of all the things I could have said . . .

The woman threw her head back and burst out laughing as if she'd just been told the funniest joke in the world. I stood there not knowing quite what to do apart from stare at the spider tattoo on the side of her neck. Then she gave some kind of signal and within an instant I found myself surrounded.

There were at least five of them and they crowded around, taunting and teasing, stabbing their fingers into my chest and pushing me this way and that while chuckling like schoolgirls and pointing at my boots.

'You're not going to intimidate me,' I mumbled, utterly intimidated. I knew exactly what was happening and that made it even more terrifying: they were sizing me up to see if I was someone they could bully and take advantage of. If I couldn't find some way of making a stand, then it was only a matter of time before they dragged me off to the toilets, beat the shit out of me and took my boots by force.

I had to do something. I fixed my gaze at the leader of the gang, took in a deep breath and forced myself to shout out: 'Listen, love, the only way you're getting these boots is up your fucking arse.'

For a split second, the group fell silent with shock. I knew they were looking at me through new eyes, wondering if they'd underestimated my potential as their latest victim. If I could front it out for a few more minutes, I just might be able to get through it. But then it all went horribly wrong.

'Is everything all right?'

I turned in the direction of the voice to see a male screw standing at the edge of the group. The woman with the spider tattoo answered him first. 'We're just talking, fuck off and mind your own business.' The screw looked at me, waiting for my confirmation. He was a young, thin man with dark hair, eager eyes and a slight Geordie accent. He looked like the sort of bloke who became a screw out of some deep-seated desire to help people at the bottom of society's ladder. It was pretty obvious what was going on but he couldn't do anything without my say-so. And the one thing I knew that I absolutely could not do was to ask for help. 'Yeah,' I said softly, 'it's all fine. Fuck off.'

But he didn't. The little bastard hovered around as I returned to my place in the queue, loitered as I collected my breakfast and then followed a few paces behind as I carried my tray of lukewarm beans, greasy eggs and murky tea back to my cell. All the while the girls who had been after my boots stood and watched from afar, their arms folded across their chests.

'For crying out loud, leave me alone will you,' I whispered out of the corner of my mouth as I walked down the corridor.

'I just want to make sure you're not going to have a problem.'

'But you're giving me a problem, you're making me look bad. Look at them. They think I'm talking to you. You're really putting it on me.'

'It's OK. I'm here to look after you, I can make things better.'

'But you're making it worse. You're making it a million times worse. I haven't asked for your help and I don't want it. Please, just leave me alone.'

'Don't worry, pet, I'll keep an eye on you.'

'For God's sake don't do that. You're gonna get me killed. You're really going to cause me problems. Just leave it. I can handle this.'

'Don't worry, I'll sort it.'

'No, for God's sake, don't do anything.'

'Don't worry, I'll make sure it's all sorted out.'

As I scuttled back into the relative safety of my cell, I couldn't help but fear the worst. This really was just like being back in the playground and now I was going to be accused of having told teacher. Even if the screw said nothing, the gang would be convinced I'd grassed them up. But my biggest worry was that he would try to intervene. In my mind's eye I could just imagine the look on his worthy little face as he approached the woman with the spider tattoo and tried to appeal to her non-existent sense of reason: 'Hey, pet, you must have a lot of anger, right? I bet you come from a broken home. I want you to know I understand your rage. Can't we just get along?'

She'd tear his head off. Then at lunchtime she and her friends would come after me.

I'd been staring at the wall and quivering with fear for an hour when a key turned in the door of my cell and a tall female screw who I'd never seen before appeared.

'OK, Kirby,' she said, 'get your shit together. You're being moved.'

'Again? Another new cell? Are you planning on moving me every day?'

'Not a new cell, a new wing. We're moving you out of here. You're going to D3.'

There were two reasons to feel relieved. One was that I wouldn't have to face the boot gang again. The second was that, because I would remain on level 3, I would still be able to meet up with Debbie, Jan and Sylvie each morning. Although they were on different wings to me, each level throughout the prison used the same courtyard for the morning exercise session.

But any relief I felt evaporated the moment I learned that, rather than a single cell, I would be moving into a dormitory with three other girls. Clutching all my belongings in two brown paper bags, I watched the screw push open the door to my new home.

The first thing I saw was two women breaking off from a passionate kiss. They were standing together in the middle of the room, so close that their bodies were squashed up against each other. As I moved towards them they turned and stared at me, each keeping one arm around the other's shoulder. I could now see their faces properly. The one on my left was tall and thin with long dark hair and a tiny beauty spot on the side of her nose. The other had short brown hair and glowing olive skin with bright green eyes. Her complexion was perfect and it crossed my mind that she too might once have been a model.

'Hello,' I said gingerly, 'I'm Tracy.'

The women stared back blankly, slowly looking me up and down. Then I heard a rough voice from behind me: 'You're wasting your time – they don't speak English.'

I turned to see a thin girl squatting over the toilet, her knickers and jeans bundled around her ankles, and a floppy roll-up hanging from her lips. This was Julie.

She stood and dressed herself, flushed the toilet then gesticulated wildly towards the two girls while putting on a fake Italian accent: 'No speaka de English, eh? Shuduppa your face, quattro formaggi.'

The green-eyed girl said something I didn't understand and rolled her eyes.

'Oh, are they Italian?' I asked, then, turning to the girls, 'Are you Italian?'

Julie gave them no time to reply. 'Nah, they're Spanish, but I can't do a Spanish accent.'

Julie flopped on to her bed and asked what I was in for. I mumbled something about waiting for a bail hearing and this sparked her off into a rant about the legal system. She told me that she was on remand for fraud but that her team had 'fucked it up big time' and that she shouldn't have been there at all. Her solicitor was a wanker, her QC was a bastard and the man heading the prosecution was a total cunt. The judge, she added, was a wanker, a bastard *and* a cunt.

Julie seemed to have a lot to say and was clearly delighted at having someone new to talk to. She rarely paused for breath as she proceeded to recount the disgusting and horrifying things she had seen and done throughout her troubled life. With her weather-beaten features and all she had been through, including having two children who'd both been given up for adoption, I'd assumed she was close to my own age. In fact she was just twenty-two.

At tea, I ate and drank very little. It was nothing to do with a lack of hunger – my stomach was crying out for a decent meal – but I simply couldn't face the humiliation of having to use the toilet in front of so many people, and wanted to delay the inevitable as long as possible.

As it turned out, I needn't have worried. Once we were locked up for the evening the two Spanish girls climbed on to one bed and proceeded to kiss and stroke one another as if I wasn't there. Julie, in the mean time, continued ranting and raving about her case and her life, even while she was using the toilet, and only quietened down when it grew dark outside and she began idly flicking through the pages of a magazine before finally drifting off.

When I woke early the following morning, I was back at my parents' house.

The soft light of dawn was filtering in through the window, the crisp white linen on my bed was smooth against my skin, the smell of fresh coffee and grilled bacon wafted up from the kitchen, birds sat on the branches of trees in the back garden singing their little hearts out and I could hear our beloved dog, Kelly, lapping away at her water bowl.

I half opened my eyes and reality slapped me. The crisp sheets had been replaced with a filthy, stinking, stained blanket, the birdsong gave way to the grunts and cackles of inmates shouting to one another from their cell windows and the smell of fresh coffee became the stale odour of shit and sweat. Only the sound of Kelly at her water bowl remained.

I rolled over to the direction of the noise and saw the two Spanish girls on the bed in the corner, half naked and locked in a noisy 69 position. Turning away, I pulled my pillow over my head and tried to get back to sleep.

One of the most frightening and surprising things about prison is how quickly you find yourself falling into step with the daily routine. With only a handful of notable exceptions and a few stark differences at weekends, one day in prison is exactly the same as any other.

Life inside is so regimented, so controlled, that it leaves little space for individual thought or action. From the time of day that you are woken to the number of minutes you are allowed to spend exercising, from the exact amount of chicken stew you are allowed to consume for lunch to the number of sanitary towels you are given during your period, every single aspect of your existence has been calculated, co-ordinated and considered in your absence and without consultation.

By Friday I realised that I could accurately predict what any inmate would be doing at any time on any date as far forward as I cared or dared to think. It made me thankful I only had to put up with it for a few days; I didn't know how anyone could cope with the monotony for any longer.

Weekdays begin at 7.30 a.m. with the unlocking of the cells and the slow march to a quick breakfast. This is followed by what is misleadingly called 'exercise' but in reality is nothing more than walking around the courtyard for twenty minutes or so. In the event of rain, the session is cancelled and inmates have to spend the whole day inside the building. Within the space of a few months, this lack of exposure to natural light manifests itself as a pale, ghostly complexion known as 'prison pallor'.

At 9 a.m. it is time for 'free flow', during which every inmate makes her way to her work or education assignments. As I had signed up for neither, I would be locked in my cell with nothing to do except listen to the scores of people noisily shuffling past.

At 11.30 inmates are let out for lunch – which always consisted of either a bowl of soup or a sandwich, nothing more. If I was quick and got to the head of the queue, there might be time for a quick phone call to my mum. By 12.15 I would be back in my cell until 1 p.m. when I would be taken down for my daily visit. This was supposed to last an hour but that rarely happened because of staff shortages. Sometimes the visit would last as little as fifteen minutes and I would spend the remainder of the time cooped up in Cunts' Corner.

By 2.45 I would be back in my cell once more and

remain there until around 4.45 when inmates are let out for tea, which has to be eaten by 5.30. That is also the time to fill in a slip of paper to choose what main course and dessert you'll have for tea the following day. The remainder of the afternoon is spent in 'association' until 6.45, when the screws hand out paper bags containing three teabags, powdered milk and some sugar. This is followed by a call of 'hot water,' which leads to streams of inmates queuing up outside the dining room to fill their flasks and jugs so that they can have a hot drink in their cell. By 7 p.m., they have been locked up for the night and the lights in the corridor have been switched off.

Weekends were tougher. We would be woken up half an hour later, eat our last meal even earlier and be locked up for the evening by 4.30 p.m. It was ridiculously early. No matter how much I tried to eat for tea, I would always be ravenous by the time I was ready to go to sleep.

I spent every waking moment of that first week counting down the seconds until my next bail hearing, supremely confident that I'd be able to return home and start sorting out the mess I'd got myself into.

The day before the hearing, I packed up all my things and even drew up a list of all the things I wanted to eat – the things I'd missed most since I'd been inside. I had no reason to doubt that I was going home – I believed in the judicial system and knew that, whatever else had been going on behind my back, I had nothing to do with any drugs. I wondered how long it would be before I was sharing the stories of my crazy week in prison with friends at the local wine bar. I'd be dining out on it for weeks.

The following morning, the dormitory was opened up at 6.30 and two screws asked me to join a group of four other inmates on their way to court. Julie, only half awake, told me she hoped that she wouldn't have to listen to me whining any more – her way of wishing me good luck – while the two Spanish girls, who had been up and at it all night long, continued sleeping.

I knew I had to make an effort to look my best before the magistrate. As we entered the holding room to wait for the sweatboxes, I took out my lipstick and started to apply it as best I could with no mirror, putting it back in my paper bag when I'd finished. A pale girl with bright red hair strolled over.

'Oh, you won't be able to take that with you, love,' she said, genuine concern in her voice. 'They'll take it off you during the search and you won't get it back.'

'Fuck off, it's Versace.'

'Nah, you don't understand. You're only allowed to take out a book and your court papers. You can take cigarettes, but if you don't smoke them all you're not allowed to bring them back.'

'But that's ridiculous.'

'Hey, don't worry, it's not a problem – just crotch it.'

I didn't want to admit that I had no idea what she was talking about. I'd spent the whole week fronting it out on D3, trying my hardest to come across like someone who had serious time behind her, the sort that no one would want to fuck with. It was bad enough having made a mistake with the lipstick. Asking her to translate the prison jargon would put me right back to square one.

Instead, I decided to play it cool and try to work it out for myself. Crotch it. Hmmm. Well, I guessed it meant hiding it in your knickers. Yeah, that must be it. My theory seemed to be confirmed when, out of the corner of my eye, I saw the girl who had been talking to me drop her jeans and knickers. I hitched up my skirt and got ready to do the same, removing the lipstick from the bag and lining it up with the gusset of my knickers as I wondered how best to position it.

The girl moved into a half-squat. She had a packet of cigarettes in her left hand and then, all of a sudden, wallop! They had vanished. There was no trace of them, not in her hand, not in her knickers or anywhere else. And all at once I realised what crotching really meant. The girl beside me looked over and gave me a cheeky grin, nodding towards the lipstick in my hand as if to say, 'Go on then.'

I looked around the room and could scarcely believe my eyes. Girls were crotching like crazy – Mars Bars, cigarettes, lighters, packets of drugs and all sorts were all vanishing up their nether regions. My eyes went back to the redhead, who was staring hard, wondering why I was hesitating. What I wanted to say was, 'You must be fucking kidding,' but I had an image to maintain. I took a deep breath. 'You're not going to believe this,' I said, holding the lipstick up to the light, 'I've only gone and brought the wrong colour. I think I'll leave it here.'

The journey to court in the sweatbox was horrendous but I comforted myself with the knowledge that it would be the last time I'd have to endure it.

Shortly before the hearing opened, David, my solicitor came to see me in the cells. He was full of smiles and enthusiasm. His absolute belief that I was going to get bail was infectious and I couldn't help but feel confident.

After that, everything happened so quickly that I could barely keep up. One minute I was in my cell below the court, the next, Sylvie, Debbie, Jan and myself had been taken upstairs and were all sitting in the dock together. I could see my parents and some of my friends sitting in the public gallery, smiling down and waving. Then the lawyer acting for Customs got up and started saying a few things and almost immediately we were told that we had to go back down to the cells and wait.

David appeared some twenty minutes later. As soon as I saw his face, I knew that I wouldn't be going home. 'I'm so sorry, Tracy, they said no. You're going back to Holloway.'

I couldn't believe it. David couldn't believe it. Sylvie, Debbie and Jan had all been turned down too. David could see the distress building up within me and immediately set out to dispel it. 'First of all, I want you to know that I believe everything you're telling me and that you knew nothing about the drug-trafficking—'

'That's right, I didn't, I really didn't—'

'I know, I know. Now, Customs won't tell me everything, but it's clear that they think you're involved in much more than you're saying. I don't know why and I don't know how, but that's what they think and that's why they're refusing bail.'

'I don't understand it.'

'You really need to think. There must be something

you did or something that happened that gave them that impression. Because I can tell you now, whatever it is, that's what they're going to be putting to the jury when this case comes to trial. And what worries me is that if it's convincing enough for a judge to deny you bail . . .'

His voice trailed off but he didn't need to finish the sentence. I knew exactly what he meant.

Unless I could work out exactly what was going on, there was a good chance that I'd spend the next eighteen years of my life behind bars.

Back at Holloway, no one seemed at all surprised that I had returned, and my place in the dormitory had been kept for me. I couldn't face anyone during association but I desperately needed to hear a friendly voice.

I hadn't seen Maria at court but I'd been in and out so quickly that perhaps I'd missed her. I tried to call her at home and got no reply. I called her mobile, even though I knew I'd only be able to talk for a few minutes before all the credit on my precious phone card was used up.

She answered straight away. It was great to hear her voice again and she immediately apologised for not having been in touch. 'This whole thing, it's been a real shock. I . . . I really want to come and see you, but I don't know if I could face going inside a prison. I don't think I could handle seeing you locked up like that, not yet anyway. But I'll write to you. I've already started a letter and I'll send it tomorrow. And I will come and see you, I just don't know when. Maybe next week. I'm still trying to take it all in.'

I could understand how she was feeling, but that didn't make it any less painful. I was still getting visits every day and friends were rallying round, but Maria was the best friend I had and I really needed her support.

When I got back to the dormitory Julie was propped up on the bed, waiting for me. 'I knew you'd be back, you poor cow,' she snorted. 'I was reading about that bastard in the papers. Fucking grasses, should all be lined up and fucking well shot if you ask me.'

She wasn't making much sense. 'What are you talking about, Julie?'

'That story in the paper. That fucking grass. You must be well gutted. No wonder they turned you down. If there's a fucking grass in the case you don't know what they've said. They sell their own fucking grandmothers to get time off. They can say anything and everyone believes them. You can't trust the fuckers. I tell you, I'm only here because some lying wanker-bastard-cunt-grass grassed me up. They take one little fact, make up the rest and everyone treats it as gospel.'

I finally got her to pause long enough to explain that I really didn't have a clue what she was talking about. There had been a couple of pieces in the papers, but they had said little more than that I had been arrested and accused of being part of a drugs gang. Julie jumped up and dashed out of the door, telling me to wait. She returned with a copy of the previous day's *Mail on Sunday*, flicked through until she found the article, then spread it out on the bed before me.

I sat down, leaned forward and started to read.

DETECTIVE ARRESTED BY £10M DRUG RAID POLICE
A detective in Scotland Yard's élite Criminal Intelligence Branch has been arrested by police

investigating tip-offs that have kept drug gangs one step ahead of the law.

The detection of the officer, who handles the most sensitive information from police informants and undercover agents, has sparked a furious row between the Yard and Customs investigators. He was held last Sunday at the end of a four-month surveillance operation by Customs which led to the recovery of cocaine and cannabis worth more than £10 million from a warehouse near Hatfield, Hertfordshire.

Among the 13 people arrested during the raid was former topless model Tracy Kirby and a man, thought to be a major drugs baron, who had been the arrested officer's main informant for years. He had received regular large payments for information received.

After the raid it emerged that members of the Customs National Investigation Service had been suspicious of the detective because of information they had picked up during surveillance operations. They asked Scotland Yard's Complaints Investigation Bureau to investigate but the Yard refused, fearing leaks which might alert the suspected officer. Instead they left it to Customs to monitor the man's activities and it is understood it was their information which led to the arrest last weekend. Now senior Customs officers are angry that the situation was allowed to continue undetected for so long. They trusted the detective, they say, and now believe he may have been betraying their secrets to the underworld for years. Detectives are

investigating allegations that he tipped off criminals about operations in return for information
which would make him look good with his
superiors and may even have taken a share of reward
money. The raid was triggered by the arrival of a
car, driven by a French woman, through the
Channel Tunnel. Undercover customs men tailed
the car until it arrived at the warehouse. They
found more than 60lb of cocaine hidden inside
the car and a further 20 tons of cannabis in the
building. In raids on homes in London and the
Home Counties, Customs men recovered large
sums of money, several handguns and ammunition.

As I worked my way through the story I could feel
my blood running cold. It was becoming increasingly
clear that I had got myself mixed up in something way
beyond my imagining, something utterly terrifying.

My mind went back to the day I had gone to see
Michael and he had begun ranting about Lynn: 'It's not
what she's done, it's what she's gonna do. She'll grass me
up, anything happens and she'll grass me up straight away
. . . I'll teach the fucking cow . . . I'll shoot her in the
head.'

At the time I had wondered what he was talking
about, what secret he might have held that would be
worth killing his own wife for. If Michael was anywhere
near as big a criminal as the police and Customs were
making him out to be, I now knew the answer only
too well. He was concerned that Lynn would tell people
that he was a grass.

'But surely that doesn't affect me, does it? It doesn't

change anything to do with my case.'

Julie leaned back against the wall and took a long drag on the cigarette she'd rolled while I'd been reading the story. 'You don't understand, do you? Once a grass, always a grass. If he was doing it before, now he's been arrested he'll roll over again to get himself off. He'll put you right in it.

'I'll tell you what happened to my ex. Then you'll get it. He had a market stall, right, selling electrical stuff. One night he's down the pub and some bloke offers him a video, off the back of a lorry. Still in the box and a good price. My bloke says, "Yeah, all right, I'll take five of 'em." They do the deal. No problem, all sorted. A week later, the bloke selling the videos gets nicked with what's left of his stock.

'Now normally that wouldn't be a cause for concern. There's a code, ain't there? The bloke who gets nicked keeps his mouth shut and does his time. The problem was that this bloke was a fucking grass. He'd been at it for years, giving the police tip-offs and the like. So when he gets pulled up with the videos, he starts singing, naming names. "Yeah, they're stolen. And these are the blokes I bought them off and these are the blokes I sold them to." He names everyone. Only he lies, says my bloke bought twenty, not five, just to protect some of his mates. My bloke gets nicked, gets bird. The gang that hijacked the lorry get nicked, get bird. Everyone gets bird apart from the fucking grass. He gets a fucking thank-you from the police and no further action. I'm telling you, Tracy, if there's a grass in your case, you're fucked.'

The following morning I met up with Debbie, Jan

and Sylvie in the exercise yard. They too had seen the story and we stood huddled in a corner discussing it.

'No way,' said Jan. 'It's bollocks. No way is Michael a grass. They've just put that in the paper to get him in trouble. They're trying to put pressure on him. Bastards.'

I said nothing. Jan had known him best and I could only hope she was right. But I couldn't help thinking about what Julie had said. If it was true and Michael had been talking, possibly even lying about what we knew and what we had done, it would certainly go some way to explaining why none of us had been given bail. My last shreds of faith in the criminal justice system began to evaporate.

After ten days in prison without proper exercise I was starting to feel seriously unfit. I made a few enquiries about getting access to the facilities, including the swimming pool I had noticed on my first visit, and learned that I'd be able to attend a session first thing in the morning.

The daily rota looked promising: circuit training, swimming, step classes and aerobics. Still slightly delicate after the operation, I decided that swimming was by far the best option.

I never even made it into the pool. I arrived in the changing room to find it full of girls who were either known drug addicts or who had spent weeks sleeping on the streets before coming to prison. Many had open sores and abscesses covering their bodies. Others were openly spitting or urinating in the water as they swam around. The thought of having the water touch my skin, let alone accidentally swallowing some, made me sick to my stomach. I decided to give it a miss and signed up for the next day's step class instead.

I had never done step aerobics before, and late the following morning I was starting to regret my decision. The class itself had been fine but towards the end I had noticed a painful twinge developing in my right shin.

I stopped and rested but the pain – something akin to a badly pulled muscle – seemed to get worse and worse. Shortly before midday my calf felt both tight and swollen and was so tender that it could no longer support my weight. I couldn't even change out of my tracksuit bottoms.

I wasn't hugely concerned – I thought I'd just over-done things, having not had any proper exercise for so long, and also I'd had a similar pain while jogging a couple of years earlier. I knew that if I could get hold of some Deep Heat to rub into it, I'd feel a lot better. But the only way to get it would be to go and see the doctor, and at Holloway that's a bit of a palaver. He attends only two mornings each week and every inmate who wants to see him has to put her name down in advance and hope she is able to see him.

I knew the doctor was in the prison that morning and managed to convince one of the screws that my symptoms were serious enough to warrant being seen immediately rather than waiting until the following week.

It was the same man who had examined me when I had arrived at Holloway and he instantly remembered me as the girl who had subjected herself to the fat-sucking torture machine. I told him my symptoms, then he began examining both my calves.

Suddenly, he became very concerned and started measuring the width of each of my legs. There was a definite note of panic mixed in with his thick Indian accent as he gasped, 'Quickly, lie down on the couch.'

'What for? Look, mate, I only came in for some Deep Heat.'

'You must lie down, right now.'

I did as he said, thinking that maybe I wasn't allowed to take the Deep Heat away and he was going to apply it there and then, but something in his manner told me he had something else on his mind.

'What is it, doctor? What's going on?'

He paused momentarily then looked me straight in the eye. 'You must rest. You are in great danger. You are going to have a heart attack.'

My first thought was that this diagnosis was coming from the same man who did not know what liposuction was and whose nickname among the inmates was 'Dr No No'. I felt the best thing to do was dismiss him out of hand.

'You're off your head,' I said. 'I've just pulled a muscle, that's all. I've done it before.'

The doctor ignored my protests and continued. 'You see, you have one calf bigger than the other. This is very bad. It means you are going to have a heart attack.'

'What are you on? I've got one tit bigger than the other as well – does that mean I'm going to have a brain tumour? You're having me on aren't you?'

I started to get up from the table and suddenly Dr No No was screaming at me. 'Good God, woman. What are you trying to do? Are you trying to kill yourself? You're sick, you're very, very sick. You could have a heart attack at any moment! Don't you understand? At any moment!'

This time the doctor sounded really scared, and his panic quickly spread to me. 'Oh my God. Why? What's happening to me?'

'It's the anaesthetic. You had general anaesthetic for this fat-sucking, yes?'

'Yeah, but . . .'

'Yes, yes. This is the danger. Great danger. Up to two weeks afterwards, there is danger of deep-vein thrombosis. Blood clot. They start in the leg, make the leg swell.' His fingers traced a line up my body. 'Travel up here through vein to heart and then—' he clapped his hands dramatically – 'bang. Heart attack. Dead like doorknob.'

'Oh my God! Do something!'

'There is nothing I can do.'

'What do you mean? Why not? You're a doctor. Help me!'

'No, no, no,' the doctor said, shaking his head furiously. 'You don't understand. I cannot help you. You must go to hospital. Immediately. But stay calm. Stay very, very calm or, bang! Heart attack.'

He dashed to his desk and became a blur of activity. He was making phone calls, scribbling letters, flicking through textbooks and still trying to talk to me, all at the same time. The worst thing I could do, he explained, would be to walk around as that would make the clot move. So long as I stayed immobile, I would be all right. He gave the example of people on long flights who develop clots in their legs. They are usually fine on the plane but often collapse and die on the way to collect their baggage.

I still didn't want to believe him – I was sure I'd just pulled a muscle – but he kept going on and was really getting to me. Within minutes I was in a terrible state, shivering and hyperventilating as I lay on the couch, wondering if I was going to die in prison.

A nurse appeared with a wheelchair, gently transferred me to it and then took me to reception. There I was shackled – not just handcuffed but shackled with heavy wrist irons – to the biggest screw in the entire prison, a fearsome woman who went by the name of Vinegar Tits, and her slightly smaller colleague, known as Mighty Mouse. Both women were totally humourless and absolutely terrifying.

'Is this really necessary?' I gasped. 'What do you think I'm going to do? I can hardly walk, let alone make a run for it.'

Vinegar Tits didn't even look at me to reply. 'Rules is rules,' she said.

More rules meant that, despite being classed as a medical emergency, I couldn't leave the prison without being strip-searched. Once that was completed I was placed in the back of a car between the two screws for the journey to the Whittington Hospital accident and emergency department. My mother and sister were due to arrive for a visit later that day but I was not allowed to call and tell them what was happening. Apparently, there had been cases in the past where prisoners had faked illnesses and got themselves taken to hospital as part of an elaborate escape plan.

Twenty minutes later we burst through the double doors into the hospital's packed waiting room. We sat on the edge of a line of seats as all around us people started pointing, whispering and nudging one another.

They could see that Vinegar Tits and Mighty Mouse were screws and realised that I was a prisoner. One woman pulled her young child away from me; another moved to sit somewhere else.

I was so embarrassed and so confused. Half the time I was convinced the doctor had been right and felt I was on the verge of a nervous breakdown. The rest of the time I was certain I'd done nothing more than pulled a muscle. It was during one of these calmer moments that I noticed a woman who had come in just after me and sat nearby. Out of the corner of my eye I could see her staring hard, looking me up and down, while sipping from a can of Diet Coke. All of a sudden I turned to face her and shouted, 'Boo!' The woman leaped out of her skin, and her can of drink flew up in the air, spilling its contents over her clothes. Vinegar Tits and Mighty Mouse burst out laughing and I started giggling so hard that I almost fell out of the wheelchair.

It took nearly half an hour before the doctors arranged for an ultrasound scan of my legs and gave me a clean bill of health. I had pulled a muscle quite badly, but there was nothing more to it than that. By then it was lunchtime, and I begged the screws to let me eat in the hospital restaurant. They too were eager for something other than prison food and readily agreed.

Trying to eat while shackled proved to be a bit of a laugh and pretty soon Vinegar Tits, Mighty Mouse and I were all giggling away like schoolgirls. Then things got even more bizarre.

'Excuse me,' said a male voice. I looked up to see a tall man in his early thirties with his arm in a cast.

'You're Tracy Kirby aren't you? Do you think I could have your autograph?'

I couldn't believe anyone had recognised me. I had no make-up, my hair was pulled back in a tight pony-tail and I was wearing a tatty tracksuit top over prison-issue overalls. I was mortified.

It happened twice more. One bloke, seeing the way I had been chained up, even started having a go at Vinegar Tits. 'Leave her alone! You don't have to have her chained up like that. She is a human being, you know.'

After lunch Vinegar Tits wheeled me outside so that I could have a cigarette while Mighty Mouse went to find a phone to tell the driver of the car to come and pick us up. Just as I was lighting my second fag, I heard my mum's voice shouting at me and saw her running over, tears streaming down her face.

She was completely terrified. 'Oh my God, oh my God! Tracy, are you all right? Oh my God. I thought you were dead. What are you doing to my daughter? Why are you doing this to her?' It took a few minutes for her to calm down and be assured that I was fine. She'd been in a right state after arriving at the prison for our visit only to be told that I'd had a heart attack and had been taken to hospital.

Then Mighty Mouse came running up the path, panting for breath. 'Fuck, oh fuck. We're in big, big trouble,' she said.

It turned out that Dr No No had arranged for me to be seen by one specific doctor but the screws had ignored his instructions and taken me in to see someone else. The doctor who had been expecting me then called No No to find out where I was and all hell broke loose. While I was quietly having lunch and smoking my cigarette, the prison had gone on full alert. They were convinced I had somehow escaped my shackles and run off, possibly taking both guards as hostages. The alarm had been raised and security guards were scouring the hospital grounds in a bid to track me down.

The two screws had been treating me fairly all day long so I felt the least I could do was help them out. 'Don't worry,' I said. 'I know what we can do. I'm down on the books as having IBS so just tell your bosses that I was on the toilet for an hour. It wouldn't be the first time and there's really nothing they can say about that.' Vinegar Tits and Mighty Mouse breathed a joint sigh of relief. They were so grateful they even let me spend time with my mum to make up for the lost visit before we finally headed back.

Although there had been times when I had felt in mortal danger, the very worst part of the whole day was the journey back to prison. On the way to hospital I had been too scared to notice my surroundings, but this time I looked out of the windows as the world whizzed by.

The only time I had been out of prison before had been in a sweatbox where the windows are so small and dim, you can hardly make anything out. This was the first time in nearly two weeks that I had seen the outside world. I could see people going about their lives, enjoying their freedom, and the grim realisation that I could no longer do that, that I had no idea how long it would be before I'd be able to do it again, tore me to pieces.

I arrived back at Holloway to find I had been moved

yet again. Rather than a dormitory, I would be moving into a double cell and I was hugely excited to learn that I'd be sharing with Debbie.

We spent the rest of association just sitting on our beds, discussing our worries about the case and sharing our disbelief that we had failed to get bail. Then, just before the end of the evening shift, the face of the Vulture appeared at our hatch and beckoned me over. 'Looks like you'll be staying with us a little longer than you thought,' she said sarcastically. 'So do you want to spend your time moping around in your cell or do you want to get a job?'

For a second I was confused by the question. I was about to tell her that I already had a job, as a presenter on a new TV chat show, but I caught myself just in the nick of time. The show went live in four days and my next bail hearing was at least a week away. I realised I hadn't yet accepted that everything I'd been working towards for the past year had fallen to pieces right before my eyes.

'I . . . I don't know,' I stuttered. 'I suppose so.'

The vulture smiled broadly. 'OK. There's a vacancy for a cleaner. We'll get you started tomorrow.'

Chapter Eleven

There are two main reasons inmates agree to go to work. The first is the money. Prison jobs pay only a few pence per hour – on average around £10 per week – but the income is handy when it comes to supplementing the very basic prison diet. If you want to drink anything other than water, tea or coffee, you have to buy it. And if you want 'treats' like chocolate or essentials like Pot Noodle to stop you from starving to death at the week-end, you have to buy those too. The same goes for decent shampoo, soap and tampons. The prices in the prison canteen are exactly the same as they are on the outside so the money never goes very far, especially once you've bought some cigarettes and a phone card.

The second, and ultimately far more important reason, is the chance to spend time out of their cells. Inmates who are 'unemployed' or who have not signed up to an education course will often find themselves locked up for up to twenty hours a day, enough to drive even the most hardened jailbird stir-crazy.

Having a job also gives you the chance to 'hustle' by pilfering supplies, or taking advantage of services that are normally out of bounds to prisoners.

The best-paid post on offer – you earn £20 per week – is to become a Womble. That's the name given to the prisoners who patrol the courtyards and perimeters, picking up all the discarded used tampons, parcels of faeces and piles of rotting food that have been thrown out of windows by the inmates. The work is absolutely filthy and most of the people who sign up can't bear it for more than a few weeks.

Aside from the money and the chance to spend time in the fresh air (other inmates are restricted to half an hour a day in the exercise yard, *if* there are enough staff available to supervise them), there are other benefits for Wombles. They all wear special passes on ribbons around their necks, which give them access to most parts of the prison without supervision. It's particularly handy for those who have friends or lovers on other wings. Without a red band, you are automatically confined to your own wing. Wombles are therefore often used to pass messages and the like around the prison.

An equally desirable but far less grimy job involves working on reception, helping to process new arrivals and also established prisoners who are on their way to and from court. The weekly pay is only £8 but you get to spend almost all day out of your cell and get access to extra food from the kitchens. There are also laundry facilities at reception, so workers get to put their own clothes through whenever they want rather than waiting for the weekly wash and having their stuff mixed up with everyone else's.

Fitness junkies usually try to get jobs in the gym. The duties there involve looking after the equipment and helping to set it up each morning, but the downside is that they also have to clean the showers and swimming pool, and all for the princely sum of £11 per week.

I was a little disappointed to learn that as a wing

cleaner on D3 I would earn just £9 per week, but it didn't take long for me to realise that I had managed to get one of the most sought-after jobs in the whole prison.

Wing cleaners do far more than just clean. Their cells are opened twenty minutes earlier than other inmates' to give them time to get to the kitchen and serve up breakfast. Afterwards, everyone else gets locked back up while the cleaners clear away the dishes and wash up.

It's not easy. The serving trays are so thick with grease that they can only be cleaned by being immersed in a large industrial sink at the back of the serving area filled to the brim with boiling hot water. It's sweaty, uncomfortable work and the cleaners have to wear special thick black rubber gloves that extend all the way to their elbows so they can wash up without scalding themselves.

After free flow, the cleaners mop the corridors and association area — a small room with a TV and pool table — and clean out any empty cells to prepare them for new inmates. Considering the state of some of the cells, that's not a job for the faint-hearted. It doesn't stop there. Once a week the wing cleaners collect the sheets and send them off to the laundry. It isn't nearly often enough, especially considering the state of some of the inmates, but it's far better than the situation with the blankets, which are washed only once every three months. By that time they have become so rank and stained that it would be better to just throw them away.

If the prison finds itself short of staff — something which happens on a regular basis — the officers go to 'lock-down' mode, where everyone is confined to their cells for twenty-three hours a day. On such days, only the wing cleaners are allowed out, taking trolleys up and down the corridors to serve meals to the inmates through the hatches. It's also the wing cleaners who organise the handing-out of the hot water at the end of each evening, either from a table in the dining room or by going round from cell to cell if everyone has been locked up.

Being a wing cleaner is hard work and often quite gross, but there are numerous advantages. The main one is that you get permanent access to all kinds of disinfectant and cleaning materials forbidden to other inmates in case they try to poison themselves or others. This means you can keep your cell relatively clean. You also get to do your washing – including your blanket – far more often than everyone else.

Best of all, the wing cleaners occupy cells in a small annexe off the main landing. Entered through a door marked NO INMATES ALLOWED, the area consists of a narrow corridor with five cells, and a small sitting area with a fridge, television and sofa. It also contains two offices, one for the wing governor and another for the senior wing officer, a screws' toilet and a room full of stores like sanitary towels and toilet rolls, which the cleaners are allowed to give out to inmates as and when they need them.

Having learned my new responsibilities, after breakfast I was taken through to the annexe to meet the women I'd be working and living with.

First up was Carol, a slender black woman in her late twenties who made her living as a shoplifter. She viewed being caught as something of an occupational hazard and up until then had managed to get away with fines or community service. Being locked up in prison for the first time didn't seem to have fazed her at all – I could tell she would be right back at it the moment she got out. Carol was due to leave a few weeks later and the Vulture had offered Debbie her job. Once Carol had gone, Debbie would move into the annexe as well, though she would start working as an extra wing cleaner straight away.

Then there was Linda, a genial forty-something grandmother who had found herself serving thirteen years for selling ecstasy, even though all the drugs the police had seized actually belonged to her boyfriend and were nothing to do with her. With her soft voice and warm smile, she looked completely out of place within the prison environment.

Sandra was short and round, with a strong Irish accent and flame-red hair to match. When she smiled she showed more gums than teeth. She was right at the end of her sentence for burglary and counting the few remaining days before she went home. She was due to leave over the weekend and I'd be moving into her cell on the Monday morning.

Linda, Carol and Sandra were lovely, but they were just the underlings – the undisputed rulers of the annexe were Maggie and Vanessa. Alone, either one of them would have been a formidable opponent: together, they were more than a match for anyone in the prison.

Vanessa was in her late forties and was a cross between something out of *Absolutely Fabulous* and *Only Fools and Horses*. There were times when she would spend ages doing her hair and make-up and end up looking really classy, but the second she opened her mouth she left you in no doubt that she was a real rough old bird. She was the wife of a notorious armed robber and had lived the high life, driving around in a brand-new Mercedes, living in a lavish bungalow and going on dozens of expensive holidays. She had assisted in the planning of several robberies and even helped to disguise members of the gang, for which she had been given three years. Physically, she wasn't particularly big or scary but there was just something about her that made me feel incredibly vulnerable right from the start.

Maggie was the opposite of Vanessa. Tall and stocky, she was a cross between a rugby player and an all-in wrestler. Her face in particular was really stony, like a champion poker player. Humourless. She had made a fortune selling drugs across south London before being caught by the police and had a long record stretching back to her teens which included assault, affray and fraud. More than once she had punched out police officers or store detectives who had tried to arrest her.

Maggie was related to some of the most notorious criminal clans around and time and again had proved herself to be every bit as tough and ruthless as the men she worked alongside. She was feared and respected throughout Holloway, and she made the most of it.

To say that Maggie and Vanessa were hard would be the understatement of the century. They were way beyond that. They were so tough that the F-word had lost all meaning for them and the notion of polite communication been long forgotten. Instead, whenever you tried to make conversation with them, every other word would be 'cunt' or some variation, and every sentence would be barked out like an order.

'Get us a cunting cup of tea, will you?'

'Sweep the cunting floor for cunt's sake, will you?'

'Change the cunting blankets on that cunting bed.'

Or, if they were angry: 'Get your fucking cunting hands off my cunting orange drink, you cunt.'

Out of context, it sounds almost funny but the way they spoke – every syllable loaded with spite and menace – was incredibly intimidating. As I shook their hands and they showed me around the unit, I knew that of all the scary women I had met since I had arrived at prison, these two were the ones I was most afraid of falling out with.

That Friday night, an hour into lock-up, Debbie and I were having another depressing conversation about our prospects for bail at our next hearing when the hatch to our cell dropped down and a smiling male face appeared.

It was Matt, the prison officer who had come into my cell and comforted me the day after I had arrived at Holloway. I had seen him at a few of my visits – that was the area he usually worked in – and waved hello, but we hadn't had a chance for a proper conversation since our first one.

'Hello, ladies,' he said cheerily. 'Sorry to disturb you but I'm on my way to the kitchen and I wanted to know if there was anything I can get you?'

'Oooh,' squealed Debbie, 'I'd love some hot water, then we can have a nice cup of tea.'

'That would be great,' I added.

Matt performed a little bow at the hatch. 'Ladies, I'm on my way.'

He'd managed only a few paces when I remembered

something and pressed the call button to bring him scuttling back. 'Actually, I just realised that I left my orange drink in the fridge in the wing cleaners' annexe. Do you think you could get it for me.'

'No problem at all, Tracy,' he said with what might have been a little wink. 'It would be my pleasure.'

Once he was out of earshot, Debbie leaned over to me. 'You know, I reckon if we ask him really nicely, he might dig us a tunnel.'

I nodded. 'It's worth a try, isn't it? I mean, he can only say no.'

Matt returned with my drink and some hot water then leaned against the hatch and started chatting away.

'How come you're on night patrol?' I asked. 'I thought you normally did visits.'

'I do,' he replied, nodding his head. 'But they like to swap us around every now and then to make sure we don't forget how to do the jobs.'

Before too long the three of us were having a real giggle. It was like three old mates down at the pub rather than two inmates and a screw having a natter through the hatch of a cell door; it felt like a lifetime since I'd had such a good laugh.

I got Matt to translate some of the prison jargon that I still hadn't managed to figure out and to go over some of the rules and regulations I was struggling to comprehend. I also told him about my new job and that I would be moving to the wing cleaners' annexe the following week.

After twenty minutes or so, the conversation began to dry up and Debbie and I decided it was time to get ready for bed.

'OK,' said Matt. 'I'll leave you two lovely ladies to your privacy. But if you want any more favours, you'd better get them right now.'

'How come?' I asked.

'Well, I'm off for a week after tonight. Actually, this might be the last time I'll see you – you'll probably be out on bail by the time I get back.'

'I'm keeping my fingers crossed.'

'I'll do the same. You have a good night now.'

And then he was gone. 'Seems like a nice bloke,' I said.

'Yeah,' agreed Debbie. 'Nice to know not all the screws are complete bastards.'

The new cell was little better than the ones I had been in before, but having access to all the proper cleaning materials meant that I no longer felt I was taking my life in my hands every time I sat on the toilet or touched one of the walls. It was also nice to be on my own and therefore not suffer the embarrassment that went along with my IBS. Debbie had been really understanding and sympathetic but it was still humiliating to have someone in the cell when I was trying to use the loo.

I hadn't suffered too badly from claustrophobia in the dormitory or double cells because they were quite large. Being on my own proved a double-edged sword: on the one hand I loved the extra privacy, but the smaller space made my symptoms much worse.

After working out the procedure for making requests to the governor, I had finally got the prison to recognise the fact that I suffered from claustrophobia. There was little they could do that didn't involve keeping me in a cell but they at least agreed to leave the hatch open at all times. For some reason that seemed to make all the difference and I felt much calmer. I guess it made me feel less trapped.

As soon as I'd finished putting my belongings away, Maggie appeared at my doorway and greeted me in her unique style. 'OK, you're in there. Put down your stuff, sort yourself out and then get us a cunting cup of tea.'

'Yeah,' said Vanessa, 'I'll have a cunting cuppa as well.'

Over the weekend I had helped serve up breakfast and done some of the washing-up for the first time, but now that it was Monday morning the real work could begin. Once we'd finished our teas we set about mopping the corridors and cleaning out the empty cells.

As D3 was a reception wing, that was always a particularly grim task. Many of the girls who passed through there would have been on the streets for weeks, months or even years. They would be infested with lice or infected with scabies and all sorts of conditions, as well as being caked in dirt and shit. It didn't take me long to realise why the prison employed inmates to do the cleaning – no ordinary person would do the job, no matter how much they were paid.

We were there to clean up every kind of mess. If someone slashed their wrists and sprayed blood up the walls, they would call us. If someone suffering chronic diarrhoea failed to get to the toilet on time, they would call us. If someone threw up in the corridor and ended up sitting in a festering pile of their own puke, they would call us.

Actually to be more specific, they would call me, or rather the Vulture would. At first I'd wondered why she had been so keen for me to have the job. Now I realised that it was her way of tormenting me and controlling me, reducing me down to the lowest possible level.

Most of the time I'd just put up with it, but every now and then the things she asked me to do were just beyond my tolerance. On one occasion she told me to help bathe a new inmate, a slightly disturbed middle-aged woman who had been living on the streets for several months and was afraid of soap and water.

By the time I got to the showers she was standing there completely naked. At first I thought there was something wrong with my eyes – she seemed all blurry – but as I peered more closely I realised what was wrong. Her hair was moving. Her eyebrows were moving. Her pubic hair was moving. Her entire body was a mass of insects and worms and maggots, all creeping and crawling across her back and her breasts. It is a sight I will never forget. I turned around and rushed to the toilets to throw up.

The Vulture wasn't alone by any means – a small group of the screws seemed to go out of their way to make people suffer; they appeared to derive great pleasure from it. Acts of sadistic cruelty were frighteningly commonplace.

I refused to let her get to me, and whilst it was hard, exhausting work, Linda and Carol were jovial enough to make it bearable; most of the time Vanessa and Maggie were a pretty good laugh too, though occasionally they seemed to turn nasty for no reason. By the time we had cleared away the dinner things and returned to our cells at the end of my first full day, I was completely shattered.

* * *

About an hour after lights-out, I became vaguely aware of someone shining a torch through my hatch. I was half asleep and ignored the intrusion – the guards checked on all the inmates during the night and had been told to pay me special attention because of my claustrophobia. Then I heard someone softly calling my name. It was Matt.

'Surprise!'

I sat up in bed and blinked myself awake. 'Oh, hello. I thought you were off?'

'Supposed to be, but I swapped my shift – someone didn't want to do their nights this week so I said I'd do them for them. It means I get two weeks off in a row, plus I've got a week's holiday owing so I'll be away for three weeks after this.'

'All right for some. Are you going to go anywhere?'

'Nah, I'll just stay at home and put my feet up.'

I got out of bed – there was no need to feel shy, I was still wearing every item of clothing I owned in an attempt to combat the cold – and made my way over to the hatch, balancing precariously on the edge of the toilet bowl by the door so that I could speak to Matt without having to shout across the length of the cell.

We started talking about prison life – how I was coping with the loss of freedom, what I thought of the other girls, and so on – but we quickly moved on to other topics. As the conversation flowed and laughter echoed around the walls of my cell, I again found myself almost able to forget where I really was and just enjoy the chance of a nice conversation. We weren't worried about noise. With their cell doors closed and hatches up, any sounds from the corridor were pretty muffled.

Besides, inmates would spend hours shouting at one another from their windows, passing messages from wing to wing and the people staying in the medical wing would be screaming and banging all night long. At first it had kept me awake but after a week or so I'd gotten so used to it that I could actually sleep through it.

At times Matt had me in fits of giggles as he told me about some of the weird and wonderful things that had happened at Holloway over the years. 'Honestly, Tracy, you wouldn't believe half the stuff that goes on in here; it's a right madhouse. One time I had to escort a prisoner into court and, twenty minutes into the hearing, this mobile phone goes off. The judge gets really angry and says if it happens again, someone will end up spending a night in the cells. Ten minutes later, the phone goes off again, but there's so much echo in the courtroom that no one can work out where it's coming from. All the barristers and the clerks and everyone in the public gallery starts searching through their bags and in their pockets, wondering if it's them. The judge was going apeshit. It was only later that we found out what had happened. The girl had crotched it! A whole mobile phone. Not only that, she'd left it on.'

Tears of laughter were streaming down my cheeks as Matt recounted the story. I had to hold myself up against the back wall of the toilet to stop myself collapsing on the ground. 'Now, personally I think that if she went to all that trouble,' Matt continued, 'the least she could have done is put it on vibrate. That way she wouldn't have been disturbing anyone and she could have had fun all the way through the case.'

When Matt glanced at his watch we were both

shocked to learn that more than two hours had passed. 'I guess it's true what they say,' he whispered, his lips curling up into a cheeky grin: 'time really does fly when you're having fun. I'm going to have to go and do my rounds, make sure the other prisoners are OK. I guess I'll have to say good-night.'

Although I was now feeling quite tired and keen to get back to bed, I was almost sad to see him go. I drifted off to sleep thinking how nice it was to have someone else on the staff, besides Vinegar Tits and Mighty Mouse, that I was able to get on with. I'd only been inside for a few weeks but I could already see that prison was a place where you needed all the friends you could get.

The next night, after what Maggie had described as 'a right old cunt of a day', Matt appeared at my hatch a couple of hours after the corridor lights had been switched off and just as I was about to get changed.

'Hey, Tracy, how are you doing tonight?'

'Aren't you supposed to knock first? I was about to get undressed.'

'Sorry, it's just that I have something for you. Take a look at this.'

Matt pushed his arm through the hatch and held out a piece of paper. I walked over and took it from him. It was a menu from a local Chinese takeaway. 'I'm order-ing myself some dinner for a bit later,' he continued, 'and I wondered if you fancied something for yourself. It's on me, of course.'

Did I ever! Three weeks of ultra-bland prison food had made me absolutely desperate for something with a bit of flavour. On top of that Chinese was one of my favourites and had topped my list of the things that I wanted to eat as soon as I got bail.

An hour or so later Matt stood outside my cell, tucking into his dishes while I curled up on the floor by the hatch, savouring wonderful mouthfuls of succulent chicken in oyster sauce and egg-fried rice. I was in heaven.

By the time I'd finished eating I was so stuffed that all I wanted to do was go to sleep, but Matt was eager to continue our chat and it would have been downright rude not to spend at least some time talking to him, especially as he'd gone to the extra trouble of getting me a piece of carrot cake for dessert.

Matt was still being pleasant and amusing, but then we started talking about my time as a Page Three girl. He started telling me once more how I'd been his favourite and how sad he was when my pictures stopped appearing in the papers. Then he said something that made all the hairs on the back of my neck stand to attention.

'Hey, Tracy, remember that picture of you with the boots?'

'What picture?'

'You know, it was in the *Sun* and you had this pair of black boots on. You were sitting on a little stool covered in a sheet with this black thong, the boots and nothing else. Oh hang on, you had some leather jewellery, a necklace and this bracelet that looked a bit like bondage straps. I think that's my all-time favourite picture of you.'

'Blimey, you've got a good memory.' I could only assume he'd cut out the page and had it in his locker

for years. Why else would he recall a picture that had
to be at least ten years old in such fine detail? He was
starting to sound like the weirdos who had written fan
letters at the height of my Page Three career.

'Or how about the picture with the woolly jumper?'
he continued. 'You must remember that one. Your hair
was all moussed up and big and your eyes looked really
gorgeous. It was like you were looking right at me. And
you had this big woolly cardigan draped over your shoulders so that your t . . .'. He paused to give his brain time
to think of a better word. 'So that your breasts were
showing. That's a lovely picture that one.'

It was all a little bit spooky and it didn't help that,
in the pitch black of the prison corridor, Matt had
chosen to illuminate his face by pointing the beam of
his torch upwards from his chin, the way people do
when they're telling ghost stories around a campfire. He
was standing there with his eyes closed and his head
tilted back, as if he were seeing the images of me in his
mind. I could almost hear the theme tune from *The
Twilight Zone* playing in the background.

I decided it was time to cut the evening short. I
yawned big and loud and close enough to the hatch so
there was no way he could miss it. 'Goodness, I'm really,
really exhausted,' I said, not altogether convincingly. 'I
should get some sleep. Thanks ever so for the food, that
was great. Good-night.'

'Oh, OK,' came the reply. Matt sounded a little hurt.
'Yeah, I guess I should do my rounds. See you tomorrow then. Bye.'

Half an hour later I became aware of a bright light
shining on to my face. The torchbeam had returned. I

sat up in bed and rubbed my weary eyes.

'Sorry, didn't mean to wake you up.'

'Then why did you shine the torch in my eyes?'

'Well I have to come back and check up on you, you're down here as being claustrophobic. You might have been having a panic attack.'

'Believe me, if I was, you'd know all about it. But I'm fine, just as long as the hatch stays open I'm fine.'

'Well, I'm just checking.'

I couldn't help wondering how long he had been there, how long he had been looking at me. 'Well, to be honest, you're making me a bit uncomfortable, and when that happens my claustrophobia gets worse.'

'No, don't be silly. I'm just doing my job. Of course I'm not making you worse.'

'I'm sorry, but you are.'

'Well . . . it's not my fault, I'm a bit bored. There's bugger-all to do on the night shift. It's nice to have someone to talk to. Are you sure you don't want to stay up a bit longer?'

'I was asleep. I really need to sleep. I'll talk to you tomorrow.'

What I really wanted to do was tell him to stop being so creepy and to fuck off and leave me alone, but he was a screw and I was just a prisoner. I felt powerless.

At work the following day, I told the girls all about my unexpected late-night snack. Vanessa was green with envy.

'Cunting carrot cake! You lucky cunt! He's obviously got a soft spot for you. You should take advantage of it.'

'What do you mean?'

'Honestly, were you born yesterday? Try and get stuff off of him. He's already given you Chinese food and cake. He'll probably go much further. Try to get some alcohol.'

Maggie joined in. 'Yeah, get him to give you some cunting vodka. Get some good stuff, no rubbish. But don't keep it all for yourself, share it around, you cunt.'

Vanessa nodded enthusiastically. 'Brilliant idea. Get him to give you vodka.'

'I can't do that . . .'

'Of course you can, you daft cunt.' Maggie sounded like she was losing patience. She took a deep breath to calm herself. 'Look, it's not going to be you who gets in trouble, is it? If you've got a way of making things easier, like getting decent cunting food and a bit of drink, you should go for it. And remember who your friends are.'

'But Maggie, it's not as simple as that.'

Then I told them all about the things Matt had said about my Page Three pictures and that I suspected he spent time watching me sleep. I told them that the nice-guy act was only on the surface. Underneath he seemed to be a bit of a weirdo and was starting to make me nervous. All the girls on the annexe agreed that, if he turned up again that evening, they would make their presence known so that I didn't feel as if I were on my own.

That night, Matt turned up at my hatch a couple of hours into his shift. We started to talk but were constantly interrupted by the other girls:

'Matt, sorry to bother you but I left my newspaper on the sofa. Could you get it for me please?'

'Matt, I've run out of <u>bog</u> roll. Could I have another one?'

'Matt, are you still there? I've got some chocolate in the fridge; it would be really great if you could fetch it for me.'

It didn't take long for Matt to get mildly irritated and tell me that he had to go off and do his rounds. He didn't return for nearly three hours, by which time I and all the other girls were asleep. But as soon as he started talking, the others woke up and the requests started up again.

I felt grateful to Maggie and the others. Matt had been asking me to list the things that I missed most while I was in prison. I talked about my family and friends but I knew what he was really driving at − he wanted me to talk about my sex life − and there was no way in the world I was going to do that with him.

When the questions from the other girls got too much for him to bear, he left and did not come back. For the first time that week, I managed to get a decent night's sleep.

At work the following day, the Vulture was supervising while Debbie and I cleaned the corridors. As she examined our work, she suddenly became agitated, ran off to find the senior officer on the wing and then called us over. She produced a dog end and told the SO she had found it behind the radiator. 'You obviously aren't cleaning properly,' the Vulture told us triumphantly. 'If you two don't buck your ideas up, I'm going to have to talk to the governor about it. There's little point in us handing out good money if you two aren't up to the job.'

I said nothing, but I remembered cleaning the radiator in question only a few minutes earlier. There was simply no way I would have missed the cigarette. I was absolutely certain that she'd planted it out of spite.

I felt as though I was living on a knife edge. If the Vulture ever found out about the Chinese food I'd eaten – a direct breach of dozens of prison rules – I'd be in all sorts of trouble. I knew I had to do something to stop Matt from harassing me but I was wary of doing anything to piss him off. I already had the Vulture after my blood; the last thing I needed was another enemy on the staff.

That evening, Matt appeared at my hatch right at the start of the night shift. He was trying hard to be funny and entertaining, even flirtatious, but I just found him irritating. He left to do his rounds on a regular basis but I never knew how long it would be before he returned, which meant I couldn't get changed into my nightclothes. It was the same when it came to using the toilet, which sat directly below the hatch. After an hour or so, I could feel my stomach start to tighten and a fierce throbbing pain in my intestine. I desperately wanted to go but the thought of Matt catching me in such a compromising position was even more painful.

To Matt the whole thing was one big joke. One time I asked him to leave so I could use the toilet and he did, only to pop his head back through the hatch thirty seconds later and say, 'You on the bog yet, then?' It might have been vaguely funny the first time but the joke very quickly wore thin as he did it again and again.

Before long I'd had enough. I knew that if I carried

on playing ball this was going to go on for ever. When he shone his torch through the hatch in the early hours of the following morning, I ignored it until he went away.

An hour later he returned and made the beam of his torch dance repeatedly over my eyes until I had no choice but to open them. But this time, unlike every other night that we had spoken, I stayed in bed.

'Come over to the hatch; I can't talk to you when you're all the way over there.' He was giggling like a schoolboy. It irritated the hell out of me.

'You shouldn't be talking to me at all. I'm trying to get some sleep. I really need to get some sleep.'

'Oh go on, Tracy, don't be silly. Just come up for a little while. Go on, please.'

'The only thing I want to do is sleep.'

'But I've got a treat for you,' he said. 'I know you'll really like it.'

I said nothing. I sensed something being thrown through the hatch and felt it land with a light thump on the bed.

'I've been keeping it in the fridge so it's nice and firm,' he added.

I looked down and squinted at the object sitting on the end of my blanket. It was a banana.

'It's in case you need to . . . you know . . . relieve yourself. I know the kind of urges you sort of women get. I'll just stay here and keep guard.'

'Look, Matt, I really don't think you should be saying things like that to me. This isn't right.'

'Things like what? What do you think I'm trying to say?'

I knew his game: he was trying to get me to feed his sick fantasies by describing what was in his mind. I refused to take the bait.

'Look, I don't know who you think I am, but I'm not someone you can talk to like that. You're overstepping the mark.'

And that's when he turned nasty.

'Who the fuck do you think you are? I'll talk to you how I like, you bitch. Now come to the hatch.'

All the schoolboy giggles had gone and there was real venom in his voice. With each new outburst, he became more and more angry until he was almost shouting. Standing in the pitch-black hallway with the orange glow of the torchbeam pointing up from his chin, his face looked like it was on fire. He looked like the devil himself. I was petrified.

'Come on, look sharp! Come to the fucking hatch.'

'No way.'

'Don't fuck me about, Tracy, come to the hatch.'

'No, I don't want to.'

'Yes you do. I've seen the way you look at me. I know what's on your mind. Now come to the fucking hatch.'

The panic attack started. My heart started beating faster and faster – I was sure it was going to explode. My throat closed so tight that I couldn't get any air into my lungs. My hands began sweating and I got so dizzy that even though I was lying down I thought I was going to hit the floor. I needed to get away, to get out of there. But I was in prison. I was locked in a cell. I was trapped.

I managed to force out a few more words. 'Leave me alone. Please, just leave me alone.'

'Leave you alone? Don't be fucking stupid. Don't try and make out you're some kind of innocent. I've seen your picture in the paper, standing there in your knickers with your tits hanging out for everyone to see. You're a fucking slag, that's what you are. You're gagging for it.'

'Please . . . go . . . Just go away.'

'Don't play hard to get. I know you want it. You're loving this, aren't you? Loving it, you slut.'

'Why are you saying this? Are you mad? Just because my picture . . . It doesn't . . . I'm not a slut . . .'

'Yes you are. Of course you are. I've seen you naked. I've seen your tits and I've seen your arse. I haven't seen your pussy but I know it's gorgeous. You love getting fucked, don't you? I bet you love getting fucked by strangers. How long has it been, eh? Three weeks? Four weeks? I bet that's the longest time you've gone without a fuck in years. I bet you used to do it every night, all night long, eh. Different bloke every night. I'd love to fuck you. I bet you're really dirty. I'd fuck you all night long, you dirty slut, you fucking dirty bitch.'

There was no escape. Even in the darkness I could feel the walls closing in. My whole body was shaking with fear, bile was rising in my throat, and still he kept on.

'I bet you'd love my cock in your cunt, wouldn't you? I bet you're really tight. I could turn you on, I could. I bet you'd love to suck my cock too, wouldn't you? Do you like it up the arse? I don't know why they call you Page Three girls, they should call you Page Three sluts. That's what you are, you're all fucking sluts – the lot of you. Now come on, get over here. Come to the hatch.'

This time I said nothing. I had my eyes tightly shut and the covers pulled up over my face. I thought if I ignored him for long enough he might just go away. I could hear his breathing getting shorter and sharper as his anger grew. What he said next turned me inside-out.

'Stupid slag. Right, if you're not coming out, then I'm coming in.'

His face vanished from the hatch and I heard the bunch of keys jangling in his fingers as he sorted through them, swearing softly to himself. The door was my only protection. I had to do something, fast. I leaped out of bed and rushed over to the hatch.

'It's OK,' I gasped. 'I'm here, you don't need to come in, I'm right here.'

Slowly his face reappeared, followed by the light from the torch. Then the fingers of his right hand danced back and forth as he beckoned me to come closer.

I took half a step forward. I was trying to look over his shoulder, to look past him to the cells opposite to see if Vanessa or Linda were up and could see what was happening. At the same time I was desperately trying to calm him down. 'Look. I'm here. There's no need for you to come in. Now please, just leave me alone. Just go. I won't say anything, but just go.'

As soon as I was within reach his arm shot through the hatch and clamped around my neck, too fast and too tight for me to scream. Instinctively my own hands rose to my throat, trying to claw his fingers away, but they had already snaked around the back of my head and taken hold of a handful of hair.

With a sudden sharp pain I felt myself being pulled towards the metal door. I thought he was trying to smash my head against the inside. He was pulling harder and harder and I shut my eyes and started to scream while waiting for the impact. Then my cries were suddenly muffled and I felt his cold greasy lips mashing up against mine while his thick tongue tried to force its way into my mouth. He wasn't trying to kill me; he was trying to kiss me.

I couldn't punch or kick because the door was in the way. The hatch was just big enough to fit my head through. Dropping the torch to the floor, he held my hair with both hands and began licking my face. I wanted to throw up.

'Don't fuck about, Tracy, it's what you've been waiting for.'

'No, fuck off, leave me alone.' The more I struggled, the harder he tugged on my hair. Then he broke off and switched his grip on my hair back to one hand, forcing my head into an awkward downward angle.

'Look at this, look what I've got for you.'

I kept my eyes firmly closed. 'I don't want to look. Please, just let me go.'

'But I want you to see what I've got for you. Just have a look and I'll let you go.'

I half opened my eyes. He took a step back so I could see his flies were open and his underpants had been pushed down. He was using his free hand to mastur-bate. 'You like that, huh, you dirty slut, do you like it?' he groaned, his excitement growing rapidly.

I turned my head away so far that he lost his grip for a split second. We started fighting through the hatch, me desperate to get away, him trying to pull me closer. 'Get the fuck away from me, you filthy pervert,' I screamed. 'Just fuck off, leave me alone.'

Somehow he managed to restore his grip on me again and pulled me towards him with both hands, slamming my body against the inside of the door. I now had my back to him. One of his arms was tight around my throat, the other forcing its way down to my breasts. I grabbed it, forced it into my mouth and bit as hard as I could. He screamed and I raced across to the other side of the cell, a searing pain in the back of my head where I'd left a large clump of hair behind.

There was no point in pressing the alarm button – Matt was the night patrol officer, so it would be him they would send to answer the call. I was completely isolated. I curled up on the bed as far away from him as possible, convinced that he would burst through the cell door at any second. I shut my eyes and started to pray: Please God, get me through this, please God, get me through this, please God, get me through this.

Then somewhere out in the darkness of the corridor I heard Vanessa's voice – my screams had finally woken her up. 'What the fuck is going on out here? Tracy, are you all right?'

I was frozen, too scared to speak, too scared to move. By the time I felt brave enough to open my eyes, Matt was nowhere to be seen.

I was still curled up in the foetal position at the far end of the bed when half an hour later he returned. This time he kept his voice low, a kind of hiss. He sounded smug, self-satisfied. It was painful to listen to.

'I know what you're thinking, but let me tell you right now there's no point in you saying anything. No one's going to believe you anyway. And if you do tell on me, your life won't be worth living. I've got a lot of friends in here and us screws stick together. I'm gonna be away for a few weeks but you're still going to be in prison. You don't stand a chance, I'll still know everything that goes on.

'If you fuck with me I could even do a story on you, sell it to the papers for big money. And it doesn't matter what you say, they'll only want to hear my side. After all, you're just an ex-Page Three girl, which means you're a slag, and on top of that you're part of some fucking drugs gang.

'It's happened before, you know. Some girl here told people I'd been touching her up, trying to fuck her. No one believed her. She was some stupid druggy convict. Whose gonna believe someone like that? I got suspended on full pay for six months and then I came back. A nice long holiday, that's all it was. Did me a favour.'

Matt then told me his friend was a policewoman and that unless I kept quiet he'd use her to get to me through my family. 'Wouldn't it be terrible if your mum or dad got stopped for some stupid motoring offence and the police found a load of drugs in their car? Just imagine how nice it would be to have your mum in here with you.'

I said nothing.

'You don't believe me, do you? You wait there, I'll show you.' He vanished again. A few minutes later he returned. From the safety of my bed I watched as he unfolded a slip of paper and began to read out the names, birthdays and addresses of each and every member of my family. The message was crystal clear: if I didn't play ball, he'd make them all suffer.

I wanted to cry again but there was nothing left to come out. I just sat there staring at the wall and watching the dark turn to light as the sun started to rise.

Just after seven I heard the door to the annexe open and a few seconds later his face appeared at the hatch. 'All right, babe?' This time his voice was gentle, cautious, almost caring. 'I think we had a little misunderstanding last night, but it's no problem. I won't be here for three weeks but we can sort it all out when I get back.'

I heard the annexe door open again as the officer taking over the day shift carried out the first part of his rounds. Matt stopped what he was saying and began to walk away, trying to give the impression that we had been having a normal conversation. 'You take care, love. Bye now.'

For a microsecond I began to wonder if the whole thing had been some horrific nightmare, just a figment of my imagination. But then as Matt passed his colleague, he couldn't resist one final remark, couldn't resist showing his true colours. 'I'll tell you what,' he said, nodding towards my cell, 'that one there ain't half got a fucking lovely pair of tits.'

Chapter Twelve

As we made our way towards the dining room the following morning, Maggie and Vanessa buzzed around me like flies, eager to share the drama of the night before. Maggie had heard some things Matt had said while Vanessa, whose cell was almost directly opposite my own, had actually seen him masturbating.

'I thought someone was having a heart attack at first,' said Vanessa. 'All that moaning and groaning. I couldn't believe it when I looked out and saw what he was up to. The dirty bastard. You've got to report this, Tracy. You've got to tell them what he did to you.'

They couldn't understand why all I wanted to do was forget about it and put it behind me, but then neither seemed to have heard the threats Matt had made against my family. I couldn't bring myself to tell them – even talking about any of it brought the horrors of the night back and I was doing my best to block it all out.

There was also no reason to doubt that, if I did complain, the screws would all stick together, gang up and make my life hell. It was hard enough living with the worry of what might happen when Matt returned, without having to worry about what his colleagues might do in the mean time.

Up until that point, the only time I had felt truly

safe in prison was when I was locked up in my cell – quite something for someone suffering from claustrophobia. But now I realised I was as vulnerable there as I was anywhere else at Holloway.

Over the course of the next few days, Maggie and Vanessa continued their quest to get me to report the incident to the senior officer on the wing. First they tried being sympathetic and understanding, but when that didn't work they tried to bully me into doing it.

It took me a while to realise what was going on. Maggie and Vanessa were both serving time as convicted prisoners and had long sentences stretching before them. The unease I had felt at being able to predict what I would be doing at any point in the future was nothing compared to what they were facing, especially Maggie, whose earliest release date was still six years away. With little to distinguish one day from another, the two of them desperately craved some drama in their lives. They wanted the attack to come out because it represented something new and different. But to me, the experience had been a nightmare, one that I partly relived every time I was locked up in my cell and heard the night officer going about his patrol. I simply wanted to forget all about it.

But Maggie and Vanessa would have none of it and soon they were being openly aggressive, constantly in my face about making the report. Maggie in particular veered from one extreme to another, either blanking me completely or calling me a 'stupid cunt' every time I was within earshot. In the end they got so frustrated at my lack of cooperation that they decided to do something about it themselves.

On the fourth day after the attack I was on a break in the annexe watching TV with Maggie, Vanessa, Linda and Debbie when Maureen, the senior officer on D3, came in and walked up to me.

Maureen was one of the most popular screws in the whole of Holloway. Everyone got on with her because she genuinely loved all the inmates, whether they were good or bad, druggies or killers; she was there for them all. She was like everybody's granny.

'Tracy, can I have a word with you?'

I shot a glance at Maggie and Vanessa and saw the mixture of excitement and guilt on their faces. I instantly knew what they'd done and I couldn't believe they'd betrayed me like that. I was furious. As Maureen led me down the corridor, Maggie whispered: 'Go on, it'll be OK.'

We walked into my cell and sat on the bed. Then Maureen put her arm around me. 'Tracy, is there something you want to tell me?'

'No.'

'I think there is.'

'No, there's nothing.'

'Listen, I'll make it easier for you. Vanessa and Maggie have already told me everything. I know exactly what happened. I just need to hear it from you.'

I was mortified, but at the same time hearing that Maureen already knew was as if someone had finally given me permission to let it all out. Although I'd been trying to forget it, the attack haunted me and I really needed to talk about it. I collapsed into her shoulder and, sobbing hysterically, told her what had happened.

Maureen listened intently, then escorted me out of

the annexe to the office of one of the prison governors, a Mr McCauley, where I had to go through the whole story all over again, from my first meeting with Matt to the time he brought me Chinese food to the events of the final night. He was appalled; shocked to learn that such a thing could have happened right under his nose.

McCauley wanted to bring in some detectives to investigate, but as soon as he mentioned the word 'police' I started to panic. For one thing there were the warnings Matt had given me, coupled with the fact his friend was a policewoman. Then there was the recent revelation that Michael had been a long-term police informant and therefore had friends on the force. I was convinced that if the police were called something would happen to my family.

'No police, please, no police,' I gasped. 'I'm not talking to the police, no way.' McCauley was a little taken aback and I think for a moment he must have doubted whether my story was true. But what I didn't know at the time was that Maureen had already received evidence to support my claims. Unbeknown to me, Maggie and Vanessa had searched my cell, retrieved the wrapper from the carrot cake and passed it on. As no such cake was on sale within the prison, it supported the idea that Matt had indeed broken the rules by sharing his food with an inmate.

McCauley had other reasons to believe me. For a start I wasn't typical of the inmates at Holloway, most of whom were hardened criminals or repeat offenders and some of whom occasionally made false accusations against the staff – particularly the male staff – in a bid to get them into trouble. Furthermore, there were witnesses to what had happened to me. Finally, I hadn't actually reported the incident myself.

McCauley finally agreed not to call the police on condition that I made a full statement about what had happened. That way, he explained, he would be able to get Matt moved out of the prison to somewhere else and I'd never have to face him again. I was still unsure of whom I could trust, but I felt I'd been backed into a corner. I agreed to make the statement, so long as it was made clear that I had not made the initial report so that Matt couldn't lay the blame on me alone. I hoped that in some small way that might persuade him not to go ahead and carry out his threats, especially now that people would be on the lookout.

The following morning I spent two hours reliving one of the most horrific experiences of my life in excruciatingly fine detail. When it was finally over, McCauley read through my statement and called me into his office.

'Tracy, I just wanted to let you know,' he said softly, 'that we absolutely and fully believe what you have been telling us.'

'So what happens now?'

'Well, because the police are not involved it remains an internal inquiry. We will question him about what happened, but we'll have to wait until he returns to work.'

McCauley's words slowed down towards the end of the sentence. There was a hesitation in his voice, as if there was something he didn't really want to tell me.

I spoke, partly to show him I was still listening and also to fill the awkward silence: 'Right.'

'The only problem is that he does have a few friends here. It's possible that someone might warn him that you've made a complaint. In which case, he might . . . erm . . . try to get to you.'

'I see . . .'

'So on the day he comes back to work, it's probably best if you avoid him. Don't let him get you on your own.'

'Avoid him?' I interrupted, filling with rage. 'I'm in fucking prison. I'm trapped. He can go where he wants; he's got the keys. I'm in a cell. How the fuck am I supposed to avoid him?'

I'd spent two and a half weeks living on a knife-edge, waiting for the day Matt was due back at work.

My nerves were shot to hell. The nightmares had got worse and worse. I'd be in my cell and Matt would suddenly be pushing his weight down on me, his fingers would be locked around my throat, so tight I couldn't scream. 'I told you not to tell,' he'd say as he squeezed the life out of me. 'I told you not to tell.' It always seemed so real. Again and again I'd wake up in the middle of the night and start throwing up from sheer fright. Some days I'd be so exhausted that I'd find it almost impossible to get out of bed in the morning, let alone go to work, but the other wing cleaners, even Maggie and Vanessa, rallied round to support me as best they could.

When I learned that Matt would be back, working in the visits room, my big fear was that he would say or do something awful when my parents were around or plant something on them or in their house to get them arrested.

It was a little after seven and my visit wasn't until 11.30 a.m. I tried to block it out of my thoughts and concentrate on cleaning the grease from the serving trays, but it was no use. I couldn't get the worry out of my mind.

Then Debbie came running in from the corridor, screaming in panic, 'Tracy, he's on the landing, he's on the fucking landing.'

Her words hit me like bullets. The muscles in my arms and legs turned to jelly. I was in the top corner of the room, wedged between the open door and the industrial sinks. I knew I had to move but I couldn't, I just couldn't. My limbs had turned to lead, nothing worked.

Time seemed to slow down. I saw a rough hand grasp Debbie by the shoulder and yank her to one side. She went flying across the room, ending up in a crumpled heap by the wall. And then Matt was standing directly in front of me.

His mouth was moving, his fingers were jabbing the air in my direction, but I couldn't make out his words. It was if someone was playing a record at the wrong speed: his voice was one continuous furious rumble. His face was twisted with hatred and the fires of hell burned in his eyes. I read his lips: 'What the fuck have you been saying, you stupid cow? What the fuck have you done?'

I was all on my own, trapped behind the doorway and all my nightmares were about to come true. He was going to finish what he'd started the night he attacked me, and this time there was nothing I could do to stop him.

Matt took a step towards me and reached for my neck. My heart was pounding so hard that my whole chest hurt. I was convinced I was going to die. I had to do something. I was still wearing the washing up gloves so, plunging my arms deep into the sink, I scooped up a handful of boiling water and threw it into his face.

Matt screamed and staggered back, his hands clasped over his face. 'You fucking bitch. Fucking hell.'

As the pain forced him to drop to his knees, I saw Maggie run into the room with a heavy metal slop bucket in her hands, ready to smash Matt over the head the second he got up. Debbie was nowhere to be seen.

Matt moved his hands from his face which was now red raw and looking more evil than ever. He stood. Maggie raised the bucket. Then I heard the sound of heavy boots and male voices in the hallways. Debbie had run off to get help and the cavalry had arrived.

The screws filled the dining room, grabbed Matt by the arms and elbows and tried to move him to the centre of the room. 'Hey, Matt, what's going on?' asked Patel.

'Oh nothing,' he said, trying hard to sound completely innocent and struggling against their efforts to move him. 'Nothing at all.' Then he forced his way forward and pushed his face at mine, so close I could feel his breath on my face. 'I'll see you on your visit,' he sneered before he was dragged out.

The second Matt was gone I collapsed on the ground and shrank up into the foetal position. I could feel my bowels twisting up as well as the bile rising in my throat; I knew what was going to come next.

More screws had come into the room and surrounded me, all of them talking at once: 'What did he say to you, what did he say? Try to remember what he said to you.' Someone thrust a pen and a scrap of paper into my hand: 'Write it down, Tracy, quick, write it all down before you forget it.'

My hands were shaking so much the pen simply fell to the floor. I tried to speak but I had been struck dumb with shock and the effort to stop myself throwing up and shitting myself. The screws kept talking and shouting and demanding that I do this and that but I just couldn't handle it. I swallowed hard, forcing the sick back down inside me, took a deep breath and screamed as loud as I could, 'Get me out of here, someone get me to the loo, for fuck's sake. And someone get me a bucket. '

I started throwing up immediately, and once I'd been taken to the loo it was all coming out of me from both ends at the same time.

Patel came to see me in my cell a little later. He told me that, when he was questioned, Matt had started insisting that he had done nothing wrong, that he'd just been checking up on me because of my claustrophobia. But he didn't fool anyone.

'Don't worry, Tracy,' Patel told me. 'It's all over. He's been taken off the premises and he won't be working at Holloway any more. We've got him. He's history.'

In the days that followed, virtually every prison officer and member of Holloway's nursing staff that I encountered urged me to begin a course of tranquillisers or anti-depressants. Time and again they waxed lyrical about the benefits the drugs would bring and many and varied ways in which they would ease my life at the prison. Each and every time I refused point-blank.

During the eighties Holloway became famous for massively over-subscribing mood-altering drugs to its inmates, principally to keep them quiet and obedient and therefore make life easy for the prison officers. This is known as the 'liquid cosh'. Since that time successive crackdowns by new governors had supposedly eliminated the excessive use of drugs, but in the short time I'd been at Holloway it seemed to me that it was as common as ever.

You could spot the druggies a mile away. Their eyes would be dead and their mouths would hang open and dribble saliva. Most of them were unable to speak and the few that could made no sense at all. Some of the drugs would leave people physically restless, unable to sit or stand still, constantly rocking backwards and forwards. But they made even walking difficult – those using them would drag both feet along the ground in a characteristic gait called the 'Largactil shuffle'. At times wandering around the corridors of Holloway was like something out of *One Flew Over The Cuckoo's Nest*. The last thing I wanted was to become like them.

Midway through my seventh week in prison I was making my way to Cunts' Corner with a group of other inmates to wait for our visitors. As usual I scanned my surroundings to check for friends and foes and saw a rough-looking blonde girl with unwashed hair and grubby skin sobbing and shaking as we walked along. She was in such a state that I ended up staring a little too long. She turned, saw me looking, and began shuffling towards me.

Shit. I didn't want to get into a confrontation just before a visit – even the drugged up girls were sometimes prone to outbursts of violence. I kept my eyes to the floor but I could feel her getting closer. I clenched my fists and braced myself, convinced that she was about to grab my head and start smashing it against the wall. Her feet came into my field of view, both of them dragging across the floor, as she moved. She was almost on top of me now and I took a deep breath and got ready for my counter-strike.

Then she said something that made me look up. She was still sobbing so hysterically that it was hard to make out her words, but I was sure she had said my name. Who was she? I stared into her dead eyes. She was two feet away from me but I still didn't recognise her. Then it hit me: it was Lynn and Karen's sister.

'Jill, is that you?'

She tried to answer but all that came out of her mouth was a stream of gibberish. She collapsed forward into my arms, nodding her head gently.

I tried to talk to her but nothing she said made any sense and I knew I wasn't getting through to her. The drugs had robbed her of all sense of reason or reality. Later that afternoon I spoke to the SO and asked if she could become a wing cleaner and move to my unit so that I'd be able to look after her. He said she would only be able to move if she came off the medication.

The following day I managed to track her down again. She was still drugged up to the eyeballs but this time made a little more sense. She told me that Karen was very scared but otherwise holding up fairly well. She explained that she had given herself up after Lynn had got in touch with her and told her that she would be fine, that she had nothing to worry about.

She said that Customs had interviewed her about the one courier trip she had made for Michael but wouldn't tell her anything more about the case. In Holloway the other inmates and some of the guards had already bullied her and she didn't feel she could take much more. The only thing that made any difference was the drugs – they helped to deaden the pain.

I grabbed her shoulders and spoke slowly so she would understand me. 'Jill, listen to me. You've got to stop taking the drugs; they're ruining you. If you do that, I can get you transferred to my unit. I'll be able to look after you.' I had no idea whether she had understood me or not.

The next day, Jill was granted bail and left Holloway. I was happy that she was out of the hellhole but I couldn't help feeling miffed that I was still being kept in prison. Although I had made many more trips than Jill, my crime had been no different. What on earth did they think I had done?

It was around the time Jill appeared that I noticed Jan was starting to behave quite oddly. She was having regular panic attacks and seemed to be suffering from massive amounts of stress, as if something big was playing on her mind. At first she dismissed all my enquiries but eventually during association one afternoon, she confessed that several Customs officers had come to see her and told her that they were planning to take her out of prison the following week to interview her in more depth.

I moved a little closer and lowered my voice. 'Interview you about what? What the hell's going on, Jan? You know something about all this, don't you? I think you owe it to me to tell me what the hell is going on.'

She stared at me for a long time, as though she were trying to work out from my eyes whether or not she could trust me. Then she looked away. 'I can't say anything. I don't know anything. I'm sure everything is going to get sorted out. I really don't think you have anything to worry about. None of us do.'

Jan vanished the following week, and soon afterwards I told Maggie what she had said.

'It's all a load of bollocks,' she said. 'Believe me, you won't be seeing her again.'

'No way, she'll be back in a day or two.'

Maggie shook her head and sighed. 'Don't be so fucking stupid. You've got a lot to learn, Tracy. She's going to turn QE and end up giving evidence against you. I've seen it happen a thousand times. All your co-defendants will turn – they'll all go grass. You'll see. Jesus, Tracy, sometimes you act like a complete fucking moron.'

I didn't want to believe it – I still clung to the hope that Jan was just a courier like me who had been innocently caught up in everything. I also didn't want to believe that Maggie and Vanessa were slowly becoming more and more aggressive towards me. But I had to believe it – Debbie had noticed it too.

Five days later Jan had still not returned and I was forced to eat a large slice of humble pie. 'Told you so,' sniggered Maggie. 'Now fetch us a cunting cup of tea.'

★　★　★

When my third bail application was turned down and David told me that it was more than likely that I'd spend at least eight months in Holloway awaiting trial, I felt a powerful urge to speak to someone really special in my life to help me through the crushing disappointment I felt.

I'd written a dozen letters to Maria but received only one or two back. The last had been more than a month ago and she had promised faithfully to come and see me. Time and time again she had built up my hopes and then let me down. I realised that, when you go to prison, you find out who your real friends are.

Before I had gone inside I'd always thought there were a lot of people in my life who would be there for me if I needed them. Certainly whenever I'd had parties, there was never any shortage of people I wanted to invite. But now my life had changed and only a tiny handful of the people I had thought of as friends were still around. Of those, two childhood pals, Tracy and Joanne, proved the most supportive. Without fail they came to visit me every Saturday morning.

I phoned Maria and explained that I simply couldn't afford to keep calling on her mobile – I would use up a week's worth of phone card units in a matter of minutes. It was great to talk to her and we finished the conversation with her promising to come to Holloway the following week. That was the last time we ever spoke.

Making and maintaining friendships in prison was equally problematic. Linda had become a kind of surrogate-mother figure and I thought the world of her, while Debbie and I had become kindred spirits, mainly because we were both in the same boat.

Maggie and Vanessa could be friendly when it suited them but most of the time they were vicious bullies. Debbie and I still had the occasional laugh with them while we were working, but we couldn't help noticing that they seemed to be ordering us about more and more, using their reputations and physical presence to intimidate us. The only good thing about being a wing cleaner was getting a cell on the little annexe. But if I didn't get on with my co-workers, it would be worse than anywhere else in the prison.

Things came to a head with Maggie when she was shipped out of Holloway for several weeks in order to give evidence in a case of police corruption. While she was gone, the senior officer decided I should move into her cell. It made little difference to me where in the annexe I was, though in some ways it was nice to be away from the scene of the attack by Morris.

However, when Maggie returned a few weeks later, she was furious. I tried to explain that it hadn't been my choice, I'd been ordered to move, but it made no difference. From that day she seemed to dedicate herself to making my life a misery and also directed her anger at Debbie

It got so bad that even Vanessa had noticed it and occasionally tried to intervene. 'Maggie is just a bully, you shouldn't let her get to you.' But I couldn't help it. She did get to me. And then Vanessa was released and I was left to face Maggie on my own.

Just after lunchtime a few weeks later I heard a famil-iar voice shouting out my name again and again. Karen and I ran along the corridor towards one another and embraced, quickly bursting into big floods of tears.

I hated the idea that she was in prison too – reading her letters and thinking of her on the run always brought a smile to my face – but at the same time I was eager to speak to her because I hoped she might be able to shed some light on what was going on.

The first opportunity we had, she sat me down and told me the story of how she had narrowly avoided being arrested along with the rest of us and ended up on the run.

The day before the raids Karen had made a courier trip to Paris with Jan and stayed overnight. The following morning she had flown back and gone straight to Michael's house to pick up her payment. As she didn't have to collect Paige until later in the day, she hung around for the afternoon, talking to Michael and her sister.

'On the way home I stopped off at Tesco's to pick up a few things,' she told me. 'And that was when I got a phone call from a friend saying that something had happened to Jill and that there were dozens of police cars lined up outside Lynn and Michael's house.

'I didn't know what was going on – I thought maybe there had been some sort of accident – so I pulled over and called Jill's mobile. The phone was answered but all I could hear was loads of crying and screaming; her kids were going absolutely mad. I was calling out Jill's name but no one was replying. What I didn't know was that Jill had her phone in her bag, out of sight of the Customs officers, and every time I rang she reached inside and pressed the answer key, hoping I'd be able to work out what was going on. But I didn't have a clue.

'I tried Lynn's phone and Michael's phone – both of which were switched off. I got into a real panic and turned around to drive back to my mum's house. That's the reason I wasn't arrested – Customs were waiting for me at my house but I didn't turn up.'

When she arrived at her mum's house, Jill was there with her kids but she also had Lynn and Michael's kids with her. 'They were all petrified. They had been in the house when Customs had raided it and they thought they were being attacked by robbers or something. The officers refused to tell Jill what was going on so she took the kids and left.

'Jill's boyfriend, Glen, arrived and we decided to go and see Sue Richards, Lynn's best friend, who lived round the corner. I knocked on her door and her mum answered, telling me she couldn't come to the door. As she was saying it, I saw two or three men coming down the stairs and a couple milling about at the back of the house. I realised they were being raided, ran back to the car and shouted to Glen, "Go, go, go!"

'That's when I realised they were after loads of people and that's when I called you. We ended up round a friend's house for the night, watching *Sky News* to see if we could find out what the hell was going on. Finally they ran an item about the raid on the warehouse and the millions of pounds of drugs that were found. And all I could say was "Oh my God," over and over again.'

Unable to go back home, Karen had spent the next few weeks at different caravan sites around the country. She had always known she would eventually give herself up but she was mortified at the thought of having to leave her daughter behind. She had been trying for a child for years without any success and only had Paige after several courses of cripplingly expensive fertility treatment.

The end finally came in Bognor Regis, of all places. 'We went down to Butlins for a week and while I was there I realised I couldn't go on, I had to give myself up. We decided to leave a day early and as I was packing up the car I heard my name being called. In the split second before I turned around, I knew they'd found me. They let me get my things from the car and gave me a chance to say goodbye to Paige and then took me off. That was last night, and now I'm here with you.'

Karen had given no comment throughout her interview, but Customs had let a lot of information slip out, none of which gave me any confidence about my chances of getting bail.

For one thing, Michael had kept enormous ledgers and notebooks with details of every single trip we had ever made as well as the amounts we had carried. For another, he had not only told Customs that the money had been going out specifically to pay for drugs, which were then smuggled into the country, he also told them that Karen and I and the other couriers were fully aware of this right from the start. He said he had told us exactly what the money was for. No wonder they were keeping me in prison.

The biggest surprises were still to come. 'How much money do you think we've taken out of the country since we started working for Michael?' Karen asked me. This was something I'd already gone over in my mind several times. On my first trip to Dublin I knew for a fact that I'd carried £5,000. On subsequent trips I'd taken what I'd assumed was roughly the same amount of money – two or three inch-thick wads, albeit in foreign currency. Overall, I guessed I'd carried about £150,000.

Karen shook her head. 'At the end of my interview they said that in the last ten months I had taken out just under nine million . . .'

'Fucking hell . . .'

'That's what I thought.'

'But that's impossible. How could that be?'

In total, Karen had made thirty-one trips for Michael and I had made twenty-nine. On at least fifteen occasions we had travelled together and split the bundles of cash between us. If they were claiming Karen had taken out millions of pounds, then somehow I must have as well.

It would be some time before we learned that Michael had almost always given us guilders, a currency favoured by drug dealers and money launderers because it is available in high-denomination notes. A 1,000-guilder note was worth nearly £400. Karen and I had been carrying up to £200,000 each on our trips without even knowing it.

'If I'd realised how much money I had on me,' Karen confided in me, 'I would have told Michael that I'd been mugged and it had been nicked. Then I would have spent the rest of my life living off it.'

'If someone had told me how much money I had on me,' I replied, 'I'd never have got off the toilet at the airport.'

Up until that point I'd been clinging to the hope that the bureau de change had been genuine. After all, I'd driven past it enough times and we even had those authorisation notes for the money we were carrying. I'd been hoping that whatever else Michael Michael had been involved in, it wouldn't take Customs long to work out that Karen and I weren't part of it. Now that pipe dream had well and truly come to an end.

One thing troubled me. Karen was a million times more streetwise than I was. She was also Lynn's sister. Had Michael really managed to pull the wool over her eyes too? Had Michael really been that clever, or had I just been incredibly naïve?

'I'm starting to think I must be the world's biggest moron.'

'Well, if you are, Tracy,' she said, 'what does that make me? Honestly, if I'd believed for even a minute that something like this was going on, I would have told you. I would have got out of it ages ago.'

Looking back over the things we had been told and the way events had unfolded, we realised that at times it had seemed as though Michael had been reading our minds and making moves to reassure us before our fears could get out of hand. When I'd felt the first twinges of doubt whether the money was really coming from the bureau de change, Sam had magically appeared with the authentic-looking authorisation notes. When I'd started to worry that Michael was involved in drugs, he had launched into his anti-drug tirade over Freddie, the dealer I had met out in Spain. There were dozens of other similar incidents. I realised that while to some extent I had turned a blind eye to some of what was going on around me, Michael had clearly been orchestrating events as well.

But still I didn't know the half of it.

The full picture emerged over the course of the next few weeks as bundles and bundles of statements and court papers arrived at the prison. After six months of interviews, Customs were finally ready to release the information that Michael had provided to them. At the same time we learned that Lynn, Sonny and Jan had also become 'supergrasses', giving information about every aspect of their involvement in the drugs ring in exchange for dramatic reductions in their final sentences.

There were thousands of pages, dozens of files stuffed full of paper. I would spend every spare hour reading until my eyes hurt and I had a splitting headache. What I read amazed and terrified me. The full extent of what I'd got myself caught up in was quite incredible. And slowly but surely I finally learned the awful truth not only about Michael Michael but also exactly what I was up against.

Chapter Thirteen

Constantine Michael Michael emerged into an unsuspecting world on 25 November 1957, the eldest son of Greek Cypriots who had travelled to England in search of a better life. By the time his brother Xanthos came along in 1962, Michael's shoemaker father, John, and mother Maria had moved to north London to run a small fish-and-chip shop.

Michael attended the notoriously rough Highbury Grove School in Islington and quickly dropped his 'sissy-sounding' first name. His teachers remember him as an affable and well-mannered boy who, despite an obvious talent for mathematics, showed little interest in studying. None was surprised when he left school without gaining a single qualification.

Under intense pressure from his family to make something of himself, Michael enrolled at Southgate Technical College to study fashion, 'like a good Greek boy', but found the subject tedious and dropped out after falling madly in love with Georgina, a Greek Cypriot girl from Leicester. They thought they had plenty in common – her parents also ran a fish-and-chip shop – and within six months Georgina had become Mrs Michael.

The newlyweds moved to the Midlands and set up home with Georgina's parents, but almost as quickly as it had started, the marriage fell to pieces. Within eight months Michael had returned to London and was back living with his own parents. 'I couldn't stand her,' he told them. 'We weren't compatible.'

Having had enough of the fast-food trade, Michael started work as a driver for a local VW dealer, doing little more than moving vehicles about. Keen to boost his earnings, he did a little buying and selling in his own time but soon came a cropper. He sold a 928 Porsche for a tidy profit, only to discover that he had never actually owned it. Charged and convicted within the space of a few weeks, Michael spent four months at Brixton Prison as Prisoner B15772.

It was his first brush with the law and the experience left him shell-shocked. But all the same, Michael found himself irresistibly and inexplicably drawn to the characters that populated the criminal underworld. He made a number of firm friends and would later brag that he had broken all three elements of his gangland virginity – first arrest, first charge and first time in prison – in one fell swoop.

Soon after his release he met and married yet another Greek Cypriot girl, Alexandra, following a second whirlwind romance. Around the same time he joined forces with a friend who was launching an accountancy business and they set up a partnership, trading under the name Michael & Co. and specialising in arranging mortgages and pensions. For a short while it seemed that he might be on the verge of settling down and becoming a respectable citizen, but it was not to be.

Although the firm he worked for was legitimate, Michael's private clients were not. Through the network of contacts he had made while in prison, he began keeping the books of cash-rich businesses that were not always on the right side of the law. There were pubs and bars that got their alcohol off the back of lorries from the Continent; car dealers who sold the odd ringer; and brothels masquerading as saunas or massage parlours.

Before long the second Mrs Michael got sick of it all and left. Michael didn't seem to mind at all. For one thing, Alexandra was starting to bore him; for another he was making more money than he had ever known and using it to live life to the full. Most importantly, though, he had just been introduced to a woman called Lynn Baker.

He had met her while working for Ruth, a madam who ran a brothel in Highgate and employed Michael to keep her books. For a man who had always chosen his girlfriends at least partly to please his mother, Lynn was an odd choice. A former vice girl, blonde, busty and cocky with it, Lynn had many unsavoury friends and acquaintances who had grown up on the edge of the world of organised crime. More to the point, she wasn't Greek. Lynn was exciting, dangerous and every mother's worst nightmare, but Michael was utterly smitten.

Within three months they were living together. As his relationship with Lynn developed, so Michael became more and more involved in the day-to-day running of the sauna, which Lynn co-owned. Seeing an opportunity for expansion and even greater profit, the pair soon went into business together, pooling their resources to buy more saunas and start their own little empire.

But Michael had plenty of other work to keep him

busy. He specialised in giving references and providing fake paperwork for people who didn't have legitimate jobs but needed to show banks that they had a steady income, in order to get a mortgage. From there it was a short leap to arranging mortgages for people who didn't exist at all. In 1989 Michael set up a scam in which he helped arrange £3 million worth of bogus loans, earning himself a commission of around £30,000.

The fraud was soon uncovered and, just as Lynn announced she was pregnant, Michael was arrested once again.

And that was when he began travelling down the path which would make him a multi-millionaire and one of the most powerful figures in the British under-world, but would ultimately lead to a £4 million contract on his life.

Michael had no fears of returning to prison, but was concerned about the business that he and Lynn were building up. By now they had four saunas and the money was starting to roll in. 'Some of them were registered as companies and I declared profits which I paid tax on. I even paid VAT. But everyone knows that saunas and massage parlours are just whore-houses. The police knew what went on in all these places and they used to raid them on a regular basis.'

With dozens of detectives poring over his financial records in the aftermath of the mortgage-fraud case, Michael was terrified that the police would soon begin a concerted effort to shut all his saunas down. Desperate to sustain what was fast becoming his chief source of income, Michael met up with the police officer who had first arrested him. 'Even though he was the one who nicked me, I didn't bear a grudge: I thought the guy had been fair to me. I actually quite liked him.'

The feeling proved mutual and, as the pair began a cautious friendship, Michael saw a way of striking a bargain. Through his work and his time in prison he had got to know a number of mid-ranking criminals – armed robbers, drug dealers and the like. He would often get to hear about raids that were being planned, drug shipments that were arriving and even underworld murders that were being set up. This was because Michael was seen as a man with good connections, the gangland equivalent of the Yellow Pages. If you needed a fake passport, a stolen car or a few kilos of cocaine, Michael was a good man to ask. He didn't actually get involved in anything himself, but he always knew some-one who did, and would be happy to make the intro-duction.

Although most people imagine the underworld is very secretive and closed, that's not always the case. If, for example, you come into possession of a large quan-tity of gold bars, the only way to convert them to money is to find people willing to buy them. And the only way to do that is to put the word out. Once you achieve a certain level of trust and credibility, usually by having been in prison, you are aware of all the requests for information, buyers, drivers for robberies and so on. Michael had access to the kind of information any policeman worth his salt would give his right arm for, and he knew it.

A deal was soon struck: Michael would become an informant, passing on details of the criminal enterprises of those around him. His main reward would be a virtual guarantee that his sauna business would be left to flourish.

A top-secret file was opened and, working first under the code name 'Andrew Ridgley' and later a 'Chris Stevens', Michael began to talk. As the information began to flow it became clear that, far from being something to worry about, the brothels were a valuable source of intelligence. Whenever Michael met big-time drug traffickers he would get them drunk and treat them to a session with his prostitutes. 'I'd introduce them to the girls and make sure they had a good time,' he says. 'The saunas were a very good cover. When people are totally relaxed in a steam bath, they drop their guard and tell you things they'd never tell you anywhere else.'

Michael threw himself into his new role with surprising amounts of enthusiasm. In his first few weeks he gave the police details of the people who had laundered the proceeds of his mortgage-fraud scam; he told them about being approached to nobble a juror in the Guinness trial; and he told them all about a group of burglars who were committing violent robberies, and the identities of the men believed to have killed a prostitute whose body had been found in Epping Forest.

Meanwhile he continued expanding his chain of brothels and broadening the range of financial services his company offered. 'Maintaining the saunas and the accountancy office were an integral part of my ability to provide. The way the police viewed it was that I lived the right sort of lifestyle, drove the right sort of cars. I could converse with criminals on their level so it was a good opportunity for me to get bits and pieces which I would then pass on to the police.'

Right from the start he demonstrated a considerable talent for deceit and a remarkable ability to get people to do his bidding. When two of his accountancy clients who made their living from drug-smuggling lost their supplier, they asked Michael if he knew anyone who might help. He told them he would set up a meeting with some friends of his, but insisted it should take place at his office. The gang met; only Michael was aware that the police had placed microphones around the office and were monitoring every word.

The flow of information continued for eight months while Michael awaited trial. Then, when the case was drawing to a close, it was payback time. The public and press were sent out of court and the police made private representations to the judge about what an important asset Michael had become. Despite the serious nature of his crime and the fact that it was his second offence, he served just two months in prison.

By the time he was released and their first child was born, Lynn and Michael's sauna business was flourishing. They now had several branches spread out across London and, with no police interference, were making profits of tens of thousands of pounds each year. Some of the money they spent on property, buying ever bigger and more elaborate houses. The rest they spent on luxuries.

Michael continued to sing like a canary at every opportunity. Every little piece of information he came across he would use. Only occasionally was the information acted on directly; most of the time it was placed in police files and used to boost their intelligence about what was going on in the underworld, giving them an unprecedented insight into the workings of the country's top gangsters. But if the police felt they could make an arrest or prevent a crime from taking place without compromising the source of their information they would do so. As the months ticked by, many of Michael's underworld associates began to suffer occasional spates of bad luck. Vehicles carrying shipments of drugs would get pulled over by the traffic police because of a faulty light or broken mirror, only for the officer to notice an 'odd smell' and uncover the booty; gangs who had spent weeks casing a location for an armed robbery would arrive to find the cash truck had started taking a new route; budding contract killers would find their homes being searched on a pretext and all their weapons being confiscated.

On other occasions, asked if he knew any prospective customers for shipments of heroin or cocaine, Michael would agree to find someone and then introduce the gang to a man who would later turn out to be an undercover police officer. This first officer would introduce the gang to another man, and then another, so that by the time they were arrested, it would be impossible to link their downfall back to Michael, and his position as an informant would not be compromised.

To Michael, the concept of 'honour among thieves' didn't exist. In May 1991 he gave information about a flat in Northolt where up to a thousand ecstasy tablets were being made each day. The police report recorded the name of the suspect and noted: 'Ridgley is in a position to assist us heavily with info in this matter and it would appear the Northolt address is a major outlet.' It would be many years before anyone realised that Michael had informed on his own brother-in-law.

In the offices of senior police officers up and down the country, Michael was soon being talked about as one of the best and most reliable informants in the country. He was proving to be an absolute goldmine. No other informant had such good access to, or was so trusted by, the senior figures in the British underworld.

So when the police wanted to run an undercover sting operation against the Adams family, a notorious gang based in north London, Michael was the man they chose to help set it up. The police wanted to find out what the family did with their money, so they transferred tens of thousands of pounds into Michael's own bank account and taught him how to launder it.

Michael told the Adamses that the money was profit he had made on drug deals and transferred it to a bent solicitor who often acted on their behalf. He in turn transferred the cash into an offshore company. The idea was to use the same trick that the FBI had used against Al Capone – to prosecute the family for attempting to evade tax.

But the scheme fell apart when Michael himself came under the scrutiny of the tax authorities. 'They said they had information that had been passed on by the police that I was involved with the Adams family, that I owned a yacht in Cyprus, which I never did, that I was a front man for the Adamses, which I never was.

'Then they said that I owed them £750,000 in taxes. The police tried to sort it out and tell them to forget it because I was part of an operation, but they wouldn't listen. In the end I became an informant for the Inland Revenue as well and they agreed to reduce the amount down to £125,000, of which I paid around £20,000.'

Although the débâcle temporarily soured his relationship with the police, things were soon back on track and the tip-offs began to flow once more.

It was around this time that Michael started providing information about a shadowy underworld figure known as 'the Pimpernel'. Originally hailing from north London, the Pimpernel switched from bank robbery to the drug trade in the seventies and never looked back. He is alleged to have amassed a £100 million fortune from his global drug-smuggling empire, appears in the Top Ten Most Wanted list of at least a dozen countries and has spent almost half his life on the run.

He got his nickname from his ability to evade the best efforts of the police to track him down. When the police in Britain got a little too close, he fled to Marbella, leaving behind speedboats, yachts, Rolls-Royces, a Porsche, a Ferrari, gold bullion, cash and cocaine. The loss seemed to have little effect on his wealth and he soon became a well-known figure in Marbella, driving around in a white Rolls-Royce and enjoying the millionaire lifestyle.

He then travelled to France and is said to have made millions more smuggling cocaine, fleeing just before the police raided his apartment in Paris. He next turned up in America, where he had extensive contacts with the Mafia and the Colombian cocaine cartels. He was lounging by the pool in Rod Stewart's former home in Beverly Hills when he was arrested by the FBI.

Imprisoned in San Francisco, the Pimpernel needed someone to sell one of his properties in Spain to help fund his escalating legal bills, which could only be paid with money that could be shown to come from a legitimate source.

His estranged wife, Ann, was a friend of Lynn and, having heard all about Michael's formidable accounting skills, asked if he would be interested in helping out. Michael readily agreed and was soon working on behalf of one of the most powerful and dangerous criminals in the world.

It took two years and a dramatic escape from custody – the Pimpernel was being flown to France but slipped off the plane during a refuelling stop and fled to Ireland – before they could finally meet in person. By now Michael had all the trappings of the successful criminal. He and Lynn had moved into their £1 million house at Radlett, and Michael had a Porsche and a Rolls-Royce. Their two sons both attended private school. To the Pimpernel, Michael seemed to be cast from the same mould as himself.

Of course, the Pimpernel had no idea that details of everything that he said and every new criminal enterprise he planned were being reported back to the police.

Michael was playing an increasingly dangerous game, but he loved every single minute of it.

The link with the Pimpernel boosted the value of Michael's stock even higher. The bigwigs of police intelligence were so impressed that there was talk of making Michael the central figure in a sting that would be carried out jointly with the FBI. The idea was for Michael to travel to Chicago and link up with some of his Mafia contacts. He would be provided with thirty kilos of cocaine, using this as a lure to get the Americans to agree to make a deal while being secretly filmed.

That particular deal fell apart, but the stakes were dramatically raised in the mid-nineties when, due to his old contacts being promoted, Michael was given a new 'handler', a detective called Paul, who worked at Scotland Yard's élite Criminal Intelligence Branch and was responsible for handling top-secret information between informants and undercover officers. While previous officers had played things strictly by the book, Paul, according to Michael, spent all his time pushing him to get more and more involved. He wanted Michael to take an even more active role in the criminal activities of his new associates in order to gather more detailed information.

It wasn't the only change. Rather than simply guaranteeing a quiet life for the saunas, Michael's tip-offs were now generating cash rewards, often several thousand pounds at a time. The money would be shared with Paul, and soon the relationship between the two had become what would later be described in court as 'completely corrupt'.

The basic deal was that Michael would do pretty much what he wanted – sell drugs, launder money, trade in guns, anything – and Paul would make sure the police never went anywhere near him. In return, Michael would provide Paul with enough titbits to create a few arrests and make him look good in front of his bosses, but also share the vast wealth his criminal activities were generating.

The arrangement suited both parties down to the

ground and when the Pimpernel offered Michael the chance to become the British head of his new drug-distribution ring, he accepted right away. He didn't have to worry about not knowing how to run a drug-smuggling operation – Paul promised he would give him all the help he needed.

Michael claimed his first drug job for the Pimpernel was to arrange the collection and storage of several hundred kilos of cannabis resin which had been imported to Britain hidden in soap-powder boxes. It was the first of several shipments that would arrive in this way.

Michael first stored the drugs at Jan's house – he had met her while she was working at Lynn's brothel – and then brought in some other friends to help with the distribution and sale of the drugs.

The money for the drugs came back in sterling but the Pimpernel wanted payment in Dutch currency, so he could pay his suppliers without having to first change the money over. Michael spoke to a friend about the problem and was soon introduced to a man called Housam, who liked to be called Sam for short.

They met in the central London office where Sam conducted his finance business and hit it off immediately. Michael then handed over £76,000 in cash, taking Sam's Lebanese passport as security, and waited.

Sam returned, having changed all the money into Dutch guilders. His contacts in the world of international finance meant he was able to do so without arousing suspicion. Normally, any cash transaction of more than £10,000 has to be reported to the police.

The process was repeated several more times until the £250,000 Michael had made selling the cannabis had all been exchanged. Sam had made a small commission on each transaction, but he and Michael soon realised that the best way to maximise their profits would be to set up their own bureau de change.

Michael and Paul then sat down to address the problem of how to get the money out of the country and back to the Pimpernel. One technique they devised was to place up to £400,000 in the spare tyre of a car and simply drive it to Spain. The warehouse where the drug loads were delivered to was equipped with a tyre-removal machine especially for this purpose and millions of pounds were smuggled out of the country in this way, though it was very time-consuming.

For smaller amounts, Paul and Michael decided to use couriers. 'What you need to do,' explained Paul, 'is recruit a bunch of pretty girls, but don't let them know what's really going on. That way they can stroll through Customs and no one will be any the wiser.'

As their experience grew, so they adjusted elements of the scheme. They worked out that it was best if as few couriers as possible knew about the existence of one another. That way, the suspicious among them would be more likely to believe they were part of a small scam rather than some massive international operation.

Another rule was that the couriers were not allowed to know how much money they were carrying. There had been a disaster early on when a courier had vanished with £150,000 after discovering just how much those funny foreign notes were worth.

Michael changed tactics. By wrapping the notes tightly in clingfilm he found he could squeeze up to £200,000 into a package only two inches thick. The wrapping also meant there was little chance the money could be interfered with.

Michael was equally proactive when it came to finding new and better ways to smuggle drugs. The Pimpernel put him in touch with Richard Jones, the lorry driver I had met at Michael's birthday party, who claimed to have a foolproof method of bringing cannabis into the UK. The drugs would be placed in blue barrels, which would be hidden inside tankers carrying paraffin wax or other products. The paraffin would hide any odour from the drugs and, because the tanker still appeared to be full, there was nothing to arouse any suspicions.

Jones's claims proved to be right on the money. Of the twenty-one cannabis-laden tankers that came into the UK, the only one that was discovered was the one that remained in the warehouse the day it was raided.

While his deals with the Pimpernel continued, Michael claimed that he also began working with other major European drug dealers, much to the delight of Paul. One was a dapper Frenchman by the name of André Caddoux. His technique was to use French-registered cars that had been specially adapted to create a hiding place for drugs in the fuel tank. The cars could smuggle up to ten kilos of cocaine on each trip.

Michael didn't stop there. He hatched a plan with a gang based in Spain to buy a typical tourist bus and build in a secret drug-carrying compartment. The coach would be filled with tourists and even have an interpreter. It would be the perfect cover. As regular shipments of cannabis with the coach began, Michael dubbed it 'the fun bus'.

Michael made money from all aspects of the trade, but most of his wealth came from the money-laundering. He would charge between 1 and 5 per cent of the total amount laundered to hand the money back to the European dealers. Within months he had become a millionaire many times over and hardly knew what to do with all the money.

Paul kept the police away and was rewarded accordingly. At least once a week he would arrive at the house in Radlett and Michael would hand over up to £10,000 in cash. The money would be brought down from the loft, where Michael kept a cash stash of between £30,000 and £1 million. In all, Paul is said to have received more than £250,000. And suddenly I knew what Jan had meant when she had said, 'This should never have happened.'

Most of the time, reading through the statements would fill me with a mixture of nausea and sheer terror. It was hard to swallow the fact that almost everyone I had met in the year before my arrest – Jan, Sonny, Richard and André, to name but a few – had been involved in the drugs gang, but there were a few small things I could take some comfort in.

There was the fact that during his first few trips abroad, Sonny had truly believed that his brother was simply running a tax-evasion scheme. Once he found out the truth, he was more than happy to continue in the family business, but at least it showed that Karen and I were not the only ones who had been deceived.

The same was true of Sue Richards, one of Lynn's best friends with whom Michael was having a passionate affair. Michael got her to take tens of thousands of pounds abroad under the pretext that he was having some property built in Spain. During her police interviews she broke down in tears when she realised the man she had loved had constantly lied and completely betrayed her. Even though she had taken cocaine with Michael on a number of occasions, she had had no inkling that he was dealing on such a grand scale. Michael had often talked about 'shipments' arriving on the 'fun bus', but the one time she asked him what it meant he told her it was loaded with cigarettes and alcohol.

Michael even managed to persuade his elderly mother to take a package to France for him on the pretext that it was part of a business deal. She had no way of knowing that the package – £200,000 in Spanish currency – would ultimately be used to buy drugs.

The only person who knew exactly what was going on from the start was Jan Marlborough. Even Lynn was kept in the dark about many aspects of Michael's lifestyle, hence his panic-stricken rant to me that afternoon at his house when he told me she would grass him up. At long last I understood exactly what he had meant.

Then there were the Chicago Mafia, the members of top Colombian drug cartels and many of the brightest and most successful criminals operating in Britain and Europe, including the Pimpernel, a man who managed to avoid getting caught by the police for fifteen years. All of them were taken in by Michael, all of them believed every word that he said. None of them knew he was giving away each and every one of their secrets.

Even the National Westminster Bank were taken in. When the money-laundering scam got too big for their own bureau de change, Sam struck a deal with one in the Lebanon, where he already had an account. Sam would phone through an order to Beirut for batches of foreign currency and then Michael would meet the courier at an airport or hotel to swap the foreign notes for the sterling he had received from drug deals. The couriers would then deposit the money at a London branch of Nat West as if it had come directly from Beirut. It meant that the money seemed to be coming from a legitimate source.

At one point a manager at Nat West raised questions about why some of the cash coming from Sam did not resemble the rest of the cash coming from the Lebanese bureau de change. Michael reacted by importing the same wrappings used by the Lebanese office to wrap his own cash. The questions stopped.

A few weeks later Customs officers detained some couriers carrying cash from Beirut on Michael's behalf – but he had done such a good job of convincing Nat West that the money was legitimate that the bank itself intervened and reassured Customs that there was no problem.

Between January 1997 and April 1998, Sam and Michael successfully laundered £28.2 million through Nat West right under their noses. The bank had done nothing wrong. They had followed their own rules and regulations and made genuine efforts to check the source of the cash.

The only problem was that Michael was too clever and too sophisticated for them.

Little old me never stood a chance.

Operation Draft began on 23 January 1998 when officers from Customs and Excise began a routine investigation into a Hatfield industrial unit after receiving a
tip-off that it was being used to store drugs. Within the
space of a few days they had identified Michael Michael
as the principal mover behind the organisation and
placed him and all his associates under close surveillance.

For four months they watched as tankers, tourist
buses and cars, all laden with drugs, moved in and out
of the unit. They saw Michael meeting with some of
the biggest names in organised crime and then, to their
horror, with Paul, the detective from the Central
Intelligence Branch.

They listened in on telephone calls, planted bugs in
hotel rooms (at one point catching Michael and his
lover) and recorded the comings and goings of more
than a hundred people. They filmed and photographed
me and other couriers making our way to and from the
Continent with our bundles of cash, and they identified Michael's suppliers in France, Amsterdam, Ireland
and Spain.

Most crucially for me, Customs officers had witnessed
my rushed meeting with Michael and André at the
Hilton Hotel in Watford. Even though I had been trying
to get away as quickly as possible, the pictures told
another story.

There I was, having a drink with Michael Michael,
one of Britain's biggest drug traffickers, and André, one
of the biggest coke suppliers in Europe. Not only that,

I then accepted a package from Michael and headed off to the airport. It put me into the top league of operators, which was why Customs had gone to the effort of arranging for an undercover officer to pose as a taxi driver to see if they could get any information out of me before I got on the plane.

The knock took place on 25 April. At the same time that a dozen Customs officers were running in through my front door they also surrounded the house at Radlett and moved in to arrest the main man.

Michael, out of his head on coke, believed he was being robbed by rivals and grabbed a loaded gun, pointing it at the first man in through his door. Only when the intruder identified himself as a Customs officer did he drop the weapon and give himself up.

Inside Michael's house, the investigators were staggered at what they found: it wasn't the £800,000 in cash or the original paintings worth £1 million hanging on the walls; it was the fact that, like any good bookkeeper, Michael had kept precise and detailed records of every drug transaction he had ever taken part in. The paperwork told who had bought what and how much they had paid. It listed each courier, where they had travelled to and how much money had been taken. It listed cash due from drug sales across the country and who owed what. 'We had absolutely everything,' said one Customs officer, 'all the evidence we could ever want.'

For a short while Michael was glad it was all over. The strain of living a double life was starting to get to him. He had been telling so many lies to so many people that he could no longer separate fact from fiction. He believed that at any moment Paul would walk through the door and apologise and that he would get the chance to give up the life of an informant.

Then he was told that Paul had been arrested. Furthermore, he was told that whatever arrangement he might have had with the police, it did not cut any ice with Customs. He was the head of a major drugs gang and that was all there was to it.

And that was when Michael decided to talk. And talk and talk and talk.

During the course of 250 taped interviews, he told the police absolutely everything. He told them about the suppliers, the traffickers, the smugglers, the money launderers and the mules.

Somewhere at the back of my mind, I knew that if Michael told the absolute truth, I'd probably be OK, but it wasn't just Michael I had to worry about. Jan had also turned supergrass and spoken about trips we had made abroad, giving the distinct impression that I had known she and Michael were dealing in drugs. Worst still, Sonny had recalled the time he had arrived at Michael's house and seen me straightening a pile of money, only he had told the Customs officers that I had been counting the money. 'Did she know what it was for?' the officers had asked him. 'Oh yeah, she must have known,' came his reply.

The sinking feeling that had begun when I had started reading the statements became more and more powerful with each new page. And Michael's words rarely brought any comfort. 'Even to my family I have had to tell lies and be deceitful,' he said at one point. 'I have become a polished liar. There were occasions when I informed on my family. Because of my statements my friends, my family and my lover are all awaiting trial. It is part of the business of informing and dealing – being disloyal goes with the territory.'

Chapter Fourteen

The more I read, the more horrified I became and the more I realised just how much trouble I had got myself into.

Of the tens of thousands of pages of interviews and statements that I'd gone through, one line haunted me more than any other. It was the advice that Paul, the corrupt policeman at the heart of the enterprise, had given Michael after encouraging him to get involved in drug trafficking: 'Recruit a bunch of pretty girls,' he'd said, 'but make sure you don't let them know what's really going on.'

With the benefit of hindsight, it seemed the clues had been there right from the start. But as I started to look at things from Michael's point of view, it was very clear that he'd gone to great lengths to keep certain people – people like me and Karen – very much in the dark about what he was getting up to.

This alone was a horrendous betrayal, but what hurt and scared me even more were the lies contained in his statements. Michael had obviously been promised a massive discount on his own sentence for giving information about the big organised-crime figures in Europe and America that he had been acting for, and also the small fry who formed the drugs-distribution chain in the UK.

But, in order to give himself extra credit, Michael had elaborated on some stories and completely falsified others. As Karen and I compared notes on the paperwork we found dozens of occasions where he had simply lied, and lied again, sometimes for no obvious reason. It was as if he had become drunk on the power of betrayal. He knew that if 90 per cent of what he told Customs was true, he could make up the remainder and more than likely be believed.

It didn't bode well for my future. If Michael was going to be put forward as the star witness at my trial, then the jury would be encouraged to believe that everything he said was true. My only defence – that I had no idea the money was being used to pay for drugs – would be shot to pieces if Michael took the stand and said I knew about the cocaine and cannabis right from the start.

I wasn't the only one in trouble. One morning before breakfast, I was in my cell listening to the news on the radio when an item came on about someone committing suicide in prison. I'd been idly reading the latest batch of statements but the mention of the word 'prison' ensured the rest of the bulletin had my full attention. I was thinking how sad it was, and about the times I had got that low, when they gave the name of the dead man: Richard Jones.

It was as if my heart stopped. I wanted to scream but there was no breath in my lungs. I felt hollow, terrified. I forced myself to get up to the hatch and saw that Debbie, who was now living in the cell opposite mine, was standing there with an ashen face.

'Fucking hell, did you just hear that?' she gasped. We

were in a state of shock. Richard, the lovely lorry driver I had met at Michael's party, had been accused of driving a lorry full of drugs. Whether he knew what he was doing or not and what his reasons were is anybody's guess, but now he faced years in prison because Michael had grassed him up. He had obviously decided there was only one way out. Richard was a fully grown man with a family and responsibilities. If he decided that he couldn't handle what was to come, then what chance did we have?

It was around this time, as the prospect of spending most of the best years of my life behind bars loomed larger than ever, that I had my short-lived confrontation with Mad Mandy.

We had finished the first supper serving, shut one side of the hatch and invited people up for seconds. The rules were strict: you're only allowed to have what you're down on the list for and, to prevent bullying, you're not even allowed to swap something with the other girls. Most people couldn't abide the food but the heavy drug users would go through phases of being ravenously hungry and eat as much as they could, no matter how disgusting it was.

Mandy was second in the queue and the girl I was serving decided that she didn't want any cake. When it was Mandy's turn she asked for a portion of the chicken stew and, as I was placing a piece of cake on a plate for her, she asked for a double portion. 'I want the cake that girl didn't have,' she sniffed.

'You know I can't do that now, but I'll sort you out later,' I whispered, cocking my head towards a screw at the far corner of the room.

But Mandy was still coming down off her last crack binge and in no mood for logic. 'Gimme the fucking cake, man.'

'Mandy,' I said, sliding one piece of cake towards her across the hatch, 'I said I'll sort you out later, all right?'

It wasn't all right: she exploded in a fit of rage. 'You fucking cunting white bitch, you fucking deaf or what, give me the fucking cake now you stupid motherfucker.'

I pulled the cake away. 'Right, if that's your attitude you ain't getting fuck-all.'

Mandy called me all the names under the sun, then threw her plate of chicken stew at me. I watched it come flying through the serving hatch – it seemed to be moving in slow motion – and ducked just in time for it to miss my head. It smashed on the wall behind me and the sticky mix of meat and watery sauce poured down on my head like rain. The anger shot through me like a missile. 'Come on then, you bitch,' I spat back, 'come on then.' Ripping the thick black kitchen gloves from my hands I sucked in a deep breath and charged out towards her . . .

Afterwards, in my cell, where they had dragged me to let me calm down, I collapsed on the bed and burst into tears. I hated what I'd become, hated what was happening to me. There was no way I could cope with this for the next eighteen years. I didn't see how anyone could.

In prison, you spend your whole time living on your memories. Once you're locked up in your cell and shut off from the rest of the world, they're all you have. And so it was that I started thinking back over my life, about every decision I'd ever made, every person I'd ever met and everything I'd ever done, desperate to find out where things had started going so horribly wrong.

The more deeply I thought about it, the more I could see that I'd spent much of my life going round in circles. I'd got into relationships with men that had ended badly when they had hurt me and abused my trust, but weeks later I'd fall into a new relationship that would end up being exactly the same. And more than once I'd gone into situations with my eyes half closed or having left my common sense behind, and suffered greatly as a consequence.

Desperate to get to the heart of the matter, I took up an offer Governor McCauley had made soon after Matt had attacked me: I began sessions with a psychotherapist, talking through everything that had happened in my life.

The woman, Angela, did not normally work in prisons – McCauley had rightly guessed that I'd feel far more comfortable and willing to open up with someone from outside the system – but came highly recommended. She turned out to be an absolute godsend. Through a long series of intense and often painful counselling sessions, we slowly uncovered memories and traumas that I had suppressed but which, we soon realised, had to some degree been responsible for pointing me down the rocky path my life had followed.

I'll never forget the look on my mum's face when she found out I'd been stealing money from the local corner shop where I worked on Sunday mornings. There was so much hurt and disappointment in her eyes, I thought my heart was going to shatter into a thousand pieces. I was just twelve years old.

I'd fallen victim to the oldest trick in the book. The owner had sent me out to run an errand and when I came back he was going through the till and scratching his head. 'This isn't right,' he said, talking to himself but making sure it was loud enough for me to hear. 'There seems to be £20 missing.'

I was terrified that I was about to be found out but I was also confused. I thought I'd been really clever about covering my tracks so the money I'd been taking out of the till would appear to have been spent elsewhere. Obviously I'd made some stupid mistake.

The owner looked up as if he had only just seen me and announced he was going to the toilet, asking me to watch the shop. As soon as he was out of sight I lifted my top and pulled the two £20 notes I had stolen earlier that morning out of my waistband. Opening the till gently so the bell wouldn't ring, I slipped one of the notes back in and hid the remainder of the money.

A few minutes later the owner returned and asked me to run to the local post office and get some change. When I returned he was holding the extra £20 note between his fingers. 'I think you and I need to have a talk,' he said.

As far as my parents were concerned, it was just one more black mark against my name in the big book of bad behaviour that seemed to feature me on every page. Without doubt I was the worst-behaved child of the family. I was constantly in trouble, and before too long they had almost come to expect this kind of thing from me.

I hated the idea of them being so disappointed with me and desperately wanted to tell them what was really going on. I wanted them to know that I didn't mean to be bad, that it wasn't really my fault, but there was no way. No matter how hard I tried, I just couldn't bring myself to tell them the truth.

The bullying started almost as soon as I joined my local secondary school.

An older boy whose name I have long forgotten had taken a bit of a shine to me and, in the process, unknowingly set off a chain of events that led to a horrific campaign of physical, verbal and emotional abuse that came to dominate every moment of my waking life for the next two years.

The problem was Sharon, a girl in the boy's class, who wanted him all to herself and had been consumed with jealousy after seeing the two of us talking together. Having decided that I needed to be taken down a peg or two, she made it her life's work to do just that.

Sharon was reputed to be one of the toughest, if not *the* toughest, girl in the whole school. One story circulating around the playground was that a year or so earlier she had got into a fight with a boy and bitten off part of his ear, before beating him to a pulp. On top of that she was a good four years older than me, which at that age is almost a lifetime, so it didn't take much for me to become utterly terrified of her.

Sharon and a group of her friends would seek me out at breaktimes and call me names, but the bullying soon became more physical. Within weeks I would find myself surrounded by a group of up to twenty girls who would poke, prod, slap, kick, scratch and punch me while spitting out a stream of vicious insults.

Not a single day went past without some kind of incident. If I happened to walk past one of the gang, they would make sure they bumped into me or tripped me up. The school building was on a number of levels and the first-year pupils were always at the top. The gang used to hang around the stairwells and each time I walked past they would push me down a flight. I would often go home covered in bruises and only narrowly escaped more serious injury.

Friends in my class tried to stand up for me but they were quickly intimidated into giving me a wide berth. Lunchtimes were the worst. I'd be sitting with a group of friends and the gang would turn up and suddenly all my friends would vanish.

They were after me all the time, to the extent that I was bunking off school because I was too scared to go in. The constant fear, terror and humiliation are feelings I will never forget. Just the sight of one of the girls would set me quivering and reduce me to a physical wreck.

I didn't tell my parents. All they saw was that for some inexplicable reason their bright young daughter had turned into a right little monster. At one point I got myself suspended, at another I briefly ran away from home. I put them through hell but I could never tell them what was really behind it. Like many victims of bullying, I felt it was all my fault, that no one else was having problems. I changed from being a confident, happy girl, a conscientious worker who enjoyed school, to someone who was withdrawn, weepy and experiencing constant nightmares. I'd always been the first person to volunteer in class but before too long I didn't want to be there at all. All my enthusiasm for life had gone.

By being naughty I would usually get myself placed in detention, which meant I would leave school half an hour later than everyone else. By that time the bullies would usually have gone.

That worked for a little while, but then some of the gang started waiting around for me. Then they found out where I lived and started tormenting me during evenings and weekends. Once I got the Sunday job at the shop, they took things to a new level.

A group of them would wait outside until the owner was out of sight and then come steaming in. They would produce plastic bags from their pockets which I would have to fill up with cigarettes, sweets and anything of value that they could sell, like Schaeffer pens. On top of that I had to give them money from the till as well – at least £40 – or risk being beaten up during the week. It was ludicrous. I was being paid £4 for four hours' work on a Sunday morning and making off with at least £50 worth of stock and cash while I was there.

When they had been bullying me at school, they explained that if I ever told anyone what they were doing, they would kill me. Once I was at the shop they threatened that, if I ever told, no one would believe it wasn't my idea to steal the money and the goods. They would blame everything on me and I would end up in prison. I was young, I was naïve and I believed every word. I grew up thinking that the worst crime in the world was to tell on someone. Sometimes I couldn't sleep at night from the worry of it all.

Only those who have been bullied can truly know

the horrendous effect it has on your daily existence. When I read stories of children committing suicide because they have been bullied so relentlessly, I can fully understand how they could end up feeling they had no other way out.

The torture finally stopped when I did the one thing I hadn't managed to do during the two previous years – I hit back. The gang had surrounded me and Sharon was standing directly in front of me. I remember feeling as though a wall of people was closing in on me, sucking out all the air and making me suffocate.

The gang moved in closer and closer, Sharon poking my face over and over again. I was begging her to stop but she wouldn't. She just kept on and on and on. I pushed her hand away and she slapped me hard across the face. At that moment something snapped, something inside said I wasn't going to put up with this any more. I was like a cornered animal. I stepped forward and punched Sharon square on the nose.

I don't know what came over me but it had an incredible effect. For two years I had done nothing and they were so shocked that they didn't know what to do. Sharon was stunned; she just staggered back and then walked away.

It didn't stop overnight, but after that day the bullying slowed to a trickle. Gradually the girls who had been responsible started to say hello and treat me with a grudging respect. Within a few months, it was all over.

But bullying isn't just about the physical pain: the cuts and bruises heal but the emotional scars last a lifetime. Although you try to fight it, deep inside you know you've lost your self-esteem and your confidence is not what it should be. And though you move on, the experiences slowly but surely begin to affect the decisions you make for the rest of your life.

Finn was my first real boyfriend.

We got together soon after the bullying had come to an end. He was three years older, out of school and had a job as a plumber's apprentice. He seemed like a real adult and had no trouble sweeping me off my feet. Within weeks of our first date I was besotted.

Right from the start, my parents were less than keen – they were convinced that he was much too old and could only be a bad influence on me at a time when I already seemed to be out of control – but that just strengthened my love for him. They hoped it would be typical of relationships at that age and burn itself out, but the days became weeks, and then months, and then years, and we were still together.

I finally agreed to sleep with him and afterwards I became even more convinced that this was the man I was going to marry. I'd practise signing my name with his surname, spend hours wondering what kind of wedding dress I'd wear, where we would live and what our children would look like. Finn was my Prince Charming and we were going to live happily ever after.

Soon after I'd lost my virginity, things started to change. Finn became incredibly possessive and jealous. All the tenderness evaporated and was replaced by mistrust and obsessiveness. He insisted I see him every night, not because he loved me but because he was convinced that if he didn't I'd meet someone else.

Whenever we were driving around in his car, I'd have

to spend the whole journey staring at my lap. If I dared to lift my head then Finn would immediately assume I was looking at whatever man happened to be passing by at the time. On more than one occasion he brought the car to a screeching halt, jumped out and ran over to whoever was around, screaming at them at the top of his voice, 'Are you looking at my girlfriend? Are you trying to get off with her? I saw her looking at you. She wants to fuck you.' Sometimes the men were young but sometimes they were pensioners with walking sticks and thinning grey hair. It made no difference to Finn.

Then he would get back in the car and start punching me, always on the legs and arms, never on my face. He'd call me all sorts of horrible names. I'd end up covered in bruises but I never told anyone. I just accepted that was the way things were. Somewhere deep inside, I knew I had replaced one set of bullies in my life with another.

To my shame, I stayed with him. I even blamed myself, just like I had done with the bullying before. Like many women who end up trapped in abusive relationships, I assumed it was my fault and that if only I could be a better girlfriend, I wouldn't make him so angry.

I left school and started working in the homewares department of my local branch of Tesco. The change of environment and independence of earning a full-time salary helped me come to my senses, but when I tried to get out of the relationship, Finn threatened to kill himself. He poured on the guilt so thick that I would lie awake at night worrying about it.

And then I missed my period.

It took more than a month for me to work up the courage to tell Finn and, as I'd expected, he was furious.

He accused me of having slept with someone else and said there was no way the child could be his. I had just turned seventeen but even at that early age I felt very maternal and had a powerful urge to be a mother. However Finn told me in no uncertain terms that he would never support me if I went ahead and had the baby and there was just no way I could cope on my own. I felt I had no choice but to have a termination. It was the hardest decision I have ever had to make. My parents knew nothing about it and there was no one else I felt I could talk to.

Finn wanted nothing to do with it and left me to make all the arrangements. I didn't go to my GP because I was terrified that my mum would find out. Instead I found a clinic on the other side of town and arranged to go in and see them. By then I was nearly three months gone.

It was horrific. The consultant spent almost the whole appointment shouting at me and putting me down, treating me in the most appalling fashion. I remember her calling me a 'silly girl' over and over again under her breath. When I burst into tears she just got even worse. It was as if she saw me as a loose teenage tart running around getting pregnant all the time and then expecting someone else to sort it out for me.

Thinking back, I guess the woman was just trying to scare me to make sure it would never happen again, but whatever her motivation, it was wrong, so wrong. I'll never forget her mean words for as long as I live. In years to come, I'd realise that this experience before the termination had affected me almost as much as the procedure itself.

The abortion was booked to take place four weeks

later and in the mean time I had to hide the signs of my pregnancy from my friends and family. I'd started to get big really quickly and had a noticeable bump around my middle. Luckily it was the middle of winter and I was able to disguise it with baggy jumpers, but I had to avoid hugs or people brushing up against me in case they realised.

A week before my appointment a new manageress started in my department at Tesco. Right from the start we failed to hit it off, partly because I was suffering chronic morning sickness and always running off to the toilets to throw up. When she discovered I had booked a day off she told me to cancel it because she needed to be away on that day. She explained that she was my boss and therefore she had first call. I told her I couldn't cancel it and that it was really important, but my words fell on deaf ears.

'Whatever little-girl nonsense you've got planned, you're just going to have to do it some other time.'

'But—'

'This discussion is over. Now get back to work.'

When the day came I took it off anyway; I had no choice. Finn refused to give me a lift to the hospital. I only had enough money for the cab fare in one direction so I decided to get there by public transport, taking two buses and walking at least half a mile. The constant morning sickness was making me very weak and by the time I arrived at the hospital I was ready to collapse.

The abortion itself was all of my worst nightmares come to life, a memory so horrific I can hardly bear to recall it.

The doctors wanted me to stay overnight but that would have alerted my parents. I had to get home. I felt sick and sore all over and I was bleeding profusely but I insisted on discharging myself. I signed the paperwork and made my way to the exit, only to collapse on the pavement outside.

They refused to take me back inside because I'd signed the release form and therefore any damage I was going to suffer had been self-inflicted. I got them to call Finn, who eventually turned up in his car, shouting and swearing at the doctors and nurses and making a terrible scene. Then he took me away.

He dropped me at home and I went straight to bed, feigning a migraine. The next morning I still felt incredibly ill but had to drag myself to work. As soon as I arrived my manager called me into her office for a meeting, shouted at me for taking the day off when she had told me not to, and sacked me on the spot.

I was still fuzzy-headed from the anaesthetic, so I could hardly take in what she was saying. When it finally dawned on me I refused to go. In the end the manageress and her assistant each took hold of an arm, dragged me to the door and literally threw me out into the street. I spent the next four hours walking around aimlessly, tears blurring my vision. It seemed so unfair. I'd been sacked before but this time it just wasn't my fault and I was determined to do something about it. I wasn't going to let them treat me like that.

I arranged to meet up with the representative of the local union the following day. I soon realised the only way I was going to get any justice was to tell them the truth about why I had taken the day off. Everyone at Tesco would have to know I'd got pregnant and had an abortion.

It was a humiliating ordeal, but the union man was brilliant. He arranged a meeting with the senior management and told them that unless I was reinstated all the staff would walk out and all thirty-two checkouts in the store would be closed down.

The negotiations took four weeks but in the end we won and I got my job back, including back pay for all the time I'd been off.

On my first day back, the manageress was waiting for me. If looks could kill I would have dropped dead on the spot. As I took up my usual position in the home-wares department she walked over to me.

'You don't work in this section any more,' she sneered. 'You've been reassigned.'

'To which department?'

'Babywear.' She was smiling. She was an evil cow.

I spent the morning surrounded by happy, smiling pregnant women, hand in hand with their partners as they giggled over tiny socks and vests. I kept one eye on the clock the whole time and as soon as it was lunchtime I went upstairs and barged my way into the senior manager's office.

'I just want to say: you can take this job and shove it up your arse.'

He sat back in his chair, his mouth open with disbelief. 'How can you say that, after everything that you've put us through? How can you come in here and tell us you don't want the job now?'

'I don't care about the job. I never liked the job, it

was the principle.' And with that I spun on my heels and walked out for good.

I thought the abortion would be the end of our relationship, but Finn insisted we were still together. And now he had a new ace up his sleeve. 'If you leave me, I'll tell your parents about the baby and they'll kick you out on the street.'

A bad relationship quickly turned worse. There were more beatings for no reason, and if I refused to sleep with him he would just insist until I gave in. After one particularly vicious argument I arrived home in the early hours of the morning and ended up sitting in the middle of the floor in the living room, rocking backwards and forwards and literally pulling my hair out.

When my brother arrived home after a night out and saw the state of me, he demanded to know what the hell was going on. Up until that point I hadn't told anybody about the abortion or the abuse, but now I blurted it all out.

My brother listened intently and then grabbed my hand. 'Right, we're going upstairs and you're going to tell Mum and Dad what you just told me.'

'No, I can't do that. I just can't.'

'Tracy, you've got to. You can't have this over you for the rest of your life.'

It was just after 2 a.m. when I climbed the stairs, woke my parents up and broke their hearts by telling them that seven months earlier I had got pregnant, had an abortion and kept it hidden from them.

It was one of the worst nights of my life but it was also a new beginning.

Finn was finally out of my life for ever.

So far I'd managed to hide the pain of imprisonment from my parents. I wanted to be strong for them, to give them the impression that, although it was tough, I was coping with life inside. But I knew I couldn't keep up the act for much longer.

My dad came to visit and as soon as he saw me he knew something was wrong. Normally I'd be smiling and making silly jokes, and I would have taken time to apply make-up and do my hair so that I looked as healthy and happy as possible. This time I came out looking like I'd spent a month fighting in the trenches and just sat there with my head bowed.

'Tracy, what's wrong, love?' I could hear the lump in my dad's throat.

For a long time I didn't say anything. Tears began rolling down my cheeks and splashing on to the table in front of me. Then eventually I managed, 'Dad . . . I'm being bullied. There's this woman, Maggie. It's killing me. I don't think I can take any more. I really don't think I can take any more. I just wish I was dead.'

I told him about being moved into her cell, and how since then I'd wake up each morning uncertain whether I'd be able to make it through the day. I told him about the fights, the arguments and the drugs. I told him the truth about prison life. I told him it was a living hell and that I couldn't cope.

Dad reached across and took my hand in his. He never said a word but I knew exactly what was going through his mind. I was his little princess and he wanted to protect me, but there was nothing he could do. In less than half an hour he would be gone and I would be back inside prison, on my own. It was the first time I had ever seen him cry.

When the bell sounded to signal the end of the visit, my dad stood up and hugged me tightly. He wouldn't let me go. He told me again and again and again that he loved me. Eventually the guards separated us and I watched him walk away a broken man. It was as though he had aged twenty years during the visit. I couldn't believe the pain I was putting my parents through, the agony I had forced them to endure.

And then I was angry at myself, angry for having broken down and told him what was really going on. He didn't need to know. He had enough to cope with just with the idea of me being in prison at all.

As I watched Dad walk out of the door I remembered something Angela had said after one of her counselling sessions, where we explored the fact that I was bringing things upon myself, making myself suffer for all the things that had happened earlier in my life. 'Do you think you've punished yourself enough now, Tracy?' she asked me. 'Do you think you've gone down as far as you can? After all, you're in prison now. You can't get much worse.'

When I got back to the cleaning annexe, Debbie was getting a haircut from Linda. Maggie came marching into the annexe, snatched the scissors, opened the blades and pushed them hard against my throat.

Wearily, I dragged my eyes from the television screen up to her face. 'What?'

Maggie knelt across me, forcing her bulk down on

my knees as she leaned forward, pushing her face close to mine. She nodded towards the office at the end of the corridor. 'You are going to go in there and speak to the SO and tell him you are moving out of that fucking cell.'

'I ain't doing nothing.' She pushed the scissors further forward. I could feel the cold metal biting into my flesh. 'I'll tell you what, Maggie. You do what you want to do. If you feel you have to cut me then just go ahead and fucking cut me because I really don't care any more.'

For the previous eighteen months, whatever Maggie had said, I had done. But I wasn't going to do that any more. She was completely and utterly unprepared for me to defy her.

'Erm . . . look, I ain't fucking about, you're gonna move out of that cunting room.'

I looked up, straight into Maggie's eyes, but all I could see was my father's tearstained face. 'No I ain't. You can't tell me what to do. The thing is, Maggie,' I continued, 'you don't frighten me any more.'

Out of the corner of my eye I could see Debbie, sitting on the sofa with her knees curled up to her chest and her knuckles in her mouth. She could not believe what she was hearing.

Debbie had slipped out to fetch help and returned with Mr Patel. As he walked into the annexe, Maggie put the scissors down behind her.

'What's going on?' Patel asked.

'Nothing,' Maggie said. 'One of the girls is getting her hair cut and we're just having a chat.'

'Is that right, Tracy?'

He was looking at me. He knew only too well what

was really going on, but unless I made a complaint his hands were tied. But there was no way I could tell him. 'That's right, we're just having a chat.'

Patel returned to his rounds and Maggie leaned her bulk over me again.

'It's not over,' she hissed. She moved back into the corridor.

'Whatever, Maggie,' I called after her. 'You do your best.'

It had taken a trip to rock bottom for it to happen but I had finally managed to stand up to Maggie, one of the most feared and respected inmates in the whole prison. It was as if I had gone back in time to the playground with Sharon and her friends. And just like the day that I finally hit back, from that day on, Maggie began to treat me with a grudging respect.

My trial was still months away and Holloway was as horrendous as ever, but it began to cross my mind that maybe, just maybe, I might be able to survive it. I was in for another rude awakening.

Chapter Fifteen

The senior management at Holloway Prison are a bit like baby pigeons – you know they exist, but you can't be completely sure because you never see them. The top governors, we are led to believe, are far too busy and important to get involved with the day-to-day problems of the inmates, except in exceptional circumstances. So as soon as I got the message that Mr O'Connor, otherwise known as Governor Number One, wanted to see me in his office, I immediately knew what it meant: someone in my family had died.

O'Connor greeted me with a nervous smile and a firm handshake then sent one of the screws running off to fetch me tea and biscuits. I put one hand on his desk, desperate to stop my legs from wobbling, and tried to prepare myself for what might come next. O'Connor could see the panic on my face and quickly cut to the chase, asking me to sit down as he cleared his throat ready to begin.

'The reason I wanted to see you, Tracy, is that I've had a rather disturbing phone call. From the press. From one of the Sunday tabloids. They've come to us because they've got hold of a . . . story . . . which they intend to publish tomorrow. We don't know much about it, except that it will be about . . . erm . . . the incident.'

In the few seconds that he had been speaking I had

run the full gamut of emotions: terror of the unknown; blessed relief that my family were OK; shock and dismay that the press were still hounding me; confusion over what the piece was going to be about. I felt drained and dizzy.

'What incident?'

O'Connor shifted uncomfortably in his seat. 'Erm . . . the er . . . incident with Matt.'

'Incident? You mean the time one of your officers sexually assaulted me?'

He looked at the floor and nodded sheepishly. I sat back in my chair and tried to take it all in. On the night he attacked me, Matt had said something about selling a story to the papers. It seemed he had finally made good on the threat. The bastard.

My thoughts then turned to my family. I'd never told them anything about it. Even though it had all happened nearly a year earlier and I'd seen them countless times, I'd never said a word. I'd been trying to protect them, especially my mother, who I knew was having constant nightmares imagining all sorts of things that were going on inside the prison. Having only just learned from my dad that I was being bullied by Maggie so badly that I was contemplating suicide, I dreaded to think how she'd cope with the revelation that a member of the staff had tried to sexually assault me.

O'Connor let me call my solicitor, David, who immediately sprang into action. With his best bullshitting cap on his head, he called up the editor of the paper and told him that there was a court order banning any mention of my name. If the paper breached the order, they would be in contempt of court and liable for a huge fine. The editor could even face jail.

It wasn't a complete lie. There *was* a court order banning any mention of anyone connected to the drug-smuggling case, but this story had nothing to do with that and therefore wasn't covered. But by now it was late on Saturday afternoon and the paper had no way of contacting the court to check what David was saying. It meant there was a strong chance that they'd play it safe and drop the story, at least for a week.

I spent all night pacing back and forth in my cell, unable to sleep and filled with rage against Matt. After everything he'd put me through, after all the horrible things he had said and done, he was now going to humiliate me in public. But as well as anger, there was confusion. I couldn't see how Matt could sell a story without making himself look bad. Unless, of course, he had told the press a pack of lies . . .

Morning finally arrived. Patel opened my cell with a cautious smile and the news that no story had appeared: David's plan had worked, for the time being at least. At least now I'd have a chance to explain things to my parents first.

The rest of the week passed by in a blur of fear, heartache and disappointment. I was supposed to have another bail hearing, but it was postponed. Debbie made her application on the Wednesday, only to be told the case had been put back a month. Karen went for bail on the Thursday and was turned down flat.

The heartache was reserved mostly for my parents who, after hearing the sordid details of my ordeal, became convinced that I was holding back on all sorts of other horrors, no matter how much I tried to persuade them otherwise. From that moment on, anything they saw on television or read in newspapers about prison life, whether in Holloway or elsewhere, in Britain or abroad, became part and parcel of my daily existence.

All this was interwoven with the constant fear that Matt might take his story to one of the daily papers or that it might get leaked to some tabloid TV show.

And of course, all these events were taking place against the background of preparing for a trial which, if I were found guilty, would lead to a sentence of at least eighteen years.

By the time I found myself back in O'Connor's office the following Saturday, I thought I'd prepared myself for the worst. I was wrong. 'It's definitely going in the paper tomorrow,' he told me. 'They've been on the phone again and we know a little bit more about what they're planning. They have come to us saying you were doing this and that but we have told them it's not true, that you were the victim. They're still going ahead but we don't know for sure which way they are going to play the piece.'

'When you say "doing this and that", what exactly do you mean, Mr O'Connor?' I knew he didn't want to tell me and I didn't really want to hear, but at the same time I knew I had to know.

'They seem to be implying that you led him on, that you were . . . performing.'

I left O'Connor's office numb with shock. This was even worse than anything I had imagined. And even though I'd prepared my family and friends by telling them the truth, a story that somehow suggested I had started it all would be worse than *their* fears, too. Matt was taking his revenge on my getting him kicked out of

Holloway. He was going to make sure the whole world thought of me exactly the same way he did: as a slut.

I was taken back to my cell and was sitting on my bed, staring at a spot on the wall opposite, in some kind of a trance. I suddenly realised that I hadn't moved for more than an hour, when I felt my cellmate's hand on my shoulder. Her fingers felt warm through the thick material of my blouse. 'I know things are tough, Tracy, but I can help you take the pain away. Isn't that what you want?' Her voice was deep and comforting.

'What are you talking about? Do you mean drugs?'

'No, don't be silly. Something much better than that. Look, it's all ready for you.' On the bed beside me was a length of white cotton. She had taken the laces out of my trainers and tied them together. 'All you have to do,' my cellmate continued, 'is fix them together and make a loop. You can put it through the window. That's how they all do it.'

'But what about my family?'

'What about them? Your family can't help you take the pain away. It's the only way. It's the only thing you can do.'

For a split second it seemed to be the answer to all my prayers, just the escape I'd been looking for. But then as the full horror of what I was contemplating sank in, I realised I could never go through with it. Furious, I turned on my cellmate.

'No. No way. Never. Shut up, just shut up and leave me alone! Just get out. Get out of my cell!'

My cell! I whipped round to face my cellmate but there was no one there. Then I realised that both voices had been coming out of my own mouth. I was in a single cell on my own and I'd been having an argument, out loud, with myself. Not only that, I'd somehow taken the laces out of my shoes and tied them into a makeshift noose without realising it.

I was losing my mind.

I went over to the hatch, I listened at the window, I looked under the bed and in the chest of drawers. I was shouting into the dark corners. I was desperate to find someone hiding just so I could prove that I wasn't going crazy. But there was no one. I was all alone. I started to panic – hyperventilating, crying, sweating, shaking. One minute I was burning up with heat, the next I was freezing cold.

I started running around in circles, spinning faster and faster, smashing into walls and furniture, blinded by panic and oblivious to pain. I was desperate to get away but there was nowhere to go.

Then the voices started up again, all around me. And somewhere in the middle of them I could hear someone who sounded like Linda, calling my name again and again. She was telling me that everything was going to be OK and that I should calm down, but I didn't want to listen. I didn't believe it was her; I was sure it was all coming from inside me.

Realising she had no way of getting through to me, Linda pressed the panic alarm and the screw on night patrol, Mr Coutts, came rushing over.

By the time he poked his head through my hatch, I was sprawled on the floor in a pile of my own puke. I had thrown up so much that there was nothing left inside but I continued to dry-heave again and again, convulsing as if I was having some kind of fit.

Coutts started talking to me. His voice was deep, calm and relaxed. He kept talking and talking.

Following his instructions, I slowly dragged myself over to the hatch and sat, slumped, on the toilet. Coutts reached through, took hold of my hand and began stroking it, all the while telling me that everything was going to be all right. And that was where he stayed for the next two hours. There is no doubt about it – he and Linda saved my life that night.

The following morning the door to my cell was opened up early and three officers with sympathetic looks on their faces walked in. I hadn't slept a wink, hadn't even bothered to get undressed.

'It's in the paper,' said Patel. 'Do you want to see it?'

'Well, I've got to see it sometime.'

'I've got to tell you, Tracy, it's bad, it's really bad.'

My hands were shaking as I took the paper from him and flicked through to pages 12 and 13. The headline – PAGE 3 GIRL PEELS OFF IN JAIL CELL FOR BANANAS AND VODKA – made me shudder, but what really caught my eye was a picture of Vanessa in the centre of the text. 'Oh the poor cow,' I said out loud. 'They've gone and dragged her into all this as well. As if she hasn't got enough to deal with.'

There was also a picture of Matt taken outside his home and one of the worst ever pictures of me. I was virtually naked but hiding my private parts by sitting cross-legged. My only items of clothing were a scarf and a pair of legwarmers. It was awful. It was so . . . eighties. I looked like a real dog.

But the biggest shock was still to come. I started reading the article and once I got to the third paragraph I realised with horror that it was Vanessa who had sold the story to the paper in the first place. Not only that, she had gilded the lily in order to up the selling price.

According to her version of events, I had begged Matt for alcohol and agreed to take off my clothes in return. She said I had performed a raunchy strip show for Matt, who was heard outside my cell groaning in ecstasy. The paper quoted her as saying: 'We asked her what she had to do for him in return and she showed us. It was a really raunchy performance – it almost made me blush to watch her and she had all her clothes on. The peep show continued all week. But by the end of the week Matt couldn't contain his excitement and his groaning woke up the rest of the landing.'

I couldn't believe what Vanessa had done. Never in a million years would I have dreamed that she would betray me like that.

The article soon found its way around the prison and a lot of the inmates believed it was true. They suddenly started showing me loads of respect, believing that I really had managed to get one of the screws to give me decent food and some booze by showing him my tits. Other inmates hated me for it and shouted abuse every time they saw me. I did my best to put them all straight but I knew that my life in prison – let alone my life outside – would never be the same again.

I couldn't escape the feeling that the management at Holloway would have liked the whole thing to be swept under the carpet and forgotten about. After all, the attack had taken place nine months ago. Other than Matt being moved to another prison, nothing had been done. But now the story was about to be made public, the prison had no choice but to take action.

On my third visit to Governor O'Connor's office in as many days, he explained that a tribunal would be held the following week to see whether Matt should be dismissed. It would take place in the prison's boardroom and be attended by O'Connor, McCauley, a governor from another prison, a secretary, Matt and his legal representative.

The whole thing would be just like a court case. There would be character evidence, statements from eye-witnesses and even forensic evidence. Several screws would be making an appearance, some speaking in support of Matt, others against him. Vanessa had been called but it was no great surprise to learn that she had declined to attend.

'Will I be able to have legal representation?'

O'Connor shook his head. 'No, absolutely not.'

'But how come Matt can and I can't? That's not fair.'

'I'm sorry, Tracy, I don't make the rules. That's just the way it is.'

In the end he agreed to a minor compromise. He gave permission for Linda to come into the tribunal with me as a McKenzie friend so at least I wouldn't have to go through the ordeal alone.

In a perfect world I would have liked for Karen to have been at the tribunal with me but she had enough problems of her own to deal with.

Because she was on a different wing and level, our only chance to meet would be at Cunts' Corner, but for Karen every visit was a traumatic and emotionally draining experience. She would spend the whole time with her beautiful three-year-old daughter, Paige, building towers from bricks, filling in colouring books, completing jigsaws and reading fairy tales. By the time the visit was over you could feel the love between them from the other side of the room. And that's when the screws would arrive to take Paige away.

It was always the same. Paige would throw herself around Karen's neck and refuse to leave. When the screws ran out of patience Paige's father would grab at the little girl's arms and legs to pull her away. Then Paige would start screaming, 'Mummy, mummy, mummy' at the top of her voice, again and again and again. Sometimes she'd manage to grab Karen's sleeve or trouser leg at the last minute and cling on as if her life depended on it, tears racing down her cheeks, until her fingers were prized away. 'No, no mummy, no,' she would cry, but Karen was powerless to help.

As she was being dragged or carried out, Paige would be twisting and turning, scratching and punching and kicking in a desperate bid to get away. When that failed she would crane her neck to get one last glimpse of Karen before the door to the visiting room was slammed shut. Karen would be standing there, trying to be strong. 'Don't worry darling,' she'd say, 'Mummy will be home from work soon.' But inside she was falling to pieces.

She wasn't the only one – there were at least half a dozen toddlers at every visit and each and every one of them would go through the same process when they had to be separated from their mothers.

Back in Cunts' Corner you could still hear Paige and the other kids screaming and begging not to go. Karen would sit quietly, her eyes closed and perfectly still. You couldn't comfort her or even touch her — if you did she would break down completely. It would take her hours to recover from the ordeal and there was nothing anyone could do to help.

Despite her troubles Karen still managed to be a good friend to me in the run up to the tribunal, and other support came from the most unlikely places. Two days after my meeting with O'Connor, Maggie came running up to me during association. Although the bullying had all but stopped, we hadn't spoken properly since the scissors incident. Now it was as if she wanted to be my friend again.

'I saw the article. I can't believe that Vanessa turned into such a cunt,' she said. 'It's disgusting. I've had a letter from O'Connor asking if I'll appear at the tribunal, tell them what I saw. And I just wanted you to know that I will. I'll put them straight. I know Vanessa was my friend but this is bang out of order. And that cunt Matt is a total fucking pervert. He deserves everything that's coming to him.'

On the morning of the tribunal, I had planned to get to the boardroom early to allow my nerves to settle before anyone else arrived. But as I stood outside the door and waited for the screws to let me inside, I was informed that Matt was already there. My legs turned to jelly and all the courage that I had spent days building up suddenly deserted me. Linda and the screws barely managed to catch me before I crumpled to the ground.

'Come on, Tracy, you can do this.'

'I can't. I can't face him.'

'But you have to. You can't let him win. You have to be strong. You have to get through this. This is just what he's counting on – you not being able to go through with it. If you don't, then he gets off scot-free. He could even do it to someone else.'

And then I remembered what Matt had said about having been accused of attacking a prisoner before and having returned to his job because no one believed her. At that moment I knew I had to go forward, not just to clear my own name but also for the sake of those who had gone before and to ensure that after me, there would never be another.

The door swung open and my eyes fell on Matt straight away. He was sitting at a table with a copy of the article from the Sunday paper spread out in front of him. His thin lips were curled up into an arrogant smirk and the fingers of his free hand were slowly running back and forth over the picture of my semi-naked body.

It was the best thing he could have done. As soon as I realised what he was up to a surge of anger ripped through my body. My knees stopped knocking and I stood up straight and walked to my seat. Inside I was still petrified but there was no way I was going to let the bastard know it. I was going to beat him.

Linda reached under the table and took my hand, squeezing it gently. 'You're doing fine,' she whispered, 'you're doing really well.'

The other staff and governors arrived shortly afterwards and announced that the tribunal was ready to begin. O'Connor put his elbows up on the table and looked directly at me. 'OK, Tracy, you've made some serious allegations against this officer and . . .'

I half raised my hand. 'I have to stop you there. I did not make these allegations. Vanessa did. She is the one who has gone to the papers. This story is there because of her, not me. I only made a statement after the incident had been reported by others. I've been dragged into all this.'

There was a pause and O'Connor wrote something down in his notebook.

'OK. Well, can you tell us what happened, starting from the first night of the week that the officer was working nights?'

'No.'

'No? You mean you can't tell us?'

'I've taken legal advice and I'm not prepared to do that. I'm not going to sit here and go through everything that happened while he is here. I've made my statement and everything I have to say is contained within that. If you need to ask me questions, you can, but I'm not going to just sit here and repeat all the things he said to me.'

The idea of reliving the experience in front of a bunch of strangers sickened me and I hoped my little speech would put them off. O'Connor took my statement in his hands and began working his way through it, line by line.

Matt had started out looking smug but as the statement was read out and the specific details of the things he had said and done were aired in public and in full for the first time, his face became increasingly red. Instead of staring at me, he was now looking at the floor and shielding his eyes with one hand.

I said little – everything was there in my statement and there was nothing to add apart from the occasional 'Yes, that's right.' I did my best to keep my voice clear and strong. I could see the shock and horror on the faces of the other staff as the truth came out. I began to feel as though I'd done the right thing.

But then it was the turn of Matt's legal representative, Mr Johnson, to cross-examine me. 'Miss Kirby. My client has been a prison officer for many years. He has an impeccable record of conduct. Why on earth would he behave this way towards you?'

'I don't know. Why don't you ask him?'

'Isn't it true that my client was just doing his job? That you are lying? Isn't it true that you had been having nightmares and that as part of his usual rounds my client would look into your hatch to check that you were OK? And furthermore, isn't it true that he shared his food with you out of the goodness of his heart? And I can provide evidence that he has shared food with other prisoners before, not just you. It certainly was not in return for anything. These allegations are completely false, aren't they? You have made them up, haven't you?

'The truth is that you were flirting with my client to try and make your life in prison easier. And because he failed to take your bait, you have now turned on him. Isn't that the truth, Miss Kirby?'

Regardless of the facts, the defence for a charge of any form of sexual crime always proceeds in exactly the same way. They try to discredit the victim in every possible way. They say she is promiscuous, that she led the perpetrator on. They try to unsettle her by making her go into every intimate detail of what happened, making her repeat foul language or mimic obscene actions. Reliving a brutal and traumatic attack in front of a room full of strangers is a horrendous and humiliating experience. Many victims end up getting confused, making mistakes or simply breaking down. To a jury, it can look as though they have been caught lying. Their credibility falls to pieces and the accused walks free. It's the reason why only 3 per cent of rape cases that go to trial end in conviction.

David had warned me that, even though my case with Matt was only a tribunal, not a full-blown court case with a jury, the tactics would be no less underhand. I made denial after denial, but the onslaught continued. I told them Matt had started it all, that he had clearly been obsessed with me, but everything I said was turned around and used against me.

'What, you think my client is attracted to you?'

'Well . . . yes.'

'And how do you know that? How can you possibly know the inner workings of my client's mind?'

'Well, I'm not totally ignorant. I think he made it pretty obvious from the things he was saying.'

'Things that he denies saying. Things that we only have your word for.'

'Others heard them too.'

'Oh. Like Vanessa. Well her account here certainly doesn't seem to support yours.'

'Well . . . she . . .'

'For all we know, Miss Kirby, you may have conspired with Vanessa in order to sell the story to the papers yourself.'

I wanted to get up and walk out. How dare he suggest

such a thing? I took a deep breath. 'Excuse me, but have you actually read the story? Why on earth would I do something that makes me out to be a complete slut? Don't you think I've got enough problems in here without that kind of shit to deal with as well?'

'Then why do you think Vanessa did the story?'

'For the money, of course.'

'So you deny leading my client on, performing for him?'

'That never happened. Her story is a pack of lies.'

Under the table Linda squeezed my hand again. I was so glad she was there with me.

'My client says you were flirting with him.'

'No, absolutely not. No way.'

'He says, and in your own statement you agree, that there were many long discussions, sometimes lasting through to the early hours of the next day.'

'But that doesn't mean we were flirting.'

'He says you discussed various sexual acts.'

'He was saying things, not me. It wasn't a conversation!'

'My client says he has seen your breasts.'

'Everyone has. I used to be a Page Three-girl, for Christ's sake. But he never saw them in prison.'

'We only have your word for that. Let's move on. On the last night of his shift, what do you say my client was doing outside your cell?'

'He was masturbating.'

'How can you be certain?'

'I saw him doing it.'

'Doing what exactly?'

'Masturbating.'

'Did he have his trousers down?'

'No. But his zip was undone.'

'And then what?'

'What do you want me to say? He had it in his hand.'

'What was in his hand?'

My mind was racing. I was in a room with a bunch of middle-aged men. What was the most appropriate word under the circumstances? Cock? Prick? Knob?

'His penis.'

'So he was holding his penis.'

'Yes.'

'Which hand?'

'I don't know. I don't remember.'

'But you're certain you saw this.'

'Yes.'

'Even though the lights in the corridor were switched off.'

'Yes, there was light from the torch.'

'And where was the torch?'

'In his hand.'

'Which hand? The same hand?'

'I don't know, I can't remember. This was a year ago.'

'But you claim to have nightmares about this, to have relived it many times. And now you say you can't remember.'

'It could have been either hand. I couldn't see which hand.'

'But somehow you could see his penis.'

'I saw what he was doing.'

'Holding his penis in his hand.'

'Yes.'

'Just holding?'

'No, he was moving it up and down.'

The solicitor leaned forward, placing the flats of both his palms on the table. 'Up and down. How exactly? Can you demonstrate the action? Can you describe his penis?'

I turned to O'Connor. 'Are you going to allow this? This is disgraceful. He was masturbating. That says it all. Are you just going to sit there and allow him to ask me questions like that?'

O'Connor scratched his chin, then whispered something to the governor sitting beside him. 'I have to agree, Mr Johnson. I think the allegation is clear and supported by others. I don't think we need to hear any more detail on that particular aspect. Unless you have any more questions for Miss Kirby, then I'm going to dismiss her.'

I sat on a bench outside the boardroom, waiting for the other witnesses to finish giving their evidence, in case I needed to be recalled.

It was the first time I'd ever been cross-examined and the whole experience made me realise how difficult it was going to be when I appeared on the witness stand during my own trial. Although the case was still months away, I could just imagine the questions that I'd be asked and the way the jury would respond to them. 'Didn't you ever think to count the money? Didn't you think it was odd that you were handing over the cash in restaurants, not in an office?'

I can handle that sort of situation when it happens on the spur of the moment, but when there is a long build-up, I get myself into such a state that I burst into tears, have panic attacks and develop a desperate need to go to the toilet. What worried me most was that if

I kept crying and making excuses to leave the court, the jury would be convinced that I was lying, not that I was ill.

As I sat there, Patel walked past, having finished giving his portion of evidence. 'You should have told us straight away,' he said. 'This should have happened months ago.'

'I thought you'd all stick together. That's what Matt said would happen.'

Patel smiled warmly. 'But just because we all do the same job doesn't mean we're all the same. The guy's got some friends here but a lot of us think he's an arsehole and a pervert. We're not going to protect him because we don't want to have to work with people like that.'

An hour later Mr O'Connor emerged from the boardroom and told me they had finished hearing all the evidence and that they had to go off to make their decision. Until then, I'd have to go back to my cell.

It was just starting to get dark and I'd almost given up hope of hearing anything that day when O'Connor appeared at my hatch. 'I wanted you to know as soon as possible: we found him guilty. He has been sacked. That's the end of it.'

In fact it didn't end there and then. Matt appealed against the decision of the tribunal and it took another three months before he was finally out of the job for good. I later learned that during that time his wife had left him and he had been forced to move out of his house and was having trouble finding work.

I didn't lose any sleep.

Chapter Sixteen

Losing one's liberty affects different people in different ways. As the anniversary of my arrest and arrival at Holloway approached, I could see that freedom had come to mean something different to each and every girl there.

To Julie, it was all about sitting in the corner of a smoky pub with a bunch of friends, checking out the talent and knocking back pints of lager top. Karen, on the other hand, wanted nothing more than to be able to cuddle her daughter through the night and never again to have to watch her being dragged away, kicking and screaming and crying, after just half an hour together. Debbie talked constantly about going shopping. She longed for the day she could walk down a road – any road – and walk into a shop – any shop – and look around for as long as she wanted. It really didn't matter where the shop was or what they were selling, to Debbie freedom was all about making her own decisions and having the ability to go wherever she pleased.

For me it was even simpler. I'd always hated the fact that, at the first sign of drizzle, all outdoor activity would be cancelled and we'd have to spend the whole day cooped up inside. As time went by, my frustration at being denied the opportunity to feel the rain on my face grew into an obsession.

I worked out that if I sat on the radiator in my cell and opened the window slats as far as they would go, I could push my bare legs and arms out just enough to feel a few drops on my toes and the tips of my fingers. Sometimes I'd let my hands get wet and then rub the water over my face – the closest I could get to what I really wanted.

I must have looked like a complete idiot and it soon became something of a joke on the wing, but I really didn't care. Every inmate develops their own little quirks and tricks to help them hold on to their sanity, and this was mine. A little humiliation was nothing: I sometimes thought I would have given my soul for a walk in the rain.

My trial had been due to take place in the summer but just after my anniversary the judge announced that, because there were so many defendants, he was going to split the proceedings in two. At the very earliest my trial would not take place until the following January. There was no chance of bail and I had to accept that even if I were found not guilty and allowed to go free, I would still have spent almost two years in prison.

The passage of time did nothing to make life inside any easier. In fact, the longer I spent at Holloway, the harder it became to deal with. It got to the stage where every morning, as soon as I opened my eyes, my first thought would be: Oh God no, I can't do this, I can't do this. Then I'd spend the next ten minutes trying to talk myself into getting up, getting dressed and making it through another twenty-four hours. Come on, Tracy, you can get through one more day. Just get through one more day, I'd tell myself over and over again.

It would be rare to get through a day without some kind of confrontation, especially on the reception wing, with its constant flow of new faces. Every minute outside my cell was a minute I'd have to spend battling to survive. I was always tense, anxious about what might happen, where the next threat might come from.

Every now and then I'd come across someone decent and that would be a nice surprise, but most of the time many of the prisoners were off their heads on drugs. If they even so much as looked at you for too long you'd have to rush over and give them a dose of verbal, shouting and swearing like a maniac, simply because you couldn't afford to show any sign of weakness.

At first it was all an act. Inside I'd be shaking like a leaf, dying with fear, but I couldn't afford to show it. Then, for the next few days, I'd have to have eyes in the back of my head to make sure I didn't get attacked. As time went by, it became second nature. My pretend rage got replaced with the real thing and I realised with horror that a part of me almost enjoyed the buzz it gave. A year in prison had turned me into an animal and driven me to the verge of insanity.

For some of the screws, all this tension and anger was just another excuse to play their sick mind games. They would never actively set people up against one another, but if they felt the balance of power had been disturbed, they'd give someone the nod to carry out an attack. They would either turn a blind eye, or only jump in and break it up after the person they championed had got a few good punches in.

Along with the self-loathing, dark thoughts would fill my head. It had been six months since the night I had first contemplated suicide and ever since, the idea had come back to haunt me on a regular basis. There had been a time when I could have simply dismissed the idea of it because I just wasn't the type. But once you have sunk that low, you cross a barrier and from that moment on, whenever things get on top of you, death really does seem the only way out.

I was only just managing to hold on. Others were not so lucky.

It was halfway through breakfast one morning, and dozens of girls were milling along the corridor to join the queue as I carried the hot water urn from the kitchen to the serving area.

I had to dodge sideways as a girl who had seemingly forgotten something slipped out of the queue and squeezed past me to get into the big dormitory opposite the kitchen. As soon as she got inside the door she started screaming, 'Help me, for God's sake somebody help me! She's dead, she's fucking dead!'

I dropped the urn and rushed towards the dorm. The sight that confronted me there is something that will haunt me for the rest of my life: a thin blonde girl was dying right before my eyes.

After her cellmates had left for breakfast she had knelt on the rim of the toilet, tied two shoelaces together to make a noose and managed to loop them around a rail. She had then thrown herself forward as hard as she could, tightening the noose and driving the laces deep into her neck.

It had only been a few seconds but already she looked horrific. Her eyes were bulging right out of their sockets and had swelled up to twice their normal size. Her lips were so drained of colour that they were turning blue and her tongue was hanging down limply, almost touching her chin. She was making a sound like a hoarse, rattling cough. It was coming right from her throat, along with a frothing green pus. More froth was pouring out of her nose and her whole body had gone limp and was hanging forward off the toilet. It was clear that she didn't have long left.

The girl who had been screaming for help was desperately trying to get her fingers underneath the laces, but they had been pulled far too tight and bitten into the flesh so far that it was impossible.

There was no time to think and no one else around to do anything. I knew I had to take the pressure off her neck. I turned and dived underneath her, supporting her with my back. I lay crouched on the floor, snot and bile and froth cascading down into my hair and around the sides of my face, while the other girl started frantically scrabbling at the knot holding the laces together. It was no good – that too had been pulled too tight.

Even though I was supporting her, the girl was still dying. The laces had cut off the blood and air to her brain. I could hear her breathing getting more and more shallow and slowing down. She was on her way out. The obvious thing to do would be to cut the laces but this was prison: access to knives, scissors or anything sharp is strictly controlled. I felt utterly helpless and the moment seemed to go on for ever.

Just then two screws came running into the dormitory. They were both young, quite new to the job, and had clearly never seen anything like it before. They just stood there, transfixed by the gruesome sight, like rabbits caught in the headlights of a car.

'Don't just stand there, get some fucking scissors, get me some fucking scissors,' I kept on screaming until one of them finally snapped out of his trance and went running off to the office to get a knife.

He returned with a whole bunch of other screws. They surrounded the toilet, lifted the girl up and cut the laces. As I pulled myself up off the floor they carried her to a bed in the dormitory and gave her mouth-to-mouth while others prepared a stretcher to take her down to the hospital wing.

I could hear her coughing and choking. Her breathing was still erratic but now there was a chance she was going to make it. One of the screws came over and gripped my shoulder. 'Well done, Tracy. I think you saved her life.'

Two days later Linda used her red band to go and see the girl to find out how she was getting on. She returned with a crumpled slip of paper on which the girl had scrawled a message for me. I waited until I got back to my cell before unravelling it to see what she had to say.

'You stupid fucking bitch. What gives you the right to put your nose into other people's business? You were well out of order. You should have let me die. You should have kept right out of it. Now I'm on fucking suicide watch. Thanks for nothing, you selfish cow. If I ever see you, I'll fucking kill you.' Only in prison can saving someone's life make an enemy out of them.

I later learned that the girl, who was just eighteen years old, had only two more weeks to serve before she was due to be released. Part of her parole conditions was that she had to reside at her parents' house, but the reason she had run away and got in trouble in the first place was because her father was abusing her. With her release date coming up her only choices in life were to return to the abuse or run away and live on the streets.

She'd decided that she'd rather be dead.

By the summer, Karen and I were the only members of our original group left at Holloway, though because we were on different wings I only ever saw her during visits. Although we would all face trial together, Debbie and Sylvie had been given bail, while Jan had clearly made other arrangements.

There were changes at the wing cleaners' annexe too. Maggie was gone, and there were some new faces. Of these, by far my favourite was Eileen.

In prison, everyone is innocent. It's such a standing joke that you never seriously ask anyone whether they are guilty of what they have been accused of because the answer is always no. I'd long since given up trying to explain my own situation because I just sounded like everyone else. But in Eileen's case, there was not a single person in the prison, not even the screws, who felt that she should have been there.

A beautiful black woman in her early thirties, Eileen had travelled to London from her native Jamaica, where she worked as a professional singer and songwriter with a fair degree of success. She had made a few well-received records, got quite a bit of record company interest and had been invited to come to meet up with some of the executives at one of the big labels.

Her whole family, including her five-year-old daughter, were really excited, as it seemed almost certain that she was going to be offered a deal. To help carry her music samples a close friend had given her a special case as a present while her friend's sister, who lived in London, had arranged to pick her up at the airport and give her a place to stay.

As Eileen came through Customs she was stopped on a routine search. When the officer examined her case, he discovered that several kilos of cocaine had been stitched into the lining. The whole thing was a set-up, a deal that her so-called friend and sister had put together without her knowledge, but Eileen couldn't prove any of it and she was the only one to be charged.

Back in Jamaica, Eileen had been a regular churchgoer – she had started out as a gospel singer before broadening her horizons – and she invited me to join her at the chapel in Holloway where she would be singing a couple of gospel songs. Having heard her singing bits and pieces as she went about her work, I knew she had an amazing voice and was keen to hear more.

Most people in prison occupy the bottom rung of the ladder in society. Anyone with any kind of talent – especially the kind that even the most ignorant people can appreciate – is really looked up to. People listen to what they have to say and seek out their advice. Within weeks of her arrival, Eileen had become one of the most respected women in the prison without ever having to throw a single punch.

We arrived at the chapel to find it completely packed. This often happens in prison because inmates see 'finding God' as a way of proving to the parole board that they are reformed characters and therefore ready to be released back into society. The problem, however, is that with only one chapel in the prison it also serves as the perfect meeting place for inmates from different wings, be they friends or enemies. You could feel the tension building as the service began and I leaned over to Eileen: 'I don't like this, it's going to go off in here.' Eileen agreed and we slowly began working our way towards the exit just as the first of several chairs flew overhead and the whole place exploded into a massive brawl.

Apart from finding God, the other common form of self-discovery among inmates at women's prisons is to find that they are gay. (A small number find both.) You have lesbians in prison, of course, a good number of them among the staff, and you have straight girls. Then you have straight girls who realise they have been living a lie and become gay. And then you have straight girls who, after months without sex, become what is known as 'prison bent'. That means that, rather than being fully gay, they become gay just for the duration of their time in prison.

The difficulty for the lesbians is knowing whether the people they get involved with are fully bent or just prison bent. To be with someone who is fully bent means the relationship can prosper after release or even if they are transferred to different prisons. To be with someone who is prison bent means they are setting themselves up to get their hearts broken.

Sometimes those who were curious about their own sexuality, or sitting on the fence, would be targeted by the older and more experienced inmates. It almost became a game to try and guess who would 'turn' next. It made no difference how much of a man eater the girl was, whether she was married with kids or had a boyfriend waiting for her on the outside.

Few of the relationships lasted for any length of time and they almost always ended badly. At least 80 per cent of prison fights are down to problems within relationships. The two Spanish girls I had briefly shared a cell with certainly had their problems. At one point they split up and started going out with other people. In the weeks that followed they would fight every time they saw each other, until they somehow worked out their differences and got back together.

The whole gay thing was a regular topic of conversation, especially during exercise time, when there would always be at least one couple going at each other in the corner.

'You never know,' Julie told me one day. 'If you're in here long enough, it might happen to you.'

I shook my head vigorously. 'I don't think so. Sex has never been my governor. I don't think I'll ever get that desperate.'

'Yeah,' added Julie. 'I know what you mean. I've got a right hand and a hairbrush. I don't need anything else.'

Two weeks later, Julie turned.

Another new face at the annexe and one who was to become a firm friend was Amanda.

When she turned up – stocky with short-cropped hair and looking exactly like the sort of woman who joins the police or the SAS – we were convinced she was a plant. She was supposed to be linked to the Michael

Michael trial and had been arrested as a direct result of information that Customs had gleaned from Michael's comprehensive records, but neither I nor Karen nor anyone else attached to the case had ever heard of her.

During her first few weeks no one would have anything to do with her because of the rumours that she was an undercover Customs officer, trying to pick up information about drugs cases by posing as a prisoner.

The truth, we soon discovered, was that she was pretty much in the same boat as the rest of us. We became good friends and, with Debbie out on bail, Amanda became my main work partner during my cleaning shifts. She also became a key witness to the continuing abuse I suffered at the hands of the Vulture.

One of our main jobs as wing cleaners was to clean out cells that had been vacated, so they would be ready for new inmates. We would work our way along the corridor and enter and clean any cells that had been left open (they are normally locked to protect people's personal possessions).

On one particular day I noticed the Vulture coming out of a cell a few doors down. There was no reason for her to have done anything except open the door so the cell would be ready for cleaning and I was immediately suspicious. I told Amanda what I'd seen and suggested that she come in with me to act as a witness in case anything was amiss.

Inside the cell, everything seemed normal until I looked over to the bed. On a table to one side were two small white tablets, each embossed with a symbol that resembled a small bird. It didn't take a genius to work out what they were. But it made no sense.

In the modern prison world, drugs have all but eclipsed tobacco as a form of currency. The most common way of smuggling them in is for a girl to get her boyfriend to secrete a package under his foreskin. After getting through the search, he removes the drugs while queuing up for the visiting room (it's too crowded for anyone to be able to see this happening) and places the package under his tongue. It remains there until the end of the visit when it is passed to the inmate in a French kiss who then swallows it. Once she has returned to her cell the recipient shits the package out a few days later or, for a more instant high, forces her fingers down her throat and brings it up that way.

Cannabis, cocaine, ecstasy and heroin are all widely available but prescription drugs are also popular. In fact, they are such a valuable commodity that people suffering from serious medical conditions have been known to save their medication to sell on to others. At Holloway, as with many other women's prisons, epileptic fits are a regular occurrence, because the drug used to control them has narcotic qualities and sells like hot cakes on the black market.

All such trading is strictly forbidden and anyone caught with drugs that have not been prescribed to them gets a trip to the punishment block. It means that no girl with half a brain would leave her pills on her bedside table for the entire world to see; she'd crotch them and take them with her. There was only one explanation: the Vulture had to have planted them.

I took the pills and, with Amanda as my witness, I threw them in the bin. I could have gone to one of the other screws and reported that I'd found them, but then the girl who had moved out of the cell – whoever that was – would get done for having drugs and I'd have another enemy. But even though I'd got rid of the drugs, I knew exactly what was going to happen next. 'This is one big set-up,' I told Amanda. 'She's hoping I'll take the drugs and sell them. I bet you anything in the world that I'm gonna get a visit from the DST tonight.'

The DST – dedicated search team – is by far the most feared group of screws in any prison. Rather than the traditional uniform of straight black trousers and pressed white shirts, they wear combat trousers, military-style bomber jackets and heavy boots, all of it pitch black. To see the DST march through a corridor is to know that someone is in big trouble. The team's members spend their whole time searching for drugs and other contraband. They carry specialised equipment to allow them to take apart anything they might find inside a cell in their quest for drugs, and can strip an entire room in less than half an hour.

They make sure they handle every single item of your clothing, every single thing you possess, just to be sure. Their remit includes a thorough strip search of their target, in which the person has to squat while naked, ensuring that any items which have been crotched are likely to fall out. Even for those people who have nothing to fear, a search by the DST is a humiliating and uncomfortable experience.

In my whole time at Holloway I'd never been subjected to a DST search. The nicer screws on the staff sussed out pretty quickly that I wasn't into drugs and, although I still had to undergo the regular urine tests, they were usually quite lenient with me because they always knew I would be clean.

Today was different.

Amanda had spread the news of what had happened earlier in the day around the annexe, from where it had spread around the entire wing. As the DST came into the wing cleaners' sitting area where Amanda, Eileen and I were watching television, there was a whisper echoing around the building: 'Tracy's been set up.' The atmosphere was so thick you could have cut it with a knife.

The DST consisted of two women and one man, but the Vulture was with them. 'We have reason to believe you may have drugs in your cell,' she said. 'We are going to conduct a search.'

I looked across at Amanda as if to say, 'Told you so.'

The male officer waited outside my cell while I went inside, followed by the Vulture and the two female screws.

'You know the drill,' said the Vulture, a smug, self-satisfied grin on her face. 'Drop 'em.'

I knew exactly what was going on. It was just another attempt to break me. Inside I was fuming, but there was no way in the world I was going to give her the satisfaction of knowing that she had got to me. I stripped down to my underwear and kept my voice calm and casual. We could have been discussing the weather.

'No problem. Top half or bottom half, what would you prefer?'

'Get your top off, Kirby.'

I did as she asked, doing a little spin. She checked my bra then threw it on the bed. 'Now the rest.'

'Fancy,' I said with a sigh, 'of all the days you are

doing this to me, this is the one time I don't have my matching La Perla on.' I did another little spin. 'Is that OK? Is that all right for you?'

The Vulture waved her hand towards the door. 'Just put your clothes back on and get out.'

I went back to the sitting area, where Eileen and Amanda were discussing what they could do about what had happened. It didn't take us long to come to the conclusion that we were completely powerless. Even if we made an official complaint, no one would believe us. Even if I'd kept the drugs, I could never prove that the Vulture had planted them. There was nothing to do but sit and wait.

A cell search normally takes forty-five minutes at the most. It took the Vulture and her team more than two hours before they finally accepted that the drugs were not there. Still unwilling to accept defeat, the Vulture emerged from my cell holding a pillow.

'We found this. You've got one pillow too many; I'm taking this one away,' she said, trying to make it sound like a victory.

'Well, I hope you're pleased with yourself. I've been watching TV and I've had three cups of tea.'

'Fuck you, Kirby.'

It didn't end there, of course. A month later the Vulture managed to trick me into cleaning out a cell that she knew had been infested with lice and was due to be fumigated. Another time she spread a rumour that my charges had been dropped and I was about to go home, knowing that I'd hear it from other inmates and be devastated when I learned it wasn't true.

Whenever there was bad news, like my trial being

delayed again or one of the other defendants getting a big sentence, the Vulture would be the one to tell me. That's how much she hated me.

She also continued her trick of hiding cigarette butts behind radiators and spilling coffee on floors that we had cleaned to make it look as though we weren't doing our jobs properly. Her tactics proved so effective that everyone on the annexe had their pay cut from £9 per week to just £7 as punishment for failing to come up to scratch.

Another time she grabbed me just as I was on my way to breakfast.

'Hello, Tracy, just wanted to be the first to congratulate you.'

'On what?'

'Well, you've been here for nineteen months and you still haven't gone to trial. You've just become the longest-serving remand prisoner in the history of Holloway.'

'But my trial's at least three months away.'

'I know. Isn't it great? It means no one will ever be able to take your record away.'

Somehow I managed to rise above it all, apart from one time when, already feeling low, I saw her at my hatch just before lights out. The Vulture knew only too well through her network of spies and sources that Maria and I used to be friends and that I had not seen her since being in prison. So when she offered to lend me her newspaper, she was counting on the fact that the lead story in the gossip column would upset me. And she was right.

Maria had given birth to a baby boy. She had gone

through the entire process – pregnancy and birth – without my knowing anything about it.

Not everyone hated Holloway as much as I did. One girl, Kay, had been in and out of there so many times that she considered it a second home. On average she'd come in for two weeks on some minor charge then get kicked out, only to reappear a few weeks later. During the time I was there, Kay must have come to the prison at least thirty times.

We became good friends and I soon learned there was a method in her madness. She had a bad drug habit and was living on the streets. Being in Holloway meant three meals a day and a roof over her head. Also, after two weeks in prison you are entitled to a discharge grant of £90 when you leave. Kay would smash a shop window to get herself arrested, spend a fortnight eating as much as possible then take her money, go back to the streets and blow it all on drink and drugs.

One time they tried to kick her out after only a week, which meant she'd get no grant. She refused to go and when the screws went into her cell to get her out she had stripped naked and smeared shit all over her body. She sat on her bed with her legs wide open and her unwashed and seriously rank private parts point-ing towards the door. 'Come on in and get me then you bastards,' she screamed. Not surprisingly, no one went near her.

She remained in virtually the same position for the next two days until a bunch of kindly screws working on reception had a whip round and got together enough cash to convince her to leave.

Despite such distractions and a host of other weird and wonderful characters coming in and out of the prison, by the time Christmas came around again, and with it an overbearing feeling of depression, I was starting to feel as though I'd spent my entire life at Holloway.

During my first Christmas, the Vulture had been on duty and ensured everything was miserable. This year she would be off, and I planned to make the most of it. I asked the senior wing officer whether, as the corridor in the annexe had a locking door, it would be possible to set up a table in the centre so that all the girls could have lunch together. He thought it was a great idea and agreed immediately.

I knew I was going to find another Christmas away from my family just as hard as the other prisoners would, but somehow, having something to do, trying to make things as nice as possible for everyone else, took my mind off my unhappiness.

Amanda and I spent all morning getting the annexe ready, using strips of toilet paper to make streamers and flowers to decorate the table. When the rest of the girls returned they were so impressed they gave us a standing ovation.

The only thing missing from the spread was any kind of alcohol, but no one really minded that much. A few girls throughout the prison had set up their own illicit distilleries and were knocking out hooch – fermented in a bin liner from old bits of fruit and leftover potato – at a few quid per glass, but only the most desperate hardened alcoholics would go anywhere near the stuff. I had tried it once, a few months earlier, out of a desperate desire to get drunk and make the time go faster. Big mistake. The foul-smelling black liquid that looked like a cross between shit and gravy did nothing apart from make me throw up and give me a headache. It was as if I'd missed out on the fun stage of drunkenness and gone straight to the morning after. Rather than risking it again, I was happy to face the festive season stone cold sober.

Before we sat down I joined the queue for the telephones and called my family. That was hard. I could hear all my uncles, aunts and cousins in the background, as well as my brother and sisters, and more than anything I wanted to be there with them. Christmas is a strong tradition in my family. There had been only two times when we had not all been together, both of them because I was in prison.

Back in the annexe, everyone was doing their best to put on a brave face but one of the new cleaners, Jessica, went into her cell and refused to come out. She had a couple of kids and I knew she was missing them terribly. I didn't know how to play it. In the end I decided I had to be cruel to be kind because she was bringing everybody else down.

I went into her cell. 'Listen, you're ruining this for everyone out there. You're not the only one. We're all in the same boat, we're all devastated that we're locked up on Christmas Day but we're trying to put on a brave face and you've got to do the same. So pull yourself together and get your arse out there. If you don't come out in five minutes, we're all coming in and we're going to drag you out.'

I went back into the corridor and sat at the table. I was full of anxiety, wondering if I'd done the right thing or whether I'd gone too far. Then, two minutes later,

Jessica came out of her cell, walked over and gave me a big hug. 'Thanks, Tracy,' she whispered.

We finished our meal and started playing that game where someone puts an orange under their chin and has to pass it to the next person without using their hands. Although the orange started under my chin it quickly fell down to my cleavage and then to my crotch. All the while Amanda was rolling around on top of me, desperately trying to get at the orange. It was hilarious. I couldn't remember the last time I'd laughed so much.

Then, soon after 4 p.m., a bunch of screws appeared and said it was lock-up time. In prison all public holidays are treated like weekends, which means you get banged up in your cell in the middle of the afternoon.

As a minor concession, we got the screws to leave all the hatches down so we could talk. We were soon having a no-holds-barred, full-on conversation about sex – all the things we liked, all the things we missed and all the things we were going to do when we got out. It was one of those weird prison moments when you can almost forget where you are, one of those times when you feel almost . . . human.

Then the alarm sounded and I looked out of the window of my cell to see half a dozen pissed-off screws had taken up positions throughout the courtyard. It meant there had been a suicide, though there was no way of knowing whether it had been successful or not.

It didn't take long for the whole prison to break into a screeching rendition of Queen's 'Another One Bites the Dust'. Singing it at times like this was a grisly Holloway tradition. The first time I'd heard it I was so shocked that I tried to block out the sound, pulling my pillow over my head and stuffing my fingers in my ears. But that had been twenty months ago. That had been the old Tracy Kirby.

This time I stood boldly at the window, stamping my feet and clapping my hands along with everyone else. Then I knew, without a shadow of a doubt, that I had become one of them.

Eileen's case was about as open and shut as it is possible to be. She was the only defendant and there was only one charge, so after just four months on remand, her case came to court.

We all felt confident that once the jury heard the circumstances of her case, once they found out the kind of person she was and about the amazing talent she had, they would be able to see that she would never get involved in anything like drug-smuggling.

We had become firm friends and when I said goodbye to her the day before her trial began, I fully expected that the next time I'd see her would be across the table in the visiting room.

It was not to be. The trial lasted just over a week and news of the result spread through the prison like wildfire. Eileen had been found guilty. And she had been sentenced to eleven years.

It was after lock-up when they brought her back into her cell in the annexe. She looked as though she had aged a decade in the time she had been away. She spent ages stumbling around like a zombie, her face frozen in shock. The news was being shouted from window to window, block to block, and no one could quite believe it.

Through my hatch I could see her sitting on the floor

in the middle of her cell. Her legs were tucked underneath her knees and her arms were folded tightly across the middle of her chest. She was slowly rocking back and forth, tears streaming down her cheeks. For the next three hours all she could say was: 'My daughter, my daughter, my daughter, my daughter.'

After a while I could hardly bear to look at or listen to her. Part of me wanted to rush over and console her but the rest just wanted to get as far away as possible. It was all too close to home, all too real

But there was no way to escape from it. If they could find Eileen guilty of smuggling drugs and sentence her to eleven years, then what chance did I stand?

Chapter Seventeen

The closer it got to the start of the trial, the sicker I became.

I couldn't help but fear the worst, especially after what had happened to Eileen. The growing sense of unease, combined with vivid memories of the vicious cross-examination I had suffered during the tribunal, played heavily on my mind and before long started to take its toll on my body.

A few days into the new year my IBS flared up like never before. I found I could no longer tolerate any dairy products. Even a small amount of milk in a cup of tea would lead to days of diarrhoea and stomach cramps so severe that I was often on the verge of passing out.

My claustrophobia was getting worse, too. I'd wake in the middle of the night drenched in sweat and convinced that I was about to suffocate. My nightmares became filled with images of sweatboxes and black walls closing in on me. After the few journeys I had made to court over the previous months I would arrive feeling wretched and exhausted. It had been bad enough when I had nothing more to do than sit there and listen to the judge refuse my bail application, but once the trial started I'd need to be razor sharp.

I'd have to pay attention to every word to make sure my legal team challenged anything that was incorrect, and at some point I'd have to go into the witness box and give the story from my point of view. But I knew that after an hour and a half in a sweatbox I'd be in no fit state to count to ten, let alone defend myself against drug-trafficking charges.

I made an application to the governor, who, after consulting my medical records to confirm that my condition wasn't a recent invention, agreed that I could make the journey to and from court in either a minivan or a car.

I'd hoped that having one less thing to worry about might reduce my stress levels, but two days before the trial was due to start, the judge announced that it would be postponed for at least a week. During that time my health got worse and worse. I assumed it was just pre-trial jitters and that once we actually got going things would improve. I was soon to learn, however, that the trauma of a court case would make my time at Holloway seem like a walk in the park.

My wake-up call came at 5.30 a.m., two hours ahead of normal in order to give the prison staff time to get me 'processed' and through the rush-hour traffic to Plumstead in south London.

It was far too early for the kitchens to have anything ready so instead, as for every other inmate on her way to court, the screw who woke me up passed a 'breakfast bag' through my hatch and informed me that tea or coffee would be available a little later.

Rubbing my bleary eyes, I took my bag back to the bed, sat down and emptied out the contents. There was a small plastic bowl with a matching spoon, two soggy Weetabix, a small carton of milk and a single slice of white bread. The cereal was no good to me because I couldn't tolerate the milk. Tea and coffee were off limits for the same reason. I searched through the bag looking for margarine, jam – anything to make the bread a little more palatable – but there was nothing. I ate it dry and later washed it down with a glass of tap water.

It was Monday morning and my last prison meal had been at four on Sunday afternoon. Luckily I'd had a Pot Noodle in my cell to get me through the night, but a couple of hours after my bread-and-water breakfast, sitting in the back of the minivan on my way to court, I was hungry again.

We arrived at the Woolwich court complex on the edge of Belmarsh maximum-security prison just after 9 a.m. The magistrates' and crown court sit next to one another on a grassy strip at the edge of the car park. Both are made of the same bright yellow brick used to construct the prison itself, but they are considerably more approachable thanks to the two-storey-high glass door and windows that make up the entrances. Famously, there is a tunnel between the courts and the prison so that the most dangerous inmates – terrorists, mass murderers and large-scale drug dealers – can move between the two without ever having to step into the outside world. As a lesser prisoner, I got to travel by a more conventional route: the back door.

The first three weeks of the case had been set aside for legal argument. This is where the barristers make representations about aspects of the case to decide what it is right and proper for the jury to hear. Although the jury is not allowed to be present, the defendants are required to attend throughout.

Karen and I were in the dock along with Sylvie and Debbie. It was the first time we had all been together for months and it was nice to see them again, but at the same time Karen and I felt strangely removed from them. They, after all, had been given bail while we remained in prison. A part of me found that difficult to deal with and at times I almost forgot they were there at all.

For the first week the discussions ranged from the admissibility of the surveillance evidence to the level of certainty that the prosecution could match the nicknames in Michael's records with the actual people accused of having worked for or with him.

The defence barristers were bringing up all sorts of grounds for why the case against us should have been thrown out but the judge dismissed them all and sided with the Crown Prosecution Service every time.

The debates were long and full of legal jargon and made little sense to me or any of my co-defendants, but we had to do our best to take in every word, just in case we overlooked something that might later prove crucial.

The court day usually finished at 4 p.m., but getting out of the cells and back into the van would often take another hour. That meant that the journey home would neatly coincide with the start of rush hour. On a good day we would arrive back at Holloway at seven; on a bad one, at least an hour later.

Either way, the kitchens had long closed up and the only food available for those returning from court would be one of the inedible microwave meals. I picked at what I could but my stomach seemed to be reacting badly to almost everything. I'd barely survived twenty-two months in prison. Now I started to question my ability to survive a four-month trial.

On the Monday morning at the start of the second week of legal argument, I was waiting with Karen in the prison yard when, instead of the usual two or more vehicles, a lone sweatbox rolled into view. A chill ran down my spine when I realised that the Vulture was on duty that morning.

'Come on then, Kirby, shake a leg,' she said.

'But I'm claustrophobic. It's in my medical records. I can't go in the sweatbox. The governor knows about it.'

'Well I don't. There's nothing about that down here.'

I could feel my breathing getting short and my palms growing sweaty. Oh God, please don't let me have a panic attack, please God. 'There must be a note of it somewhere, there must be,' I gasped. 'Everyone knows about it. I'm supposed to go to court in a car or a mini-van.' The Vulture shook her head. 'Well, no other transport has been ordered and it will take too long now. You'll have to go in the van.'

'No way.'

'I haven't got time to play games. Like it or not, you're going in the van.'

'No, please, no.'

The Vulture gave some kind of signal and before I had time to blink two well-built screws had appeared behind me and grabbed my arms, pulling them back until my elbows were almost touching. As I cried out in pain one pushed my head down while the other bent back the thumbs of both hands. It's the classic prison restraint position; the more you struggle against it, the more pain you feel. They started dragging me towards the van. I tried to dig in my heels but the pain in my thumbs and arms quickly became too much to bear.

Karen was going mad, screaming and shouting at the Vulture and anyone else who was near by. 'She can't go in that thing. What are you trying to do? Kill her? She's got to go to court to fight for eighteen years of her life. You can't do this to her.' But no one was listening.

My own screams of terror grew louder and louder as we approached the rear doors of the van. Somewhere in the background, I could hear the Vulture giving orders: 'Just ignore her, she's putting it on. Just get her on the van.' They put me into a cubicle and slammed the door shut. I shut my eyes and prayed. I could hardly breathe and by the time we arrived I was incoherent with fear, throwing up until my throat was burning, and unable to speak. I was delirious.

As the court guards led me through to the cells, I told them that I had to get to the toilet as soon as possible. With no toilet in the cell, that meant a trip to the lavatory with a jailer standing outside the stable-style door of the cubicle. It was a humiliating experience. For the third morning in a row the nurse had failed to get to my cell early enough to hand out my daily supply of Imodium. It meant that using the toilet left me in huge amounts of pain and that I had chronic diarrhoea. The last thing I wanted at a time like that was to have someone standing a few feet away, but I knew from bitter experience that there was no point in asking the guard to move.

By the time I'd finished I was exhausted and degraded.

I was so embarrassed that I wanted to shrivel up. Then the toilet wouldn't flush. I kept trying the handle but nothing happened. I started to get myself into such a state. It was bad enough having someone stand there while I'd been using the toilet; I didn't want anyone to see the mess I'd made. Tears of frustration welled up in my eyes. I got down on my knees and thrust my hands into the bowl, scooping up pieces of shit and depositing them in the sanitary-towel holder by the side of the toilet.

When I finally finished I came out to wash my hands, only to discover there was no soap. I washed my hands in plain water as best I could but for the rest of the day in the dock, all I would be able to smell was the shit on my fingers. Incredibly, it took a complaint from David before soap and clean towels were provided in the ladies' toilets.

By the start of the third week, the cumulative effect of the early mornings, late nights, lack of sleep and lack of food was really getting to me.

I had already lost a little weight during my time in prison; by now it began to fall off at an alarming rate. By the start of the third week I had gone from a size 12 to an 8. Going to court was slowly killing me and this was just during the legal argument. The trial itself would be far more stressful and had been predicted to go on for at least four months. Even if I somehow managed to get through it, I was becoming so mentally and physically exhausted that I'd never be able to take the stand in my own defence.

I was permanently tired and unable to concentrate.

During jury selection I was so weak and mentally exhausted that I could barely follow what was being said. In the breaks I would ask Karen to explain things to me, but within seconds her words would fade from my memory. Things got so bad that one of the jailers at the court actually took pity on me and started sharing the contents of his lunchbox – sandwiches, fruit and crisps – in a bid to keep me going.

As I listened to the legal argument, another factor came into play. The more I heard, the more I became convinced that any jury listening to the same evidence would think that I was in it all the way up to my neck.

For the first time, I started to consider pleading guilty to the drugs charges. Until that point I'd been prepared to fight them all the way, but now I wondered if it was a battle I had any hope of ever winning. If I did lose, the price would be a high one. During my twenty-two months at Holloway, I had been turned down for bail on four occasions and every attempt by my legal team to have the charges dropped had failed. I was still looking at charges connected to the large-scale trafficking of Class A and B drugs and a jail term of around eighteen years.

With time off for good behaviour and a deduction of the time I'd spent on remand, I would be eligible for parole in 2011.

My options were limited. The only way to get my sentence reduced would be to plead guilty to all the drugs-importation charges, in which case I would get an automatic discount of one-third, but then I'd still get a sentence of twelve years, of which I'd have to serve at least eight. My legal team could argue for further discounts but my chances in such an appeal were tissue-paper-thin. The problem was that, despite the fact that Michael had clearly gone to great lengths to deceive a large number of people, many of the money couriers had known exactly what they were doing. Sonny's testimony had done me no favours either. The fact that he had seen me straightening a pile of money at Michael's house, assumed I'd been helping to count it and passed on that interpretation to Customs weighed heavily against me.

The problem with both options was that I would never be able to rebuild any kind of life. I'd be for ever labelled a drug smuggler, and that meant I'd feel unable to show my face in public. I knew I was guilty of being many things – stupid, naïve, short-sighted, to name but a few – but a drug smuggler was the one thing I had never been and would never be.

While I was trying to make up my mind what I was going to do, the legal argument shifted on to a new subject. It began to revolve around DS Paul Carpenter and the spectre of police corruption. Carpenter had been charged with a variety of offences and the defence barristers wanted all the trials halted until Carpenter's had taken place. They explained that if it were to emerge that the policeman had indeed advised Michael Michael not to tell the money couriers what was really going on, then it would be unjust to charge the couriers with drugs offences.

In principle I wholeheartedly supported what they were saying, but the preliminary date for Carpenter's trial was at least fourteen months away. Customs had made it clear that they would never allow me to have bail, in which case I'd have to spend another year in Holloway.

Everything changed on the first Friday in February. The jury had been sworn in, the legal arguments had been resolved and the trial was due to start properly the following Monday.

That morning the barrister representing one of the couriers put forward a proposal on behalf of his client: he asked the judge whether he would be willing to drop the drugs charges in return for a plea of guilty to the money-laundering charge. The judge retired to his chambers to consider it.

David came to see me in the cells to ask if I would like him to make the same approach. In my half-starved, sleep-deprived state I was suffering from mild paranoia, and I suspected the whole thing was some kind of a ruse. It was all much too dangerous. If I told them I was willing to admit to laundering drugs money, they might use that as further evidence of my guilt on all the charges. I told him to do nothing and that I wanted to wait and see what happened to the girl who had made the application.

By the weekend I had begun to recover my sanity enough to inquire about the outcome. The judge had agreed to the plea bargain and had then been asked for an indication of the kind of sentence he would be handing out for the money-laundering charge alone. He said no more than five years.

David took my hand and gave it a little squeeze. 'It's up to you, Tracy. If you want to fight this, then we'll fight it all the way. But it has to be your decision.'

That night I sat in my cell and thought through my options. If I got five years, I'd have to stay in prison for a further six months at the most, but then it would all be over and I'd be able to go home. It would mean pleading guilty to having taken money abroad, but I didn't have a problem with that. I had never denied it, only the fact that I knew it was connected with the drugs trade.

One thing held me back more than any other: I wanted to clear my name and be acquitted of all the charges. Only then would I be able to hold my head up and say that I had truly had no idea of what I had been getting involved in. I didn't want my parents to be disappointed in me. I explained all this to David and he left to call my father and ask him what he thought.

My dad listened carefully and then told David: 'You go back in there and you tell her this. You tell her I will never be ashamed of my daughter. I am so proud of her, the way she has dealt with all of this, the way she has survived. I could not be more proud. Whatever she decides to do, I will stand by her.'

In the early days, my parents had supported my decision to plead innocent: to fight and clear my name. Two years on, they too had lost faith in the criminal justice system. They had seen that sometimes the guilty go free and the innocent pay the price. They would always know the truth, and because of that all they wanted was to get me out of prison and back home.

'OK then,' I told David when he returned and repeated what my father had said. 'Let's do it.'

The following morning, Karen and I sat in the dock for what seemed like an eternity as the judge shuffled his papers and flicked through a series of reports. We were both resigned to getting five years and therefore spending a few more months in Holloway, but I hadn't completely given up the hope that I might get away with a slightly lighter sentence. Karen had taken out more money and made more trips than I had. She had also spent less time in prison, having gone on the run for two months. As I pulled her closer I crossed my fingers. I was praying that both of us would have good luck.

Finally the judge looked up, asked us to stand and cleared his throat. 'There is a difference in the amount of money carried by these two defendants,' he said sombrely, 'but I am not going to quibble over a couple of million pounds. The sentence for both defendants will be the same.'

My heart sank and I shut my eyes, terrified of what might come next.

'Karen Baker, I sentence you to three years.'

I looked up to the public gallery, behind the thick glass, to where my parents were sitting. I saw my Mum looking down at the barristers, a confused expression on her face.

'Tracy Kirby, I sentence you to three years.'

I was trying to follow the action but it was happening in too many places at once. Up in the gallery my mum was mouthing, 'Is she coming home?' to the barrister, but by the time I looked at him he had already replied, and when I looked back at my mum, she was saying something to my dad. And then they were jumping up and down in the aisles and hugging each other, sobbing their hearts out. And I finally allowed myself to believe that I really was going home.

I didn't know what was going to happen next. I thought I'd be able to leave the court straight away but there were formalities. They took us back down to the cells and locked us up.

David came down to explain that, although I was going home, technically I was being released on parole, which meant there was loads of paperwork and formal procedures to be completed before I could be released. He warned me it would take at least a couple of hours.

It suddenly hit me that I would be going home. A huge weight had been lifted from my shoulders. The life I had once known – that I had lost hope of ever getting back – now stretched out before me. It was too much to take in.

Karen and I met with probation officers, who booked appointments and warned us that any breach of our parole would mean returning to prison to complete our sentences. Then letters of confirmation had to be faxed to and from Holloway.

As we were collecting the last of our possessions, I noticed a payphone in the hallway and persuaded one of the guards to lend me the money to make a quick call. I dialled the number for Holloway and asked for the D3 office. The phone was answered by Mr Patel.

'Hi, Tracy, how did you get on?'

'Well as far as I'm concerned, Mr Patel, you can just fuck right off.'

'Oh wow, you're going home. That's fantastic, I'm so happy for you.'

'Tell the girls for me, won't you?'

'I will, and with the greatest of pleasure, Tracy, with the greatest of pleasure.'

When I'd finished, one of the jailers led Karen and me through a series of gates, security doors and stair-wells until we finally reached a short corridor with a door at the end. 'This is as far as I go,' he said. 'You can get out through there.'

A single door was now all that stood between us and the outside world, but it was every bit as daunting and terrifying as a forty-foot electrified fence. After being locked in a cell every night for twenty-two months and not being able to enter a room or leave a building with-out someone else's permission, a closed door becomes the greatest barrier you can possibly imagine.

Karen and I just stood there, holding one another and staring at the door handle.

'Go on, you go first,' she said.

'I . . . I can't. I'm scared. You go first.'

In the end we each placed a hand on the door and, on the count of three, pushed it open and walked through into the lobby of the courthouse.

The first thing I saw was my mum rushing towards me, my father close behind. They swept me up in their arms and held me close. I couldn't let go, I didn't want to let go. I never wanted to be away from them again.

My eyes darted around in all directions, taking in the everyday sights and sounds of this strange new world. Through the glass walls of the courthouse, the colours of nature seemed brighter than ever, and the buses, the houses, the cars all fascinated me as if I were seeing them for the first time.

My legs were shaking and my parents had to hold me up as we walked out of the front door on to the strip of grass outside the court. Karen and I hugged each

other again and again. There was no need for words.
Each of us knew exactly what the other was thinking.
We had both survived Holloway.

My dad went off to get the car and Karen vanished
with her family, leaving my mum and me to hug and
wait.

Then I felt something brush against the back of my
head. At first I thought someone had thrown something
at me and whipped around furiously, glaring at the main
door. But there was no one there. Then I felt it again
– the lightest of feather touches against my hair. And
then on my hands. And then at the end of my nose. It
was so unexpected, such a shock that it took a few
moments for me to realise what was happening: it was
raining.

My dad appeared in the car and my mum began
racing towards it, covering her head with her handbag.
'Come and get in the car, Tracy, you're going to get all
wet.'

'Just a minute, Mum,' I said softly. 'Just give me a
minute.'

I stood on the grass in front of Woolwich Crown
Court with my eyes closed and both arms raised up
towards the heavens as the cold rain poured down,
washed away my tears and soaked me to the skin.

And at that moment, I knew I was free.

Epilogue

Shortly before I was brought up from the cells and shown that the world would allow me to rejoin society, David took my mother to one side. Based on his years of experience of the judicial system, he wanted to warn her what to expect from me once I got back home.

He explained that the initial euphoria of being released would quickly wear off and that in a matter of hours my mood would start to change. Although I'd continue to profess that I was happy to be out of prison, I'd become withdrawn, depressed and so emotionally fragile that the slightest thing would reduce me to tears. In the days that followed, I'd be uncomfortable in crowds, find conversation difficult and feel completely out of touch with the world. I'd also be virtually incapable of doing anything for myself, a phase that could last days, weeks or even months.

In the event, readjusting to life on the outside proved far harder than my parents or I could ever have imagined.

As we reached Hertfordshire at the end of the long drive home, I was struck by just how much everything had changed. There were new shops and restaurants on every street; my favourite wine bar had become a pizza parlour; and a whole new residential development had sprung up on the edge of town.

Even the house my parents were living in had changed hugely. They had bought it a year or so before I had gone inside and during my absence had built a small extension and totally redecorated every room.

It was wonderful to have my mum and dad around again, but I felt like I didn't belong in the house at all. I felt like I didn't belong anywhere, apart from back in my cell. I hated myself for feeling that way.

My brother had filled the house with balloons and hung WELCOME HOME banners from the ceiling. As I stepped through the door he produced dozens of bottles of chilled champagne and we all began to celebrate my homecoming. At first it was just my immediate family, but as the hours ticked by aunts, uncles, cousins and friends called up and asked if they could come round too. Every time the telephone rang I almost jumped out of my skin: in prison you can only make phone calls, not receive them – I just wasn't used to it.

As more and more people arrived at the house, I found myself getting quieter and quieter. I just couldn't think of what to say. I sat dumbstruck in the corner while the party in my honour continued without me. I was completely overwhelmed.

As the afternoon turned to early evening, my mum asked what I wanted to eat. I asked her to get some Indian food – after so long on prison slop, I was desperate for something with real flavour. But as soon as the first forkful went into my mouth, I started to gag and almost threw up.

It was nothing to do with the quality of the food or even the shock my taste buds felt when they encountered the mix of pungent spices – it was the fork itself.

It was made of metal. For the best part of two years I'd been using nothing but plastic cutlery and now I couldn't use anything else. I ended up eating the rest of the meal with my fingers.

Within a few days I started to feel a little more like my old self, but outwardly my behaviour must have seemed odd. I spent my first free weekend with my friends Tracy and Jo, the ones who had come to visit me every Saturday during my time at Holloway. We were chatting and giggling away like old times and every-thing seemed perfectly normal until we left the flat to head out for the evening.

Jo lived on the first floor of a small block of flats and, as she locked her front door I headed down the stairs and waited by the main entrance. Jo saw me standing there and called out to me, 'Go ahead, I'll catch you up.' When I failed to move, she called out again: 'Tracy, what are you waiting for?' Her words snapped me out of my trance and, as I realised what I was doing, my bottom lip started to quiver and I burst into tears. Jo rushed down, put her arms around me and asked what was wrong.

'I was waiting for you to come and open the door for me,' I sobbed.

When I told my parents about what had happened at Jo's they told me I'd been doing exactly the same thing ever since I'd been home. Thankfully David had warned them about it and they had been prepared; I, however, wasn't, and felt completely devastated by my unconscious actions. I collapsed in my mum's arms: 'I'm never going to be able to cope, I can't even walk through a bloody door any more.'

People talk about prison inmates becoming institutionalised and I always imagined it was a process that required decades behind bars. Now I know better: you can be in prison for a month and your behaviour will be affected by it. That's just how regimented life inside is.

David was right in other areas too. I found it hard to cope with crowds. Two weeks after getting out I went out with my mum to the local shopping centre but I got myself into a panic attack and had to come home: there were too many people and I couldn't help thinking that they were all looking at me, as if my time in prison had somehow marked me for life. I also found it hard to comprehend the idea that I could go anywhere I wanted and had no one to answer to.

The following day I decided I had to do something about it, otherwise I would be trapped at home for ever. I took a taxi and went to the shopping centre at Waltham Cross on my own. I asked the driver to wait and spent around twenty minutes wandering around the shops in a state of sheer terror. As I made my way back to the car I felt terrible but at least I'd done it. I knew I was going to be able to move on with my life.

We pulled up outside my parents' house and I noticed two youngish men in smart suits walking up the driveway. I was already pretty frazzled but now I went into full panic mode. I was convinced that they had come to take me back. It made no sense, but somehow I knew it was true. Ever since I'd got home I'd developed this ridiculous but powerful fear that at any time the prison staff could turn up and lock me up all over again.

The two men saw me in the back of the cab and

started walking over. I felt my stomach rush up into my mouth. I was certain I was going to be sick.

I turned to the cab driver. 'Who are they?'

He looked at me as if to say, 'How the bloody hell should I know, you mad cow?', but he managed to control his words better than his expression.

'I don't know, love, I don't know who they are.'

I could feel my pulse rising. 'Oh my God, oh my God, oh my God.'

'Are you all right, love?'

'Oh my God, oh my God.'

I wanted to tell him to drive off, but where would I go? I couldn't run for ever and if I tried I'd only end up making things worse. I was going to have to face the music at some point so I decided to do it there and then.

I opened the door, got out of the car and stood there with my legs wobbling as the first of the two men walked up to me.

'Tracy Kirby?'

'Yes.'

'Hello. We're from the press.'

I put my hand on the man's shoulder to stop myself collapsing forward. 'Oh thank God,' I gasped. 'I thought you were from Customs and that you'd come to take me away again.' As soon as the words left my mouth I regretted it. I couldn't believe I had said something like that to a newspaper reporter. By an amazing stroke of luck, he somehow hadn't heard me properly.

'You what?'

'Oh . . . er . . . nothing.'

'Look, we know you've just got out of prison and

we wondered if we could have a few words.'

Before he had finished his sentence, before the photographer had time to get his camera out of his bag, I was inside the house and hiding behind the curtains. It didn't stop a story appearing a few days later, complete with the following quote from yours truly: 'I am so relieved that I am out of prison at last. I can now breathe in the fresh air and look out at the view across the fields – something I wanted to do during those long days staring at prison walls.'

Completely made up – but for once I really didn't care.

The paranoia, the waiting for doors to be unlocked, the fear of being out in public – all of these things faded with time and soon I was making the mistake of assuming I had come through the experience relatively unscathed. I was in for a terrible shock.

Three weeks after my release I accepted an invitation from Terry, one of my oldest friends, to go out to dinner at a posh restaurant. It was great to see him again and we chatted away at ten to the dozen as he drove us into central London. Close to the restaurant, Terry pulled into a packed multi-storey car park and began hunting for a space. We spotted someone who was about to leave and pulled over to one side to wait for them to go. But as soon as the space became vacant, a little Fiat containing three girls dolled up to the nines whipped around the corner and took it.

And I went crazy. The anger started somewhere down in my stomach and went *whoosh* straight up into my head. I felt as if a red mist had surrounded me. I started swearing manically as I frantically tried to undo my seat belt and open the door at the same time.

I sprinted across the car park and within seconds I was beside the Fiat. I clawed at the door handles, smashed my fists against the windows and kicked the body panels as I released a tirade of obscenities at the occupants: 'You fucking bunch of cunts. Who the fuck do you think you are, you bitches? What the fuck do you think you're doing, eh? I'll fucking kill you, I'll kill the fucking lot of you. You come round here and steal our space, leave us sitting there like fucking mugs. I'll fucking kill you, I will . . .'

The three girls looked absolutely terrified. They locked the doors and cowered, one of them even pulled out her mobile phone and started calling for help. I didn't care. I was completely out of control and determined to get them. God only knows what would have happened if they had got out of the car. I was more than ready to attack all three of them. In the event Terry came rushing over and dragged me – kicking and screaming all the way – back to his car.

He bundled me into the rear seat and started trying to calm me down, his face twisted with shock and concern. In all the time he had known me, I had never so much as raised my voice in public, let alone tried to tear the faces off three complete strangers in a car park. We had been friends for years but at that moment he didn't know me at all.

'Tracy, what's going on? It doesn't matter, it's only a space in a car park, it really doesn't matter.'

I was still as vicious as hell. 'It does fucking matter,' I spat back. 'It's a fucking liberty. You can't let people take the piss out of you like that . . .'

'But Tracy, we'll never see them again. I don't understand why you're being like this.'

Then suddenly I realised what was happening. Since my first days at Holloway, I'd learned the hard way that you can never let anyone take advantage of you, even in the smallest way. If you do, then they walk all over you. That's what life is like in prison, those are the rules you have to live by. But you can't behave like that in the outside world – not without being locked up again.

In a split second my anger had been replaced by shock and shame. I couldn't believe I'd behaved like that. The idea that there was this monster, this fire-breathing dragon, sleeping inside me that could be woken by the slightest thing absolutely terrified me.

I was supposed to be going out for a quiet meal with a friend, but that one little trigger had taken me right back to the landing at Holloway where I was willing to use my fists, feet and nails to fight to the death over something as petty as the last bread roll.

I left prison with no job, no money and no home. Even my clothes didn't fit any more. Slowly but surely I have managed to rebuild my life, but I know I'll never fully put the experience behind me.

Tiny legacies are evident on a daily basis. Having spent so long owning just thirty-nine items, I now find it impossible to travel lightly. Even if I'm just going somewhere overnight, I have to take virtually everything I own. I hate having my choices restricted the way they once were.

I find it much more difficult to trust people – but

considering some of the things that have happened in the past, that's probably no bad thing.

I also find it much more difficult to relax and to be myself, because I don't really know who I am any more. All I know for sure is that I'm not exactly the same person I used to be. Before, I was always a bit wild, happy-go-lucky and eager to play the fool at any opportunity. More than anything, I wanted to make the people around me laugh. I still have my moments but a lot of that has gone.

People have always had an image of me as the ex-model, the glamorous fun-loving party girl, but that was never really me anyway, it was always a front. Before I went to prison, life was just one big game. I remember spending so much of my time laughing, proper belly laughs that would leave me in absolute hysterics. That rarely happens any more. I feel like a part of me is dead, like something has been lost. I'm a much more serious person than I used to be and I don't always see the funny side of life.

I'm not the only one. Karen and I are as close as ever. The bond that began on our trips to Spain and was cemented in prison has continued after our release. She too feels permanently scarred by the experience. 'I can't cry any more,' she told me just the other day. 'I spent so long blocking things out and can't just stop that. It's like all my emotions have gone. I had to work so hard to not feel things that I no longer know how.'

Every now and then there are disturbing reminders that some of the worst things I experienced at Holloway were by no means unique. Six months after my release, a report by an independent healthcare agency into the medical staff at the prison found their attitude towards inmates to be 'profoundly disturbing'. It was said that they 'couldn't care less' about the prisoners' welfare. The audit team actually witnessed an anorexic prisoner being refused a food supplement that was part of her treatment. The report said the request was met with 'a series of expletives' and that 'the doctor on duty appeared to condone this behaviour'.

There have been times when the whole thing seems like a bad dream, and there are others when something as simple as a sound or a smell takes me right back. Even now, I occasionally wake up in the middle of the night in a cold sweat, believing I am back in my cell and that I am living that nightmare all over again.

The feelings and the fear have faded, but I know they will never go away completely. In some ways I'm still a prisoner at Holloway and a part of me always will be.

When you're inside, you know that one day you'll be released. You live in the hope that you'll be able to get your life back together and do all the things you used to do. More than anything, you want it to be just as it was. But the reality is that when you go to prison you lose much, much more than your liberty. Though one day you go free, some parts of you disappear for ever. No matter how hard you try, you can never get them back.